Delight Thyself also in the Lord

A SIMPLE DAILY DEVOTIONAL

Delight Thyself
DESIGN MINISTRIES

delightthyself.com

*"Delight thyself also in the LORD;
and he shall give thee the desires of thine heart."*
Psalm 37:4

*"And I will delight myself in thy commandments,
which I have loved."*
Psalm 119:47

Published by Delight In Him Publications,
a division of Delight Thyself Design Ministries in Hurricane, WV.

Delight Thyself Design Ministries' mission is to design and distribute Gospel tracts for the furtherance of the Gospel of Jesus Christ. Our desire is to make tracts available to churches, while at the same time sending tracts to missionaries across the world in need of material.

Delight Thyself Design Ministries, Inc.
PO Box 725
Hurricane, WV 25526
delightthyself.com

Special thanks to those who took the time to proof read.

The contents of this book are the result of years of spiritual growth in life and ministry. Every effort has been made to give proper credit and attribution to quotes and information that is not original. It is not our intent to claim originality with any quote or thought that could not be tied to an original source.

Printed in the United States of America.

ISBN-13: 978-0999517505
ISBN-10: 0999517503

Table of Contents

Prologue

What began as a blank New York City themed 2015 calendar developed into a verse-of-the-day archive, then the Lord transformed it into a daily devotional blog. Never in a million years did I ever think this was something I would ever feel led to do, but the Lord had other plans. His ways are higher than our ways, and His thoughts higher than ours. I am so thankful the Lord has already used this project to help others as the posts appeared each day on the website, and I pray for those who will read them for years to come in this book.

This devotional is simply meant to point you to Jesus Christ through His Word. If we delight ourselves in Him, He will give us the desires that He desires for our lives.

Holidays

There are themes throughout the year that center around specific holidays. **These are meant to direct our focus toward how we can best delight in the Lord throughout the holiday season.** Since some holidays do not fall on the same date each year, listed below are the dates where these can be found.

Easter - March 18th-28th

The Plot. The Colt. The Triumphal Entry. The Rejection. The Iniquity. The Submission. The Cross. The Substitution. The Napkin. The Empty Tomb. The Commission.

Thanksgiving - November 23rd-25th

Give Him Thanks. A Thankful Heart. Thankful In Every Thing.

Christmas - December 14th-25th

The Only Reason For The Season. His Purpose. God With Us. Favoured Grace. How Shall This Be? Be It Unto Me. Great Things. Where Is He? Is There Room? Good Tidings Of Great Joy. Make Him Known. God Gave.

Dedications

In her final days, my grandmother told me she knew that one day I would write a book. I laughed. For nearly 15 years afterwards, I looked back on that day as something she had no idea what she was saying. But as always, grandmothers always know much more than we do, and their wise statements often turn out to be true. I can still see her face that day as she reassured me through my confused face that would have been obvious to anyone who knew me. I pray that she would be pleased if she knew how God orchestrated this book to come together, smiling down from Heaven at the fact that she was right once again. Nanny, I love you, and I miss you every day.

Certain days throughout the year are dedicated to some special people behind the scenes of this ministry who are the Aarons & Hurs that hold up my hands through their love, friendship and support. These people will recognize the theme or verse significance on their birthdays, days of announcement, days that hold fond memories, etc. This is just a small way of paying tribute to those who my life would not be the same without the difference they have made. You know who you are, and I love each one of you.

I pray that God will speak to you as you go through each day of this devotional, pointing you not to the words I have written, but to Him through His Word.

Allison McKay
Delight Thyself Design Ministries

A New Year, A New Thing.

Isaiah 43:18-19

"Remember ye not the former things, neither consider the things of old.
Behold, I will do a new thing; *now it shall spring forth; shall ye not know it?*
I will even make a way in the wilderness, and rivers in the desert."

As a new year begins, ask God to guide you in the days ahead. He tells us to forget and not even consider what lies behind us, while promising that He has something new for us to experience. Maybe you feel like you're at the end of your road or walking through an emotional wilderness, not knowing which way to turn. He promises that He will make a way. Are you thirsty? He can bring you to a river in the desert.

Let's use this new beginning, that God has given us, to turn the page of our lives and seek Him. He promises He will never leave us nor forsake us. He will guide us through the trials and lead us through the victories, if only we will let Him.

The theme of this entire devotional is found in Psalm 37:4:
"Delight thyself also in the LORD;
and he shall give thee the desires of thine heart."

Use this new year to delight yourself in Him, and claim the promise that He will give you the desires that fit into His perfect will for your life. It doesn't mean He will just give you what you want, but rather He will give you exactly what you need to be more like Him, and serve Him better.

Each day will have a verse or a set of verses and a short challenge or word of encouragement, followed by a suggested Bible reading for the day. The readings will allow you to read through more than the entire Bible before the year is over. The Old Testament & New Testament plus reviewing Psalms, Proverbs, Matthew, Mark, Luke, John, Romans, Hebrews, James and 1 John again.

Pray that God will work in your heart,
and use His Word to help you through each day that lies ahead.

Bible Reading
Genesis 1-2 | John 1 | Proverbs 1

The Crucified Life.

Galatians 2:20

*"**I am crucified with Christ**: nevertheless I live; yet not I, but Christ liveth in me: and the life which I now live in the flesh I live by the faith of the Son of God, who loved me, and gave himself for me."*

This verse is much easier to read than it is to live, isn't it? Life is much easier when we are dead to ourselves and Christ is living for us, but how many times do we die to ourselves only to have picked ourselves back up again before the end of the day, or even the hour?

In his book, "The Crucified Life", A.W. Tozer defined the crucified life as a life wholly given over to the Lord in absolute humility and obedience: a sacrifice pleasing to the Lord. He goes on to simplify and describe it practically as a life absolutely committed to following after Christ Jesus; to be more like Him, to think like Him, to act like Him, and to love like Him. To do that, **we must be dead to our flesh and own desires.**

Romans 6:6-7,11

"Knowing this, that our old man is crucified with him, that the body of sin might be destroyed, that henceforth we should not serve sin. For he that is dead is freed from sin…Likewise reckon ye also yourselves to be dead indeed unto sin, but alive unto God through Jesus Christ our Lord."

**Commit yourself to dying each day
so that Christ can live through you,
and make you more alive than you could ever be by yourself.**

The Urgency Of Salvation.

2 Corinthians 6:1-2

*"We then, as workers together with him, beseech you also that ye receive not the grace of God in vain. (For he saith, I have heard thee in a time accepted, and in the day of salvation have I succoured thee: **behold, now is the accepted time; behold, now is the day of salvation.**)"*

Have you ever seen someone blatantly put off accepting Christ, despite having been obviously convicted of his or her condition? There is nothing sadder to witness.

A soulwinner once asked a lady, if she died today, was she 100% sure she would go to heaven. She immediately burst into tears, ran to get her car keys and then sped away. The soulwinner and their partner stood still and speechless with their jaws open, wondering if what they saw had really happened. The soulwinner has since often wondered if Marcy ever accepted Christ, or if she was still avoiding and ignoring her need for Him.

If you haven't trusted Christ before,
and realize yourself as a sinner in need of a Saviour,
what are you waiting for?

*"...behold, **now** is the accepted time; behold, **now** is the day of salvation."*

Christian, if you have sat back and watched others spread the Good News of the Gospel of Jesus Christ, what are you waiting for?

The lady at the next drive-thru window you visit needs Christ just as much as the convicted murderer on death row. You could be her last chance of knowing Christ before she is killed in an accident on her way home. The fast pace of a drive-thru does not really allow for a full verbal Gospel presentation…but she may read a Gospel tract that was given to her before she leaves the parking lot.

Time is running out.
Now is the accepted time.
Now is the day of salvation.

Bible Reading
Genesis 5-6 | John 3 | Proverbs 3

Wait.

Psalm 37:34
"Wait on the LORD, and keep his way,
and he shall exalt thee to inherit the land:
when the wicked are cut off, thou shalt see it."

God doesn't do anything by accident.
Within the pages of Scripture we can find encouragement, direction, and commands to be patient and wait on Him.

His timing is not our timing. His thoughts are not our thoughts.
But, regardless of our impatience, our stubbornness, our need to have things our way and/or in our timing…He alone does all things well. His timing, though it may be seem inconvenient and confusing, is always, always best.

Jim Elliot, the famous missionary to Ecuador, is well known for the phrase:
"God always gives His best to those who leave the choice to Him."

If you lack patience today, you're not alone.
They say not to pray for patience, cause God is sure to give you something you won't be comfortable with in order to help you learn it, but as we read in James 4:2… *"ye have not, because ye ask not".*

Have you ever been in a hurry to get somewhere, and it seems like every traffic signal in your path is synced in shades of red? Stopping and waiting may be inconvenient, but if we ignore the warning and press the gas pedal, we risk getting hit by oncoming traffic.

God may seem to give you more red lights than green ones, but they are for your good. Standing still and waiting for Him to give you a green light, on the decision you are facing, is much better than getting blindsided by the vehicles of the enemy.

Stay on the road, and wait for Him to tell you to move.

Bible Reading
Genesis 7-8 | John 4 | Proverbs 4

Patience.

1 Peter 5:6
*"Humble yourselves therefore under the mighty hand of God,
that he may exalt you in due time:"*

Again, with the patience. If you haven't already noticed, the words "wait" and some form of "patient" occur many times in Scripture. **God wants us to be humble while we wait on Him.**

Getting ahead of the Lord will only lead to headache and heartburn. If we push open the door of opportunity too soon, we may get what we think we want and need at first, but it will never last without God's blessing.

Only by humbling ourselves under His authority will we ever reach our full potential. This is where The Crucified Life comes in. If we choose to not die to ourselves daily, we will eventually find ourselves at a crossroads not knowing where to turn, crying out to God for Him to help us correct the mess we've made. Why not do it His way to start with and avoid the heartache?

Obviously waiting is not fun. It's often more confusing and depressing. He may ask us to wait a few hours, a few days, a few weeks, a few months, a few years, or perhaps many years. Where's the hope in that? The last part of our verse today… *"that he may exalt you in due time."*

Exalting ourselves will only be temporary. **Waiting for Him to exalt us leads to eternal dividends that money can't buy.**

Mary & Martha waited for Jesus to come see Lazarus. All hope seemed gone when Lazarus died. A day passed… two days… three days…

"But He's four days late, and all hope is gone. Lord, we don't understand why you've waited so long… But His way is God's way, not yours or mine. And isn't it great, when He's four days late, He's still on time." Aaron Wilburn

Still not encouraged to wait? Need some advice on what to do while you're waiting? Read the next verse… 1 Peter 5:7.

Bible Reading
Genesis 9-10 | John 5 | Proverbs 5

Rest.

Matthew 11:28-29
*"Come unto me, all ye that labour and are heavy laden,
and **I will give you rest.** Take my yoke upon you, and learn of me,
for I am meek and lowly in heart: and ye shall find rest unto your souls."*

"There is a restlessness within us that cannot be satisfied
until we rest fully in God." A.W. Tozer

Impatience leads to restlessness. **If we remain impatient for an extended amount of time, eventually we will become restless;** physically, emotionally, and worst of all, spiritually.

Have you ever thought the day went decent, and was somewhat productive, until that moment, when you have finally gotten into bed and your mind starts to race like it's running the Boston Marathon. From thinking of the list of "to-dos" for the next day, to wondering how or when something is going to happen. From designing pieces of your next project, to daydreaming about the future. Sometimes even whether you have locked all the doors of your house or not, and put the garage door down. **Unending thoughts lead to restlessness.**

What's wrong with this picture when it happens? We haven't rested in the Lord, and put each of those racing details in His hands and His timing. We haven't rested in the One Who does all things well and is in control of everything. **When we try to do things by ourselves, and don't seek His help or involvement, we are headed for disappointment and destruction.**

As Tozer alluded to, **we will never rid ourselves of the restlessness we feel until we fully rest and trust in the God of the our Salvation.** He wants us to rest in Him. He wants us to learn from Him. He wants to lead us. He wants to give us the rest that our soul needs.

Are you heavy laden with the trials and troubles of this life?
Rest in Him today.

Do a search for the word *"rest"* in Scripture. God is sure to give you something to get you through your restlessness today.

Bible Reading
Genesis 11-12 | John 6 | Proverbs 6

A Biblical Equation.

1 Timothy 6:6
"But godliness with contentment is great gain."

Godliness + Contentment = Great Gain

Here in 1 Timothy 6:6, we see a practical Biblical equation with immense opportunity and net worth. We all want great gain. Worldly gain is rarely promised or attainable. **Great gain comes only from above.**

One day, I was reading through some Scripture after spending the first week of the New Year, and much of the previous year, impatient, restless, and confused. I wish I could remember exactly what passage I had been reading, but all I know is that the Lord convicted me of just how discontented I was. I believed I knew what God's will was, but I certainly wasn't patient while waiting for Him to allow it to happen.

After much conviction through studying the Word, I finally let it go. I decided within my heart that I would be content, and if my situation was what God wanted for me, I would make the best of it regardless of how uncomfortable I was. I had trusted Him for the past few years to lead, guide, and direct me…but not fully trusted. I had given Him one of the reins of my life, while still holding on to the other one. I was sure of my calling and my desire to serve Him, but **He can't fully use someone who isn't truly content.** I had given him the reins many times before, only to take back one of them before I left my knees. But this time was different. His Word had penetrated my discontented heart. Within just a few days of this movement of God upon my heart, my situation completely changed in a way that only He could have done.

Ask for God's help with contentment,
and He will give you great gain.

His Word promises us, and God never breaks His promises.

Bible Reading
Genesis 13-14 | John 7 | Proverbs 7

Fearful & Faithless.

Matthew 8:26
"And he saith unto them, Why are ye so fearful, O ye of little faith? Then he arose, and rebuked the winds and the sea; and there was a great calm."

Are you finding yourself full of fear and empty of faith?

Have you focused in on the winds and waves of your circumstance, and it seems that the Master of the sea is asleep?

We are either in a storm, coming out of a storm, or going into a storm.

Oftentimes in the middle of a storm, just when we think it can't get any worse, we find ourselves fearful, faithless, and incapable of saving ourselves. Jesus can speak peace to our weary souls and rescue us, if we call out to Him. He will not only save us from our surroundings; but much like the disciples did after Jesus calmed their storm, we can marvel at what the Lord has done for us.

**Call out to the Saviour today,
and allow Him to rebuke the weather of your life.**

There is nothing like the calm that Jesus can give.

Ephesians 3:20
"Now unto him that is able to do exceeding abundantly above all that we ask or think, according to the power that worketh in us."

When we finally submit to the Master of the sea, letting Him handle the storms of our lives, we can then see Him work like only He can through His infinite power.

Many times just after the calm of the storm, the Lord has a way of leaving us speechless by exceeding our requests and thoughts, so much that He is the only explanation. It might be a check in the mail for the exact amount you need to pay the mortgage. It may be a phone call for an opportunity that you had given up hope would ever come. It may be God using someone to anonymously fulfill a need in your life that only He knew about. If you are a child of God, you most certainly have had a few or several of these Ephesians 3:20 moments.

**When there is no human reasoning,
manipulation or explanation to what occurred.
It was just Him.**

Exceeding: to go beyond, to surpass
Abundantly: in great quantity, well supplied
Above All: higher than anything, beyond everything

**Next time you find yourself in awe
of how He has worked in your life,
remind yourself, "That's Him".**

Bible Reading
Genesis 17-18 | John 9 | Proverbs 9

He Is Greater.

1 John 4:4b
"…because greater is he that is in you, than he that is in the world."

Remember the song…

"Bigger than all my problems, bigger than all my fears,
God is bigger than any mountain that I can or cannot see!"

I can still hear the choir singing it from when I was a kid.

The god of this world would have you believe that the mountain in front of you is too steep, the valley you're in too deep, or the river too wide. Satan has a way of messing with our thoughts, our actions, and our attitudes. If he has you thinking that your struggle is too much for you to handle, he may be right… but if you let God take care of your problem or situation, there's nothing He can't handle - no matter how big or how small!

**No matter what problem or fear you face,
God is greater than them all.**

The devil even tempted Jesus Christ Himself when He was here on earth, so none of us are immune. Remember how Jesus defeated him?

Every time in Scripture that Satan tempted Jesus,
His reply began with four simple words…*"For it is written…"*

He simply used the Word of God to defeat His enemy.
So can we! He is Greater.

Bible Reading
Genesis 19-20 | John 10 | Proverbs 10

Be Confident.

Philippians 1:6
*"Being confident of this very thing,
that he which hath begun a good work in you will perform it
until the day of Jesus Christ:"*

You know that one person who is way too confident in themselves? Come on, if we are all honest, at least one name or face probably came to mind.

However, this isn't the type of confidence that the Scripture is talking about here. This verse doesn't refer to us being confident in ourselves or those closest to us. **We should never place any confidence in the flesh.**

Romans 7:18
"For I know that in me (that is, in my flesh,) dwelleth no good thing…"

It's been said before, "We put more faith in FedEx to make a delivery than we do in God to do what He said." How sad, but true, that often is! We have no doubt that the item we ordered will arrive at our door at its expected time and place; yet, we doubt whether or not God will supply the need we have.

Philippians 4:19
*"But my God shall supply all your need according to
his riches in glory by Christ Jesus."*

Are there some days that you forget that verse?
Have you lost confidence that He is able to deliver exactly what you need?

Thankfully, we can be confident in our Saviour & the work He alone has done in us and will do through us.

Be confident today, Christian!

Luke 21:28
"…then look up, and lift up your heads; for your redemption draweth nigh."

Bible Reading
Genesis 21-22 | John 11 | Proverbs 11

Backward & Forward.

Hebrews 13:5
"...I will never leave thee, nor forsake thee."

Joshua 1:5-6a
"…as I was with Moses, so I will be with thee: I will not fail thee, nor forsake thee. Be strong and of a good courage…"

In Hebrews 13:5 we find a backward and forward promise of God.

Forward: "I will never leave thee, nor forsake thee."
Backward: "thee forsake nor thee leave, never will I"

After Moses died, Joshua had some big shoes to fill, after he was given the responsibility of leading the children of Israel once they reached Jordan. The Lord commanded him to *"Be strong and of a good courage"* several times. I can't help but think that Joshua must have thought, "That sounds good, but how am I supposed to do that?" Can you relate with Joshua?

The direction that the Lord gave Joshua in order to *"be strong and of a good courage"* is the same direction that He wants us to use in our everyday lives.

Joshua 1:8
"This book of the law shall not depart out of thy mouth; but thou shalt meditate therein day and night, that thou mayest observe to do according to all that is written therein: for then thou shalt make thy way prosperous, and then thou shalt have good success."

Just like Joshua, God has given us the Resource to be prosperous and have true success in our lives. We must meditate and observe to do what is found within the pages of God's Word. We need to abide ourselves in the Truth of the Scripture, and we cannot do that unless we are daily partaking from the Bread of His table.

"The enduring value presented in these pages have a great meaning for each of us, and for our nation. The Bible can touch our hearts, order our minds, and refresh our souls…**Within the covers of that single Book are all the answers to all the problems that face us today, if we'd only read and believe."** Ronald Reagan

Bible Reading
Genesis 23-24 | John 12 | Proverbs 12

To The Brim.

John 2:7
*"Jesus saith unto them, Fill the waterpots with water.
And they filled them to the brim."*

Three days after Jesus was baptized by John the Baptist in Jordan, Jesus and His disciples were invited to a wedding. We all know the familiar event quite well. So well in fact, that we may skip over the details when reading through the passage. Don't skip or run through the Bible. When we skip, we miss things that we could have seen if we would simply walk through His Word.

When you grab a glass out of a kitchen cabinet, and pour your favorite drink into it, how far do you fill it? Probably not to the brim.

Mary, the Mother of Jesus, had told the servants at the feast, *"Whatsoever he saith unto you, do it."* She had told them to obey Him. So, when Jesus spoke the words in our text, they knew what they were supposed to do. *"Fill the waterpots with water."* They filled them as much as they possibly could. With the water completely level with the top of the waterpots, maybe some even spilt over because they had filled them so much out of obedience. Can't you see the water running down the side, eventually reaching the floor?

Once they were filled, Jesus commanded them to *"Draw out now."* Imagine the servants' faces when they drew out a colored liquid after knowingly filling them with water! As a colored liquid spilled down the side now, they must have looked around at each other wondering if the other servants saw what they were seeing!

Ever wonder why they filled the waterpots as much as they could? They obeyed, but perhaps it's more than that. Not only did they do what they were told, they wanted to do everything in their power in obedience to Him. They wanted to serve Him with all the resources they had. They could have filled them half full, or three-quarters full... But *"they filled them to the brim."*

How often in our service to the Lord do we give Him half of what we could? We obey, but we don't go the extra mile. We don't fill our vessel to the brim. That's not how these servants were. They filled their vessels to the brim. **Christian, fill your life to the brim today.**

Go the extra mile for the Saviour Who went the extra mile for you.
Bible Reading

Genesis 25-26 | John 13 | Proverbs 13

All Things In Common.

Acts 4:32
"And the multitude of them that believed were of one heart and of one soul: neither said any of them that ought of the things which he possessed was his own; but they had all things common."

One heart. One soul. All things in common.
If only our Biblical churches would get to this point.

1 Corinthians 14:33
"For God is not the author of confusion..."

Philippians 2:3
"Let nothing be done through strife or vainglory..."

For us to have all things in common, we must neglect any agendas or selfish desires about what should or shouldn't happen in our churches. We must submit ourselves to God and His plan for our lives and our churches.

We must seek a revival.

Revival refers to a spiritual awakening from a state of dormancy or stagnation. Everyone has felt dormant or stagnate at some point. Often times what begins as a stress reliever becomes a distraction, then a diversion and eventually we are nowhere near where we used to be in our walk with the Lord. None of us are immune to the wiles of the devil.

Finding our way back to walking with the Lord, we ask for God to move among us. **We pray for revival often not realizing its requirements.** If we do realize them, we aren't willing to do what is necessary in order to see it.

We must first see an individual revival in our own hearts before it will ever appear in our churches. Until we get on our knees privately, humbling ourselves, praying, seeking His face, and turning from our wicked ways, we will never see a public revival. Only then will we experience His forgiveness and healing of our land.

D.L. Moody, the great evangelist, said:
"Every great movement of God can be traced to a kneeling figure."

**What if you were that kneeling figure
that spawned the spark needed for true revival?**

Bible Reading
Genesis 27-28 | John 14 | Proverbs 14

Handfuls Of Purpose.

Ruth 2:16
*"And let fall also some of the handfuls of purpose for her,
and leave them, that she may glean them, and rebuke her not."*

Each day we glean from the different things we focus our mind and spirit on, whether it is intentional or not. What are you gleaning? Like Ruth, we need to find the right field to glean from…the Word of God.

Ruth was new to Bethlehem. She did not know who owned the field. God's grace had led her there. It's by God's grace we have our Bible.

Boaz gave Ruth his field to glean from, freely… God has given us His Word and He shares It freely with us, just like salvation. We must not only take our fill of gleaning from God's Harvest, we must share it with others just as Ruth shared with Naomi. What kind of Christians would we be if we didn't share what God has given us with others?

What handfuls of purpose are you leaving behind for others to find?

The Bible tells us that a man reaps what he sows. Boaz had planted and reaped, and Ruth & Naomi reaped the benefits of what Boaz had sown. Boaz had sown with a purpose. He had sown his field long before Ruth came around, and the Lord allowed Ruth to come just at right time… Harvest time. What a picture of the amazing grace of God!

God has you right where you are right now for a reason; the street you live on, the job you have, the church you attend, the children you raise. God has given you the people in your life to be a living testimony to, and to share the Gospel with them. You may be the only Bible they read, the only church they attend. **What if you are the only Christian they know?**

Saturate yourself in God's Word so that the Scripture seeps out and the people around you notice. **Leave behind some handfuls of purpose in your testimony** so that your neighbors, co-workers and children, all notice that there is something different about you.

Bible Reading
Genesis 29-30 | John 15 | Proverbs 15

Everyday Courage.

Joshua 1:9
*"Have not I commanded thee? Be strong and of a good courage:
be not afraid, neither be thou dismayed: for the LORD thy
God is with thee whithersoever thou goest."*

There's courage…then there's an Everyday Courage that only comes from the Lord. How can we obtain this Everyday Courage?

Get involved.
Esther 4:16
Esther knew the risk she was taking, but she didn't let that stop her, and neither should we. Has God placed a desire in your heart that seems impossible? Have courage, and get involved.

Don't conform.
Daniel 3:18
The three Hebrew men didn't conform to King Nebuchadnezzar's demand, despite his threat of the burning fiery furnace. Today, many so-called Christians have compromised their convictions, beliefs, doctrines, and even their Bible. Refuse to compromise today, despite the flames around you. Have courage, and don't conform.

Stand against sin.
Matthew 14:3-4
John the Baptist called Herod out for the sin he was committing. Despite what may be legal and politically correct in our world today, we as Christians should not tolerate sin. We should practice being separate and holy. Have courage, and stand against sin.

When put together, these four simple things can give us Everyday Courage to fight against the wiles of the devil. In Ephesians 6:10-18 we are given the descriptions of the armour God has provided us to assist us in the fight. All but one of them is defensive. We must only go on the offensive attack when armed with Sword of the Spirit, the Word of God. It is quick and powerful. It is sharper than any two-edged sword. It can pierce even unto the dividing asunder of the soul and spirit. It discerns the thoughts and intents of our heart. See Hebrews 4:12.

Determine to have Everyday Courage to stand for the Lord.

Bible Reading
Genesis 31-32 | John 16 | Proverbs 16

The Greatest Privilege.

John 1:12
*"But as many as received him,
to them gave he power to become the sons of God,
even to them that believe on his name:"*

By giving us His power to become the sons of God, Jesus Christ gives us the highest right, or the greatest privilege, we can ever experience in this world. But in order to receive that power, **we must receive Him.** We must believe on Him and His name as the only means by which we can reach Heaven.

"He who is made a child of God enjoys the greatest privilege which the Divine Being can confer on this side of eternity. Those who accept Jesus Christ, as he is offered to them in the Gospel, have, through His blood, a right to this sonship; for by that sacrifice this blessing was purchased; and the fullest promises of God confirm it to all who believe." Adam Clarke

We cannot reach Heaven of our own power or ability. Titus 3:5 tells us that *"Not by works of righteousness…"* Heaven can't be earned. Heaven can't be bought by worldly goods. Heaven is free to those who believe on Jesus Christ and His finished work; but Heaven is costly. It cost God the Father His only begotten Son. It cost Jesus Christ His life here on earth. **But the privilege of being a child of God is free… to all who receive Him and believe on His name.**

In John 1:10 & 11, we see that though He came, some didn't know Him. Some, even of His own, knew Him; but didn't receive Him. Isn't that much like the world today? Some have never heard the Gospel message; and many, having heard the Gospel, have not received Him and believed on His name.

Lots of people know who Jesus is, but many of them don't know Him as their personal Saviour. **Do you know someone who knows of Jesus, but doesn't know Him? Pray for them today.** Pray that God would work in their heart. Pray that God would give you an opportunity to share the Gospel with them.

The only unsuccessful Gospel witness is the one not given.

Bible Reading

Genesis 33-34 | John 17 | Proverbs 17

Exceeding Abundant Grace.

1 Timothy 1:14
"And the grace of our Lord was exceeding abundant with faith and love which is in Christ Jesus."

Sound familiar? This verse often reminds me of Ephesians 3:20 and God's all-powerful ability to do much more than we could ever desire. But here we see that power referring to the grace of God through faith and love which is in Christ Jesus.

Exceeding: to go beyond, to surpass
Abundant: in great quantity, well supplied

How would you define grace?

Many have referred to it as God's Riches At Christ's Expense.
When referring to Webster's definition of grace, you could expect something close to unmerited favor; but Webster went even further in explaining that **the ultimate purpose of grace as the unmerited divine assistance given humans for their regeneration or sanctification.** Among thousands of definitions in his dictionary sits salvation by grace. Someone had given Noah Webster the Gospel.

The grace of God is ultimately displayed by the giving of His only begotten Son so that we could become the sons of God.
Exceeding Abundant Grace.

*Amazing Grace, how sweet the sound,
That saved a wretch like me,
I once was lost, but now I'm found,
Was blind, but now, I see.
T'was Grace that taught,
My heart to fear.
And Grace, my fears relieved!
How precious did that Grace appear
The hour I first believed.
Through many dangers, toils and snares,
I have already come.
Tis Grace has brought me safe thus far,
And Grace will lead me home!*
John Newton,1779

Bible Reading
Genesis 35-36 | John 18 | Proverbs 18 | 25

Delight In The Truth.

Proverbs 12:22
*"Lying lips are abomination to the LORD:
but they that deal truly are his delight."*

Of the seven things that are listed in Proverbs 6 as abominations to the Lord, a lying tongue is the second to make the list. Jesus refers to the devil as the father of lies in John 8:44.

Therefore, we find that lying is an abomination to the Lord, and associated with the devil himself by none other than our Lord, Jesus Christ.

So why do we think it is okay to tell a "little white lie" every now and then?

I don't know about you, but I sure do not want to be associated with the devil… and I sure don't want to cause myself to take part in an abomination to my Lord. Our flesh wants us to think that the little white lie won't hurt us or anyone else. God's Word tells us differently.

God's Word tells us the Truth.

Thankfully, the Scripture doesn't just stop with telling us that lying lips are an abomination unto Him. It shows us what He delights in instead of what He hates.

Delight in the Truth today.

Let's make every effort to only deal truly, so that He can be delighted by our conduct and witness for Him.

Bible Reading
Genesis 37-38 | John 19 | Proverbs 19

Chosen & Called.

Isaiah 41:8-10
"But thou, Israel, art my servant, Jacob whom I have chosen, the seed of Abraham my friend. Thou whom I have taken from the ends of the earth, and called thee from the chief men thereof, and said unto thee,
Thou art my servant; I have chosen thee, and not cast thee away. Fear thou not; for I am with thee: be not dismayed; for I am thy God: I will strengthen thee; yea, I will help thee; yea, I will uphold thee with the right hand of my righteousness."

This is a great passage to refer to when people need encouragement. As children of God, we can claim the promises spoken by God to the children of Israel. **We are chosen. We are called.**

How blessed we are to be chosen and called by Him!
But He doesn't stop there...
He promises us that He will not cast us away.
Even when we are fearful, He is with us. When we get dismayed by our circumstances and surroundings, He reminds us that He is still our God.

He promises us that He will strengthen us when we get weak in our trials.

He promises He will help us through the struggles of life.

He promises to uphold us by the right hand of His righteousness!
Who is at the right hand of the Father?
Jesus Christ... we are upheld by God through Him!

In Psalm 16, we read about the pleasures that we have access to at the Right Hand of the Father, because that's where Jesus is!

Psalm 16:11
"Thou wilt shew me the path of life: in thy presence is fulness of joy; at thy right hand there are pleasures for evermore."

Bible Reading
Genesis 39-40 | John 20 | Proverbs 20

Suffering For Doing Right.

1 Peter 3:16-18

"Having a good conscience; that, whereas they speak evil of you, as of evildoers, they may be ashamed that falsely accuse your good conversation in Christ. For it is better, if the will of God be so, that ye suffer for well doing, than for evil doing. For Christ also hath once suffered for sins, the just for the unjust, that he might bring us to God, being put to death in the flesh, but quickened by the Spirit:"

God calls us to be separated, but not isolated. He didn't save us just to give us a home in Heaven. He has a purpose for each and every one of us to fulfill according to His perfect will for our lives. **In striving to carry out that purpose and living for Him, we are going to face opposition.**

2 Timothy 3:12

"Yea, and all that live godly in Christ Jesus shall suffer persecution."

The Apostle Paul faced some of the worst persecution ever recorded. He knew what it was like to be persecuted for Christ's sake. Simon Peter also suffered through opposition. He brought some of it on himself, but can we not all relate with him? This man went so far as to tell Jesus that he would never be offended of him, then Jesus told him what would really happen. Hearing a rooster crow must have never been the same for Peter. While the devil used some fellow townspeople to never let him forget what he did, the Lord Jesus forgot all about it. What if he would have quit after he denied the Lord? Instead, he carried the Gospel to so many people.

If you have been criticized, persecuted and/or opposed in your service for the Lord, you are not alone. Anyone who has ever tried to do something for Christ faces trouble on a routine basis, sometimes even from fellow Christians. Even saved people can allow themselves to be used by the devil to discourage someone who is trying to do right and make a difference.

Take comfort today in remembering how Christ suffered for us, and that nothing we endure while serving Him is worth quitting over. He pressed on through the pain and agony because He had a purpose to fulfill. He made it possible for us to become His children because He loved us enough to die for us and suffer that punishment. *"...the just for the unjust..."*

Press on through the pain, Christian.
Continue in your purpose, for great is our reward!

Bible Reading
Genesis 41-42 | John 21 | Proverbs 21

No Comparison.

Romans 8:18
"For I reckon that the sufferings of this present time are not worthy to be compared with the glory which shall be revealed in us."

Have you wondered if the suffering will ever end?
Are you wondering if your situation will ever change?

The Apostle Paul wondered the same thing, and even prayed repeatedly for God to remove his pain and suffering. Paul is relatable in the fact that his thorn of the flesh remained. His pain never fully went away; but instead of quitting, he pressed on while relying on Christ's grace and strength to get him through. Read 2 Corinthians 12 for the full context of Paul releasing the hold that his thorn had on him.

All of us have some type of thorn that can slow us down in our service and walk with the Lord, if we allow it to do so. It may be physical, emotional, spiritual, or unexplainable; but God knows all about it. He not only knows how it continues to affect you, but He has also allowed it for His purpose.

Be encouraged by our verse today that the sufferings of this present time are only temporary. **When comparing our sufferings to the glory that is to come, there is no comparison.** The part that encourages us the most should be that He will reveal them IN us. Since in us dwelleth no good thing, that can only mean that for the glory to be revealed in us and through us, it has to be all about Him! His power can be magnified through our pain; and, like Paul, we can claim:

2 Corinthians 12:9-10
"And he said unto me, My grace is sufficient for thee: for my strength is made perfect in weakness. Most gladly therefore will I rather glory in my infirmities, that the power of Christ may rest upon me. Therefore I take pleasure in infirmities, in reproaches, in necessities, in persecutions, in distresses for Christ's sake: for when I am weak, then am I strong."

Bible Reading
Genesis 43-44 | Matthew 1 | Proverbs 22

Partakers.

1 Peter 4:12-13
"Beloved, think it not strange concerning the fiery trial which is to try you, as though some strange thing happened unto you: But rejoice, inasmuch as ye are partakers of Christ's sufferings; that, when his glory shall be revealed, ye may by glad also with exceeding joy."

How would you define the word Christian?

A common definition is "a follower of Christ". While this is true, let's break down the word itself: Christ-ian. The "ian" is a suffix with the same meaning and properties as the prior word. So, in our case, **a Christian is someone with the same properties as Christ.** Someone who is like Him. In order to be like Him, we have to partake in His sufferings, which He suffered for us.

Not only can we see His glory revealed in us through our sufferings, but we can also find joy, exceeding joy, amidst the pain.

The fiery trial that is trying you right now isn't just some strange thing that has happened to you. Though it's hard to understand right now, it has been allowed by God, for your good.

Peter goes on to say that though we should be reproached for the name of Christ, we should be happy! Why? Because the Spirit of glory and of God resteth upon us through the trial, and we can give Him glory in it.

1 Peter 4:14
"If ye be reproached for the name of Christ, happy are ye; for the spirit of glory and of God resteth upon you: on their part he is evil spoken of, but on your part he is glorified."

What a testimony for those around us to witness His power!

Bible Reading

Genesis 45-46 | Matthew 2 | Proverbs 23

Stand In The Gap.

Ezekiel 22:30
"And I sought for a man among them, that should make up the hedge, and stand in the gap before me for the land, that I should not destroy it: but I found none."

This prophetical passage is very applicable to the world we live in today. The Lord is still seeking for His people to make up the hedge and stand in the gap to make a difference in the midst of all the turmoil around us.

Which part is more convicting…the plea to stand in the gap for the cause of Christ, or the thought that there is going to come a day when there won't be anyone willing to do so?

In chapter three of 2 Timothy, Paul talks about the apostasy that will be upon the earth in the last days. He mentions how *"men will be lovers of their own selves, covetous, boasters, proud, blasphemers, disobedient to parents, unthankful, unholy, Without natural affection, trucebreakers, false accusers, incontinent, fierce, despisers of those that are good, Traitors, heady, highminded, lovers of pleasure more than lovers of God; Having a form of godliness, but denying the power thereof…"*

The last four words of verse 5 tell us what we should do when those around us are worthy of those descriptions… *"from such turn away."*

God wants us to love the sinner while hating the sin.
He is calling for someone to stand in the gap for the land in which we live.

Jesus Christ Himself referred to such an apostasy in Luke 18 asking, *"Nevertheless when the Son of man cometh, shall he find faith on the earth?"* after He told the parable about the unjust judge.

The adjectives Paul used to describe the apostasy sound very familiar to the society that we live in. Such an apostasy has already begun here in America, and it is even creeping into our churches.

Is there anyone willing to stand in the gap today?

Is there someone who is willing to lose their life so that He may save it, someone who will make a difference for His glory?

May we all consider what we can do to stand in the gap as a witness for Him for the furtherance of the Gospel of Jesus Christ!

Bible Reading
Genesis 47-48 | Matthew 3 | Proverbs 24

Delight In Him.

Psalm 37:4-5
*"Delight thyself also in the LORD; and he shall give thee
the desires of thine heart. Commit thy way unto the LORD;
trust also in him; and he shall bring it to pass."*

This is our theme verse. Many people tend to take verse 4 out of context and adapt it to fit what they want to believe it says…usually it is something like this, "Delight yourself in the Lord, and He will give you what you want." Some of them may have an agenda, and some may just not know any better. Perhaps haven't been taught or taken the initiative to study it out for themselves. When approached in the correct context, these verses can transform your Christian life.

When we delight ourselves in the Lord, we begin to seek Him and give Him His rightful place at the center of every aspect of our lives. God then promises to begin to give us the desires that fit into His perfect will for us. He won't give us what we want, but He will help us want what He wants for us, and what is ultimately best.

Delight: a high degree of pleasure; or satisfaction of mind

In order to *"Delight thyself also in the LORD"*, we must take a high degree of pleasure in the Word of the Lord and the ways of the Lord. Then to take it a step further, have a satisfaction of the mind that only comes from putting our faith and trust in Him, the One Who knows what is best. When we do that, He will begin to give us the desires that fit His will for our lives.

A Definite Act.
A Daily Attitude.
A Divine Accomplishment.

Until we delight ourselves in Him, we will never find His direction. Once we know His will, we still have to commit ourselves to Him in order for Him to make it happen. It is only when we submit to His will that we will ever begin to see His true purpose for the life that He has given us.

Delight in Him today and everyday.

Bible Reading
Genesis 49-50 | Matthew 4 | Proverbs 25

Worship & Obedience.

Genesis 22
"...God did tempt Abraham..." - v.1
"...Take now thy son, thine only son Isaac, whom thou lovest..." - v. 2
"...will go yonder and worship..." - v. 5

If you have never studied the Bible with the law of first mention in mind, you have missed out on some nuggets of the subtle added importance of the Truth. This refers to the first time something is mentioned or referred to within the Scripture.

Obviously this happens a lot in Genesis, but especially in Genesis 22 within the account of God commanding Abraham to take his only son Isaac atop one of the mountains of Moriah and offer him as a burnt offering.

Tempt - *"...God did tempt Abraham..."*
Abraham knew exactly what it meant to offer a burnt offering. I imagine he didn't sleep a wink that night due to the agonizing pictures of Isaac that must have went through his mind. He could have ignored the command, much like we ignore God's commands each day of our lives. He could have slayed someone else's son, but he didn't. Abraham rose up early in the morning after the first God given trial, and he obeyed.

Love - *"...Take now thy son, thine only son Isaac, whom thou lovest..."*
This first mention of love declares Isaac as the only son of Abraham's who God recognized. This is a great type of the love that God the Father has for His Son, Jesus Christ. The Father's love for His Son. Where would we be today if not for the love of the Father for the Son?

Worship - *"...will go yonder and worship..."*
It is interesting that although Abraham knew what the Lord required, he described the process as worship. He was willing to accept the trial, and worship God through the pain. Worship is a word that has been tainted in today's churches. Here, it is none other than Abraham and Isaac bowing themselves in reverence to a thrice holy God. In Abraham's mind, Isaac was already sacrificed, and he must have believed that God would give him back his son, one way or another. Isaac was spared once God saw the great faith that Abraham had in Him, regardless of the cost of the trial.

Bible Reading
Exodus 1-2 | Matthew 5 | Proverbs 26 | 33

Growth.

1 Peter 2:2
*"As newborn babes, desire the sincere milk of the word,
that ye may grow thereby:"*

When speaking of her grandchild, a grandma said, "He hasn't changed, except for growing."

Oh that God could say that about us! That we haven't gotten off His path, that we haven't sat back and refused to be used. That we haven't slid back on our seeking to be more like Him. What if we just grew in the knowledge of our Saviour...

Not many Christians, if any, today could honestly say that they have only grown in the Lord, and not hurt our walk with Him at some point along the way.

Our verse today explains that our desire to grow through the Word should be that of a newborn baby who constantly needs fed milk. The baby desires it. The baby craves it. The baby cries out demanding it. If only we have that same desire about our Bible; the very Words of Almighty God, and most of the time It sits on the shelf or table.

Let's not let the dust settle on our Bible.

"A Bible falling apart usually belongs to someone who isn't."
Charles Spurgeon

Remember this children's song?
Read your Bible, pray every day, pray every day, pray every day…
Read your Bible, pray every day, and you'll grow! Grow! GROW!

Bible Reading
Exodus 3-4 | Matthew 6 | Proverbs 27

Rooted In Him.

Colossians 2:6-7
"As ye have therefore received Christ Jesus the Lord, so walk ye in him: Rooted and built up in him, and stablished in the faith, as ye have been taught, abounding therein with thanksgiving."

Having a desire for the Truth, and learning to grow in the Word is essential for our walk with the Lord. After salvation, that's where it starts.

In order to continue to grow, we must develop our roots.
A plant whose roots are not formed properly will wither away.

Jesus Himself warns of this in the parable of the sower in Matthew 13, Mark 4, & Luke 8. There were those that received the Word with joy, and then when affliction came they vanished. **May we strive to be the seeds that fall on the good ground; receiving the Word, and bringing forth fruit.**

Rooted. The only way to be *"Rooted…in him"* is to be rooted in His Word. Make an effort to grow daily in the Word.

Built Up. What builds us up? His Word. *"And now, brethren, I commend you to God, and to the word of his grace, which is able to build you up…"* Acts 20:32

Stablished. How can our faith be established? *"So then faith cometh by hearing, and hearing by the word of God."* Romans 10:17

When we are rooted...We can grow.

Jeremiah 17:7-8
"Blessed in the man that trusteth in the LORD, and whose hope the LORD is. For he shall be as a tree planted by the waters, and that spreadeth out her roots by the river, and shall not see when heat cometh, but her leaf shall be green; and shall not be careful in the year of drought, neither shall cease from yielding fruit."

The Lord has planted us right where we are.
Focus on being rooted in Him today.

Bible Reading
Exodus 5-6 | Matthew 7 | Proverbs 28

Stand In Awe.

Psalm 4:4-5
"Stand in awe, and sin not:
commune with your own heart upon your bed,
and be still. Selah.
Offer the sacrifices of righteousness,
and put your trust in the LORD."

As we are rooted in Him, we will begin to stand in awe of our Creator, the One Who has made us His children.

At first glance, this verse seems to refer to being speechless at the One that died for us, and spending time with Him in the stillness of our lives. Although that is true, this is one of the many verses that prove the importance of receiving the Word with all readiness of mind, and searching the Scriptures daily.

The phrase *"Stand in awe"* comes from the Hebrew word, *ragaz*, which means to tremble, quake, rage, to be disquieted or excited.

Matthew Henry said that one good remedy against sin is to stand in awe. A holy reverence and fear of the glory and majesty of God Himself, wrapped in a holy dread of the wrath of God will help us to keep ourselves from sin.

Proverbs 1:7
"The fear of the LORD is the beginning of knowledge..."

Proverbs 9:10
"The fear of the LORD is the beginning of wisdom:
and the knowledge of the holy is understanding."

When we begin to apply the fear of the Lord daily, we begin to give God His rightful place in our lives. **Be still, and stand in awe of Him today.**

Bible Reading
Exodus 7 | Matthew 8 | Proverbs 29

The Fear Of The Lord.

Proverbs 1:7
*"The fear of the LORD is the beginning of knowledge:
but fools despise wisdom and instruction."*

The phrase *"the fear of the LORD"* appears 30 times in the Scriptures, and 14 times in the Book of Proverbs alone. It's no wonder that the fear of the Lord is the foundation for wisdom. Let's look at how we can practically apply the fear of the Lord to our lives:

To Find Knowledge
Proverbs 2:4-5
*"If thou seekest her as silver, and searchest for her as for hid treasures;
Then shalt thou understand the fear of the LORD,
and find the knowledge of God."*

When we seek wisdom, we not only begin to understand what it means to fear the Lord; but we also begin to find the knowledge of God.

To Hate Sin
Proverbs 8:13
*"The fear of the LORD is to hate evil: pride, and arrogancy,
and the evil way, and the froward mouth, do I hate."*

When we begin to fear the Lord properly, we will develop a hatred for sin. We can then begin to separate ourselves from sin, and draw nigh to our Saviour.

To Have Confidence
Proverbs 14:26
*"In the fear of the LORD is strong confidence:
and his children shall have a place of refuge."*

Do you find yourself lacking confidence? Fearing the Lord will allow us to remember that within ourselves we are nothing, and can do nothing; but we can do all things through Christ which strengtheneth us!

These are just a few of the simple Truths that we can use in our daily lives through the fear of the Lord. Study out the rest of them. You're sure to find something else to help you live for Him.

Fear the Lord today and every day.

Bible Reading
Exodus 8-9 | Matthew 9 | Proverbs 30

Expect.

Matthew 9:28-29
*"…Jesus saith unto them, Believe ye that I am able to do this?
They said unto him, Yea, Lord. Then touched he their eyes, saying,
According to your faith be it unto you."*

"Dear friends, let us expect that God is going to use us.
Let us have courage, and go forward,
looking to God to do great things."
D.L. Moody

God will meet you at your expectation.

If the blind men had said, "No, we don't believe you are able to open our eyes", would Jesus have healed them? Not "could" Jesus have healed them, because we know He can do anything He sees fit to do. But would he have?

The Bible tells us in Hebrews 11:6 that *"without faith it is impossible to please him…"*. We must believe that He is Who He said He is. We must believe that He is a Rewarder of those that diligently seek Him. Hebrews 11 is filled with people who believed that God could help them in their situation. They sought His power, and He not only met them at their expectation, but He exceeded it. He is the same God today, and He can do the same thing with us and for us.

If we go through life asking God to do something, and then not believe that He can or will, we have greatly failed. God not only wants us to ask Him, He wants us to believe that it will happen.

Do you need something today? Ask Him.
Then believe that He will move in your situation
according to His will for your life.

Do you have a desire to be used of God?
Make yourself available.
Then believe He will use you.

Bible Reading
Exodus 10-11 | Matthew 10 | Proverbs 31

Who Have You Brought?

John 1:40-42

"One of the two which heard John speak, and followed him, was Andrew, Simon Peter's brother. He first findeth his own brother Simon, and saith unto him, We have found the Messias, which is, being interpreted, the Christ. And he brought him to Jesus..."

Andrew was not well known; but he wasn't looking for fame. He was quiet; but he was bold. Andrew was a fisherman who left his nets to follow Jesus and fish for men. Andrew was always referred to as Simon Peter's brother.

As his name means, he was strong and courageous, a warrior; maybe not in word, but definitely in deed. He may not have been known as a great preacher, or written any books, but **he brought people to Jesus.**

The first person Andrew brought to Jesus was his brother, Simon Peter. He brought the preacher of Pentecost to Jesus. Thousands upon thousands came to know the Lord… because **Andrew was a soul winner.**

After hearing of all the miracles that Jesus did, a great multitude began to follow Him. Jesus asked Philip where they could buy some bread to feed the people, knowing that He would be performing a miracle in order to feed 5,000 men plus women and children. Andrew spoke up about a lad that he knew there. He brought the boy, along with his five loaves and two fishes to Jesus, and the rest is Biblical history. From Andrew we can learn the importance of bringing others to Jesus.

Who have you brought to Jesus?

What could Jesus do through you bringing someone to Him?
Only time will tell… our job is to go and tell.

Bible Reading
Exodus 12-13 | Matthew 11 | Psalm 1

Reaction.

Philippians 2:14
"Do all things without murmurings and disputings:"

If we were all honest, we would all say that we struggle with this verse. Those that would disagree need to put their pride aside, and simply admit the truth. This includes the eye-rolls as well as the huffs and puffs that we all have a habit of doing whether we realize it or not. **Our reactions speak volumes about the condition of our hearts.**

This is one of those verses that is easy to just read on past and pretend its not there. Verses 13 & 15 are much more encouraging, aren't they? But verse 14 is just as important, and has been placed there for a purpose. It is just as inspired as the rest of the verses in chapter 2.

In verse 15 we find that we can be blameless, harmless, the sons of God, and without rebuke amidst of a perverse nation. We can shine as lights in this dark world. But in order to do that, we must do all things without murmuring and disputing. That's the conditional part of this promise.

Our flesh gets the best of us more often than not, doesn't it? Our carnality wants to make us roll our eyes when people are asked to help put up the chairs after an activity at church, or when youth workers are needed in the 4 year old class. When your boss asks you to do something that you would rather not, what is your reaction? Whether in the office, the classroom, the post office or the church house… *"Do all things without murmurings and disputings:"*

What if Jesus Christ Himself asked for people to stack chairs after an event? What if He asked for workers in the 4 year old class? People would be lining up to work, and the chairs would have never been stacked up so fast.

But according to Colossians 3:17, we are commanded to do ALL in the name of the Lord Jesus; and not only that, but to be thankful for the opportunity. **If that's not convicting about our murmurings and disputings, few things will ever reach our carnal hearts.**

Words.

Leviticus 11:44
"For I am the LORD your God: ye shall therefore sanctify yourselves, and ye shall be holy; for I am holy: neither shall ye defile yourselves with any manner of creeping thing that creepeth upon the earth."

1 Peter 1:15-16
"But as he which hath called you is holy, so be ye holy in all manner of conversation; Because it is written, Be ye holy; for I am holy."

Not only should we do all things without murmurings or disputings, but we should also be aware of our manner of conversation.

The Word has much to say about the words we speak.

1 Timothy 4:12
"…but be thou an example of the believers, in word, in conversation, in charity, in spirit, in faith, in purity."

James 3:13
"Who is a wise man and endued with knowledge among you? let him shew out of a good conversation his works with meekness of wisdom."

Psalm 19:14
"Let the words of my mouth, and the meditation of my heart, be acceptable in thy sight, O LORD, my strength, and my redeemer."

We've all heard the saying… "If you don't have any thing nice to say, don't say anything at all." **How much trouble could we avoid if we would just keep our thoughts and opinions to ourselves sometimes?**

"A closed mouth gathers no feet."
Unknown

Bible Reading
Exodus 16-17 | Matthew 13 | Psalm 3

Hated.

1 John 3:13
"Marvel not, my brethren, if the world hate you."

John 15:18
"If the world hate you, ye know that it hated me before it hated you."

Have you ever felt hated by this world? Maybe even hated by other Christians? You are not alone. In fact, **Jesus Christ Himself warns us in the Gospel of John that we will be hated by the world because it hated Him first.** We are partakers of this hatred because we follow Him.

Think of all the martyrs that gave their lives for the cause of Christ. Many died so that we could have our Bible today. **God preserved His Word through His people taking a stand amidst the hate and persecution of the world.**

Most of the disciples died at the hands of those that hated them. Peter was crucified, and demanded to be hung upside down because he didn't feel worthy to be crucified in the same form as Jesus gave His life. Andrew, Simon Peter's brother, was also crucified. Luke was hanged on an olive tree. The Romans beheaded Paul. John was thrown into a cauldron of boiling oil, but by miracle he exited without injury. He was the only apostle who escaped a violent death.

William Tyndale, a well-known Bible translator who produced the first translation of the New Testament from Greek to English, after 17 months in a gruesome prison finishing his work, he was strangled and burned at the stake. He is known for praying, "Lord, open the king of England's eyes," at his dying breath.

Christian, take comfort today in the fact that though the world may hate us, we are the called according to His purpose… and because of that He is working it together for our good.

John 16:33
"These things I have spoken unto you, that in me ye might have peace.
In the world ye shall have tribulation: but be of good cheer;
I have overcome the world."

Bible Reading
Exodus 18-19 | Matthew 14 | Psalm 4

Criticism.

Matthew 5:11-12
*"Blessed are ye, when men shall revile you, and persecute you,
and shall say all manner of evil against you falsely, for my sake.
Rejoice, and be exceeding glad: for great is your reward in heaven:
for so persecuted they the prophets which were before you."*

Criticism is disabling.
If you have tried to purposefully do anything,
especially for the cause of Christ, you are sure to have faced it.

One thing that is easy to forget during the course of a critic's attack is that God has allowed it. His sovereignty doesn't disappear while the critic's voice has your mind and ear. **The Lord prepares us for His purpose in our lives, and sometimes, He uses even criticism to mold us into what He would have us to be.** Most of the time, when it seems like criticism is all around you, God is preparing you for a season of growth in your life and ministry.

Take time to pause and discern the criticism you receive. Ask the Lord to help you decide what changes He would have you to make, or for the grace and strength to continue in your purpose despite the critics.

Jesus Christ, our High Priest, was touched with the feelings of our infirmities. He was tempted in all points like as we are, yet He was without sin. Isaiah 53 tells us that *"He was oppressed, and he was afflicted, yet he opened not his mouth…"* **He did not respond to His critics.**

Christ's example shows us that we can endure the hardness of criticism without surrendering to the fight or losing our testimony. Like a soldier, we can press on toward the mark of our high calling and rejoice in our reward with the knowledge that we are more like Christ when we are persecuted.

2 Timothy 2:3-4
*"Thou therefore endure hardness, as a good soldier of Jesus Christ.
No man that warreth entangleth himself with the affairs of this life;
that he may please him who hath chosen him to be a soldier."*

Resolve to rejoice amidst the criticism!

Bible Reading
Exodus 20-21 | Matthew 15 | Psalm 5 | 43

Responding To Critics.

Matthew 5:44
"But I say unto you, Love your enemies, bless them that curse you, do good to them that hate you, and pray for them which despitefully use you, and persecute you;"

Although we cannot avoid criticism, we can learn how to Biblically respond to those who criticize and take advantage of us.

Jesus Christ tells us to…
Love them. Bless them. Do good unto them. Pray for them.

Easier said than done, right? That is because in our flesh dwelleth no good thing, and to love those that hurt us is contrary to our fleshly desires. If we only love those who love us, what reward do we have? As hard as it is, we are to seek to love those who aren't our favorite people.

God sometimes uses the pressure of opposition to teach us the power of prayer. If we take our frustrations and disappointments to Him in prayer, we will have a much better outcome to our situation. When we pray for people, we will treat them differently. When we pray for our critics and those who tend to misuse their relationship with us, we can respond to them with grace.

Not all critics are our enemies. Sometimes our actions and attitudes require our friends to hold us accountable. We learn in Proverbs 27:6, *"Faithful are the wounds of a friend…"* Those who know us best can often see things we don't, and can help us in our efforts and purpose. If you have a friend who helps you see the bright side of things, and encourages you to do right when others fail you, be thankful for them today.

Remember that Christ Himself dealt with criticism and persecution.

Matthew 27:12-14
"And when he was accused of the chief priests and elders, he answered nothing. Then said Pilate unto him, Hearest thou not how many things they witness against thee? And he answered him to never a word; insomuch that the governor marvelled greatly."

He is the Ultimate Example of dealing with critics.

Bible Reading

Exodus 22-23 | Matthew 16 | Psalm 6

Truth & Freedom.

John 8:32
"And ye shall know the truth, and the truth shall make you free."

Have you ever felt chained to something?

Maybe not physically, but perhaps mentally, emotionally or even spiritually. It's easy to let something or someone control us to the point where we are restrained beyond our original desire. Regardless of what has you chained today, you can be released of its hold on you.

You can be free through the Truth!

Those who are addicted to a substance or situation know exactly how it feels to be chained. We are all addicted to something. It may not be alcohol or drugs; but it could be social media, television, the Internet, or even food. We need not judge those who are addicted to a substance, when we ourselves have allowed something else to grab hold of us. **We can obtain the victory over anything or anyone by simply leaning on Jesus Christ to win it for us.** True freedom is found in Him.

I heard an old, old story,
How a Saviour came from glory,
How He gave His life on Calvary
To save a wretch like me;
I heard about His groaning,
Of His precious blood's atoning,
Then I repented of my sins
And won the victory!

O victory in Jesus,
My Saviour, forever.
He sought me and bought me
With His redeeming blood;
He loved me ere I knew Him
And all my love is due Him,
He plunged me to victory,
Beneath the cleansing flood.

Eugene Bartlett, 1939

No matter what struggle we are facing in our lives, we can find victory in Jesus! Search the Truth of His Word today.

Bible Reading
Exodus 24-25 | Matthew 17 | Psalm 7

Disguised Blessings.

Matthew 24:4
*"And Jesus answered and said unto them,
Take heed that no man deceive you."*

The devil may give us what we think we want or need, disguised as a blessing supposedly sent from God. He may arrange the right thing to be given by the wrong person, which opens up the door of compromise. Before you know it, you are knee deep in compromised decisions and doctrine. **None of us are immune to the wiles of the devil.** He wants to distract us, deter us, devour us and destroy us. He can't take our salvation, but it's up to us to protect our testimony.

The devil is depicted by many as a man in a red suit, with horns and a pitchfork. This could not be any further from the truth. **Oftentimes, Satan comes to us wrapped up in exactly everything we ever wanted.** We can learn from the many examples in the Bible of the devil's subtle tactics and Someone's response to him.

Ask Eve. - Genesis 3:6,13
*"And when the woman saw that the tree was good for food, and that it was pleasant to the eyes, and a tree to be desired to make one wise…
The serpent beguiled me, and I did eat."*

Ask David. - 2 Samuel 11:2-3
"…and from the roof he saw a woman washing herself; and the woman was very beautiful to look upon. And David sent and enquired after the woman."

Ask Solomon. - Ecclesiastes 2:9-11
"So I was great, and increased more than all that were before me…And whatsoever mine eyes desired I kept not from them, I withheld not my heart from any joy…Then I looked on all the works that my hands had wrought, and on the labour that I had laboured to do: and, behold, all was vanity and vexation of spirit, and there was no profit under the sun."

Ask Jesus. - Matthew 4:10
"Get thee hence, Satan: for it is written…"

Jesus Christ was tempted by Satan himself, yet without sin.
Protect yourself from being deceived by disguised "blessings".

Bible Reading
Exodus 26-27 | Matthew 18 | Psalm 8

Enmity With God.

James 4:4
*"…know ye not that friendship of the world is enmity with God?
whosoever therefore will be a friend of the world is the enemy of God."*

So many people today, even Christians, are friends of the world not realizing the enormity of their decisions. Our verse tells us plainly that friendship with the world makes us the enemy of God. **It all starts with compromise.**

Ask a substance addict if they became one after their first drink of alcohol or hit of a drug. Ask the adulterer if it began at the first glance at someone else's husband/wife.

Compromise seems innocent at the beginning. It might begin with a friend who seems like they are a good influence. Or maybe even a pastor who changed his viewpoint on something to fit with the times.

Many think that in order to get more people to come to church, we need to lower our standards so that church will be more inviting. This happens everyday by the changing of the Scripture, the compromising of separation, and the choice of songs. Music is often the first thing that is compromised, then separation, and then the Bible.

Compromise is enmity with God.

Let's be careful who we let into our lives,
and be cautious of what they are bringing with them.

Bible Reading
Exodus 28-29 | Matthew 19 | Psalm 9

Investing.

Matthew 6:19-21
*"Lay not up for yourselves treasures upon earth,
where moth and rust doth corrupt, and where thieves break through
and steal: But lay up for yourselves treasures in heaven, where neither
moth nor rust doth corrupt, and where thieves do not break through
nor steal: For where your treasure is, there will your heart be also."*

Wall Street is known for its wealth and investment strategies. Some people work all their lives trying to accumulate goods and riches, only to leave it all behind.

1 Timothy 6:7
*"For we brought nothing into this world,
and it is certain we can carry nothing out."*

As the Lord Jesus put it in our passage today, these people lay up for themselves *"treasures"* that will be corrupted by moths and rust, or stolen by the thieves of this world.

A billionaire who dies without having placed their faith and trust in the Lord Jesus Christ's finished work on Calvary, has only made one real investment… in the Lake of Fire. **The billionaire's rejection of the free gift of God seals his eternity.**

Hebrews 9:27
*"And as it is appointed unto men once to die,
but after this the judgment:"*

Mark 8:36
*"For what shall it profit a man, if he shall gain the whole world,
and lose his own soul?"*

The true wealth of a person isn't made up of their material goods,
but rather what waits in eternity for them.

How are you investing in eternity?

Bible Reading
Exodus 30-31 | Matthew 20 | Psalm 10

Wings Of Trust.

Ruth 2:12
*"The Lord recompense thy work, and a full reward be given thee
of the Lord God of Israel, under whose wings thou art come to trust."*

If you've never seen a mother bird gather her young under her wings, you've missed out on one of the sweetest pictures in creation of the Lord's care for His children. As the mother hovers over her nest of baby birds, she gently swoops each of them closer together so that she may cover them with her feathered wings. She does this to protect and soothe her young within the secret place of her nest.

**The Bible gives us a picture of how we can find safety
beneath the Lord's Wings of Trust.**

Psalm 91:1-4
*"He that dwelleth in the secret place of the most High shall abide
under the shadow of the Almighty. I will say of the Lord, He is my refuge
and my fortress: my God; in him will I trust. Surely he shall deliver thee
from the snare of the fowler, and from the noisome pestilence.
He shall cover thee with his feathers, and under his wings shalt thou trust:
his truth shall be thy shield and buckler."*

The young birds learn to trust their mother as she swoops them into safety
with her wings. They trust in her wings. They trust her.

How has the Lord swooped you
under the shadow of His trusting wings?

Trust Him to carry you through today!

Bible Reading
Exodus 32-33 | Matthew 21 | Psalm 11

1 Peter 5:7
"Casting all your care upon him; for he careth for you."

Do you find yourself burdened down with the cares of this life?

The Apostle Peter, who God used to pin the inspired Words of this passage, speaks from experience. **He had to learn to cast all of his cares into the hands of his Saviour.** When we learn to do the same, we will find the same Truth that Peter did… that He cares of us.

Notice that the verse doesn't say cast some of your cares, or most of your cares upon Him. The small little three-letter word encompasses every single care we have ever had or ever will have…all. This shows us the ability of the One we are to cast our care upon. He is able to bare the load of every burden that we have. We were not designed to carry our own burdens. If you've ever tried to do so, you know that's the truth. **God designed us to cast all of our cares upon Him.**

It's not surprising that God is able and willing to carry our burdens. The amazing part is that in the middle of all of it, despite our weaknesses and failures, He cares for us. **The Creator of this universe cares for us.** There are over 7 billion people in this world, and He cares of you. He knows the very number of hairs on our heads, He cares for us that much. That is beyond amazing.

There is no part of your life or your family's life that God does not care about. His ears are open to our cry, and He is waiting to hear from us.

Cast your care upon Him today.
Cast it ALL!

Bible Reading
Exodus 34-35 | Matthew 22 | Psalm 12

Three Crosses.

John 19:17-18

"And he bearing his cross went forth into a place called the place of a skull, which is called in the Hebrew Golgotha: Where they crucified him, and two other with him, on either side one, and Jesus in the midst."

When driving down the interstate, have you ever noticed the clusters of three crosses sporadically placed on the hillsides, and lit up for all to see in the darkness of the night? **Three wooden crosses.** A white one on either side of a yellow one in the middle. **A reminder of Calvary, and what our Saviour did for the world.**

The story behind the existence of these roadside crosses is touching. A man named Bernard Coffindaffer, of Craigsville, WV, had a vision for the project. He began contacting landowners, and planted the first set in September 1984. His goal was to place this reminder of what Christ has done for us on the Cross of Calvary about every 50 miles on the highways of America. At one point, they crossed 29 states, and were over 2,000 in number.

After Coffindaffer died in October of 1993, the project began to decline and the crosses were not maintained. The Lord then burdened the heart of a lady in Mississippi named Sara Abraham to continue his ministry and vision. Crosses Across America, Inc. was formed in 1999, and currently repairs and maintains the clusters of crosses across America. **These silent, but effective, witnesses stand for Christ on hillsides proclaiming that there is Someone Who loves us.**

What do the three crosses mean to you?

They can be a peaceful reminder of the victory Christ won to set us free. They can remind us that He died for everyone, with no respecter of persons to all who come to Him. They can also remind us of our great responsibility to continue to spread the glorious Gospel of Jesus Christ.

Think of the thousands or millions that pass a cluster of three crosses everyday. Do they realize what they truly mean? **It's our job to tell them.**

Bible Reading
Exodus 36-37 | Matthew 23 | Psalm 13

The Love Of Christ.

Romans 5:8
*"But God commendeth his love toward us, in that,
while we were yet sinners, Christ died for us."*

This is a day when love is celebrated all around us. The love of a spouse or significant other, the love of family and friends are all God-given privileges; and they should be celebrated.

However the Ultimate Example of Love was when *"God so loved the world that he gave his only begotten Son"* to this earth for one purpose…*"that whosoever believeth in Him should not perish, but have everlasting life."*

**The Greatest Love of All should take precedence over
any earthly love that God has blessed us with.**

Few things are worse than seeing someone blatantly reject the Love of Christ and His sacrifice for us. Especially when the person is obviously under conviction, with tears in their eyes, and yet still refuses to trust Him with childlike faith. He is longsuffering and so patient. He isn't willing that any should perish, *"but that all should come to repentance"*.

2 Peter 3:9
*"The Lord is not slack concerning his promise,
as some men count slackness; but is longsuffering to us-ward,
not willing that any should perish,
but that all should come to repentance."*

Having only a head knowledge of what Jesus Christ did for us is so dangerous. We cannot make someone believe what He did for us, but it's up to us to remind them, and pray that God will convict their heart until they trust Him.
**Valentine's Day should ultimately remind us
of God's love and the willing sacrifice of Jesus Christ for us.**

May we use today to share the Love of God with others,
and tell them what Christ did for us.

Bible Reading
Exodus 38-39 | Matthew 24 | Psalm 14

John 6:35
*"And Jesus said unto them, I am the bread of life:
he that cometh to me shall never hunger;
and he that believeth on me shall never thirst."*

Do you find yourself hungered for something that food won't satisfy?

We find in our passage today that Jesus is the Bread of Life. It is great to know that He not only satisfies the hunger of those lost without a Saviour, but He also fills those who come to His Word daily hungry for answers to the problems of life.

When we come to Him, He promises that we will never leave hungry.

There are thousands upon thousands of people in this world today who struggle to find food for their tables. They have a physical need. Praise the Lord for people and churches that see their need and seek to fulfill it. Food pantries and missions offer food to those in need, only requiring for them to show up and ask for it.

Isn't that just like Jesus? He not only sees our need, but He is patiently waiting for us to show up and ask for His help. **His Word is waiting for us to pick up our Bible and find our daily bread.**

Bible Reading
Exodus 40 | Matthew 25 | Psalm 15

Enabled.

1 Timothy 1:12
"And I thank Christ Jesus our Lord, who hath enabled me,
for that he counted me faithful, putting me into the ministry;"

Many missionaries and full-time ministry workers have claimed this as their life or ministry verse. They have chosen to be thankful of their calling and that God has enabled them and counted them faithful enough to serve Him. **When we make ourselves available to be used, we are sure to given opportunity to do so.** We find a great example of this in Isaiah, when the voice of the Lord asked, *"Whom shall I send, and who will go for us?"* Isaiah simply answered, *"Here am I; send me."* He didn't question what was involved he just offered to go.

God wants our availability. He isn't interested in our abilities. We are nothing outside of what God does through us. Countless times in the Scripture we see that He chooses to use the seemingly under-qualified to accomplish His will.

Moses told God he couldn't speak fluently, yet God used him to lead the children of Israel through the wilderness. David was young and ruddy, yet God had him use a slingshot and a stone to slay a giant. Saul was known for persecuting Christians, yet God changed his life and transformed him into the Apostle Paul who He used to pin most of the New Testament.

Whether you are in the ministry or a secular line of work, **God has called us all to be full-time Christians for Him; and He promises to enable us if we will only make ourselves available.** Whatever weakness you think is preventing you from being used by the Lord will be strengthened as you yield yourself to Him so that He can get the glory. For when we are weak, He is strong. Yield yourself to Him, so that He can enable you to be used for His glory.

Thank the Lord today, and every day, for enabling you to do His will.

Compel Them.

Luke 14:23
"And the lord said unto the servant, Go out into the highways and hedges, and compel them to come in, that my house may be filled."

The context of this chapter gives light to what occurs more often today than perhaps ever before. There is a banquet being prepared, to which many of those who have been invited have made excuses of why they cannot or won't attend. Yet, the One preparing the banquet still desires to have His House full, so He commands His servants to go out into the highways and the hedges and compel them to come in. **He wants everyone to be invited.** The servant in this story obeyed, yet there was still room for more…*"for whosoever will"*.

Jesus Christ came down to this earth and gave His life so that all would be able to attend this banquet in the sky. In the last few days He walked this earth, He commanded us to go and tell others the glorious Gospel. **We are to invite others to accept Him regardless of how they respond.** That is our responsibility and our greatest purpose.

How do we compel them? We are to persuade them, but we cannot persuade someone unless we first invite them. If they reject your invitation, don't stop there. You can live your life as an example to them of God's love and how God can change someone's life. Let your testimony set you apart, so that people around you realize that there is something different about you. Then try again to invite them, and attempt to share the Gospel with them. Don't badger, but instead show them the love of Christ by displaying genuine care for them and their eternity.

The best way to compel someone is to share your testimony.

People are often willing to listen to a personal story or experience. Sharing what Jesus Christ did for you personally allows the person to relate and empathize with what you needed or were seeking. Don't be afraid to share your personal experience. It might be just what someone needs to hear to ask more questions or see their need for Jesus.

Let's compel people to come, so that the Lord's house may be filled.

Bible Reading
Leviticus 3-4 | Matthew 27 | Psalm 17

Overlooked.

Matthew 15:34
"And Jesus saith unto them, How many loaves have ye?"

The Feeding of…

Most probably finished that statement with "the 5,000". A familiar and famous passage of Scripture; a miracle. A multitude fed by five loaves of bread and two small fishes. Often in the shadow of this great miracle that Jesus did, a chapter later in Matthew, and two chapters later in Mark, is a similar yet often overlooked event.

Another multitude had gathered and followed Christ as He performed miracles and instructed the people. He again had compassion on them, and refused to send them away hungry. The disciples scoffed at the thought of finding enough bread to feed them within the wilderness. They must have already forgotten the feeding of the five thousand in recent days. Here, the crowd was a little smaller… four thousand men plus women and children. They found seven loaves of bread this time, and only a few fishes. Yet, in the Master's hand it was enough, because He is always enough.

The supply was greater, the people fewer, but it was still nothing short of a miracle. Much like the disputing disciples, **we tend to overlook this miracle and focus on the one of more people with fewer resources.** What a pity that we only focus on the seemingly "bigger" things that God performs in our lives while overlooking the countless ways He continually provided for us every day. **Christian, don't get tunnel vision to only focus on the well-known areas that God is working in.** Take time to realize and stand in wonder at every thing He does for you, and remind yourself to look for His power in every situation. No matter how big or small the matter, He is always in control.

**He does it again and again,
and He'll do it again just when you need it.**

Bible Reading
Leviticus 5-6 | Matthew 28 | Psalm 18

Much Is Required.

Luke 12:48
*"But he that knew not, and did commit things worthy of stripes,
shall be beaten with few stripes. For unto whomsoever much is given,
of him shall be much required: and to whom men have committed much,
of him they will ask the more."*

President John F. Kennedy is known for having misquoted this verse, but he still got the point across…"To whom much is given, much is required."

If God gave us only our salvation through His Son, Jesus Christ, much would be required of us; but to think of all the many undeserved gifts He has given us, **how much more is required of us?** It is our reasonable service to be a living sacrifice for Him.

As children of God, we have been entrusted with so many responsibilities. God wants us to be faithful and manage the things He has blessed us with in a well-pleasing manner. He wants us to be good stewards of our time, our talents, and our treasure.

Have you ever tried to name them one by one, as the hymn says? "Count your many blessings, name them one by one…" Stop and take the time to ponder of all the blessings that you have…it quickly becomes overwhelming.

It's only by God's grace that we have these blessings. **We do not deserve anything.** The only thing we have earned is spending eternity in Hell. But by God's mercy, He loved us so much that He sent Jesus to pay the debt we could not pay.

With all we have been given, God desires us to use those blessings for the furtherance of His kingdom and the Gospel of Jesus Christ. That is what gives Him the glory He so rightfully deserves.

He gave us everything.
We should be thankful He lets us serve Him!

Bible Reading
Leviticus 7-8 | Luke 1 | Psalm 19

Philippians 4:6
"Be careful for nothing; but in every thing by prayer and supplication with thanksgiving let your requests be made known unto God."

When we are troubled with the cares of this life, this is a verse that can help settle our spirits. If you struggle with anxiety or worry, you are not alone. Our flesh wants us to fret over the things that we have no control over. If we will develop the mindset of going to God in every thing, He tells us that we will have nothing to worry about.

He wants us to make our requests made known unto Him.
Ask for confirmation.
Ask for direction.
Ask for permission.
Ask for protection.
Ask for provision.
Ask.

Let your requests be made known unto God today.
He wants to hear from you.

As you make your requests known, be sure to thank Him not only for what He has already done, but also for what He is going to do.

What have you asked Him for today?

What have you thanked Him for today?

Bible Reading
Leviticus 9-10 | Luke 2 | Psalm 20

And God Said...

Genesis 1:3
"And God said, Let there be light: and there was light."

Each of the first six days of creation the first act of God was spoken Word.
"And God said..." - verse 3
"And God said..." - verse 6
"And God said..." - verse 9
"And God said..." - verse 14
"And God said..." - verse 20
"And God said..." - verse 24

The importance of what God has to say, was displayed each day during the Creation week. **Each day that God set out to do something, He first spoke.**

Shouldn't we live the same way? Not listening to what we ourselves have to say, but finding out what God has to say before we begin each day. Unlike the Old Testament patriarchs who lived by faith and waited for God to move or show His Almighty Power in some way, **we have been given the very Words of God Almighty at our fingertips.** We can hold It in our hands, and read with our God-given eyeballs what our Father has for us.

In verse 26, we read *"And God said, Let us make man in our image, after our likeness:"* Notice the plurality in that verse. God the Father wasn't alone when He created all things in six days, otherwise He would have said "Let me make man in my image, after my likeness". The Triune God proves that He is a Trinity just 26 verses into the first chapter of His inspired Word.

The presence of The Triune God was evident in creation. God the Father is clearly represented in this passage. God the Son, Jesus Christ is present as the very Words that God the Father spoke as He created each facet of His creation. God the Holy Spirit is the Active Agent that created all that we see in those first six days of creation.

When God speaks, things happen.

Bible Reading
Leviticus 11-12 | Luke 3 | Psalm 21

Oil For The Light.

Exodus 25:6
"Oil for the light, spices for anointing oil, and for sweet incense,"

Exodus 27:20
"And thou shalt command the children of Israel, that they bring thee pure oil olive beaten for the light, to cause the lamp to burn always."

Within the pages of Scripture, oil is used as a type of the Holy Spirit. With this in mind, we see in our passages today that in order for the light to shine, it must have oil.

We as Christians are called to be Lights for Christ in the darkness of this world.

In order for our Light to shine, we must have the Oil inside of us. **The moment we trusted Christ, the Oil of the Holy Spirit was placed within us to guide us and help shine our Light.** God is glorified when our Lights shine!

Matthew 5:16
"Let your light so shine before men, that they may see your good works, and glorify your Father which is in heaven."

We must daily yield ourselves to the power of the Holy Spirit for it is He who does the convicting. He draws people to Jesus. It is up to us to let our Light shine, so that He can do the work of salvation within a person's heart. Without the Holy Spirit's power, our witness is in vain.

We need Oil for our Light!

Bible Reading
Leviticus 13-14 | Luke 4 | Psalm 22

Hebrews 11:8
*"By faith Abraham, when he was called to go out into a place
which he should after receive for an inheritance, obeyed;
and he went out, not knowing whither he went."*

By faith Abraham obeyed.
There is no record that he questioned God, he simply obeyed.

The Bible tells us in 1 Samuel 15 after Saul and the Israelites disobeyed the Lord of Hosts' command to utterly destroy all that the Amalekites had, that *"to obey is better than sacrifice."* The children of Israel had good intentions; they had planned to use their newly found items to sacrifice unto the Lord. But God didn't want their sacrifice if it meant disobeying Him. He desires obedience from us just as much as He desired it from the Israelites.

In Genesis 22, Abraham was commanded to make a sacrifice. He knew the details of what that entailed. He knew the gruesome reality of a burnt offering; yet, he was willing to take his only son up on that mountain, and lay him on the altar.

When Isaac asked, *"where is the lamb for a burnt offering?"*
Abraham boldly responded, *"God will provide."*

What could the Lord do with us if we had faith like Abraham?

When the Lord impresses something upon your heart, do you question Him? Or do you willingly obey? Abraham rose up early in the morning after he received the command from God. His obedience is for our example.

God wants us to take a step of obedience through faith in Him so that He can work His will for our lives. If we will do God's will today, He promises to reveal His will in the future. He just asks us to trust and obey Him.

Abraham was willing to sacrifice every thing he had in obedience.
God wants our willingness to sacrifice every thing for Him, by faith.

Bible Reading
Leviticus 15-16 | Luke 5 | Psalm 23

Serve Him.

Luke 1:74
"That he would grant unto us, that we being delivered out of the hand of our enemies might serve him without fear,"

One of the worst emotions to have is fear.
Everyone fears something.

It might be an unknown future, a family member's illness, commitment, or even failure. Our flesh wants us to live in fear.

Did you know that God didn't create fear?

2 Timothy 1:7
"For God hath not given us the spirit of fear; but of power, and of love, and of a sound mind."

Instead, He gives us the spirit of power, or love, and of a sound mind. He wants us to live by His power, through His love, and by controlling ourselves through His Word.

He wants us to serve Him without fear.

This is our purpose. He redeemed us by sending His only begotten Son to die on the cross of Calvary, and pay the debt that we could not pay. The grace we have been bestowed through the Gospel of Jesus Christ is given to encourage us to serve Him without fear of what lies ahead.

He wants us to serve Him with boldness.

Regardless of the struggle, He wants us to stand boldly amidst this dark world, proclaiming Christ as the source of our strength.

Hebrews 13:6
"So that we may boldly say, The Lord is my helper, and I will not fear what man shall do unto me."

Don't give in to the fear.
Seek to serve Him today in the midst of the battle you are facing.

Bible Reading
Leviticus 17-18 | Luke 6 | Psalm 24

Every Time.

Isaiah 55:11
*"So shall my word be that goeth forth out of my mouth:
it shall not return unto me void, but it shall accomplish that which I please,
and it shall prosper in the thing whereto I sent it."*

With every Gospel tract that is handed out we have these promises:
"it shall not return unto me void…it shall accomplish…it shall prosper…"

This is not due to the paper on which It is printed, the creative thought behind the theme, or the designer/author of the content. **These promises simply apply because a Gospel tract contains the Word of God.** Every time we quote, write or read the Scriptures, He promises that It will accomplish what He pleases. **Every time.**

A Gospel tract goes through a process before it reaches those It was intended to reach. It must be written while yielded to the Holy Spirit's power. It must be printed and packaged before it reaches the distributor. And ultimately, it must then be given.

God gives the writer the Message. The writer gives the printer the Content. The printer gives the tract to the distributor. Then the distributor gives the Gospel tract to the recipient. Sometimes the initial recipient still isn't the one for which the tract was ultimately intended. A lady who initially receives the tract may not be interested, and throw it on the ground. Someone who picks it up later may read it and see their need for salvation. **God's Word does not return void.** Every time.

What could God do through you distributing the Gospel?
Every tract has a purpose.

Bible Reading
Leviticus 19-20 | Luke 7 | Psalm 25 | 63

Don't Hide It.

2 Corinthians 4:3-4
"But if our gospel be hid, it is hid to them that are lost:
In whom the god of this world hath blinded the minds of them
which believe not, lest the light of the glorious gospel of Christ,
who is the image of God, should shine unto them."

Have you ever tried to look through a set of glasses that were not your correct prescription? Your vision is blurred and out of focus. The details of the things around you are fuzzy and unclear. You are blinded.

Satan, the god of this world, has blinded those who have not received the glorious Gospel of Jesus Christ. He seeks to prevent the Light of the Gospel from shining in this dark world.

Are you hiding the Gospel?
Have you placed a veil over the Light that lives within you?

If we hide our Light for Christ, we let Satan get the victory
instead of allowing the glorious gospel of Christ
to shine into this lost and dying world.

Luke 11:33
"No man, when he hath lighted a candle,
putteth it in a secret place, neither under a bushel,
but on a candlestick, that they which come in may see the light."

Set the Light of your candle on a candlestick for the entire world to see. When we share our Light with others, not only does God get glory, but it also makes the world brighter.

Be a Light to someone today.

Matthew 5:15
"Neither do men light a candle, and put it under a bushel,
but on a candlestick; and it giveth light unto all that are in the house."

Bible Reading
Leviticus 21-22 | Luke 8 | Psalm 26

Steps.

Psalm 37:23
*"The steps of a good man are ordered by the Lord:
and he delighteth in his way."*

Have you ever had a day when you knew without a doubt that God had ordered your steps? **When we acknowledge Him, He will direct our steps.**

After the disastrous attacks of September 11th, 2001 there were many stories that came to light of people that would have been inside the towers of the World Trade Center if Something had not redirected their path. Some had doctor's appointments. Some had flat tires. Some missed their flight or Subway train. Hundreds more people would have been killed on that dreadful day if they had not been delayed or the course of their path had not been altered. God had a purpose for sparing their lives that day. Some may have not yet heard the Gospel. Some may have still had a purpose to carry out.

Perhaps you have had a similar experience where God altered your plans throughout the course of a day in order to spare you from some horrific event. On the flip side, maybe there has been a time that God crossed your paths with someone that needed your assistance or you needed theirs.

The Lord has a way of changing our lives by ordering our paths to cross with people. A spouse, a friend, a family member. One day you were that lost person who needed the Gospel, and the Lord ordered someone's steps to give you the Good News.

Why does the Lord order our steps?
For His glory!

God orders our steps according to His will, and therefore He delights in them. When we submit ourselves to Him, we not only find His will as He directs us, but we cause Him to delight in us.

As we delight in Him, He delights in His children.
Are you asking God to order your steps?

Bible Reading
Leviticus 23-24 | Luke 9 | Psalm 27

Labourers.

Matthew 9:36-38

"But when he saw the multitudes, he was moved with compassion on them, because they fainted, and were scattered abroad, as sheep having no shepherd. Then saith he unto his disciples, The harvest truly is plenteous, but the labourers are few; Pray ye therefore the Lord of the harvest, that he will send forth labourers into his harvest."

Here we see the Lord Jesus Himself commanding His disciples to pray for labourers to be sent into the harvest. At the same time He is speaking to us His children who have been given the Word of God to read this precious command. **He wants us to pray that someone will go and labour for Him.**

Romans 10:14-15a

"How then shall they call on him in whom they have not believed? and how shall they believe in him of whom they have not heard? and how shall they hear without a preacher? And how shall they preach, except they be sent?"

Before the Apostle Paul was sent out from Antioch on his first missionary journey, the people prayed. They had prayed for labourers, and God had answered their prayer through Saul and Barnabas. Paul would become the greatest missionary, outside of the Lord Jesus Christ, to reach the nations with the Gospel.

What would God do, who would He send, if we would only pray for more labourers? How many more nations could be reached? How many more children cared for with the love of Christ?

We may never know this side of heaven what fruit our prayers for labourers has yielded. As we pray, God may burden the heart of the next Charles Spurgeon to once again reach two continents for the Lord's glory. As we pray, He may raise up another soul winner to reach the forgotten peoples who have never heard the Name of Jesus. As we pray, we may also find that God burdens our own hearts to reach others for Him. **We can also be one of the labourers we have prayed that the Lord would send.**

Will you labour for Christ today?
Someone is waiting to hear about Him.

Bible Reading
Leviticus 25-26 | Luke 10 | Psalm 28

An Added Day.

Isaiah 38:2-5

"Then Hezekiah turned his face toward the wall, and prayed unto the Lord, And said, Remember now, O Lord, I beseech thee, how I have walked before thee in truth and with a perfect heart, and have done that which is good in thy sight. And Hezekiah wept sore. Then came the word of the Lord to Isaiah, saying, Go, and say to Hezekiah, Thus saith the Lord, the God of David thy father, I have heard thy prayer, I have seen thy tears: behold, I will add unto thy days fifteen years."

Hezekiah is an example for us to use our days wisely. He was sick unto death, and after he had gotten the news that he was to set his house in order, he begged God to intervene. The Lord heard his prayer and the fervency of his heart, and graciously gave Hezekiah 15 more years to live for Him.

Today, on this extra day on the calendar, the Lord has given us another day to live for and serve Him. What will you do with this "extra" time?

This is a good day to reevaluate our priorities.
What do we put first in our lives? What is our passion and purpose in life?

For some it's their career, their family, their children, their desire to be well known or famous, their need for attention or applause. All of these are temporal things.

Are you redeeming the time that God has given you?
Are you using the bulk of your days to serve Him or to serve yourself?

Let's use February 29th as a jumpstart into having an eternal perspective on how we spend our time and resources. We can use our time to lay up treasures in Heaven, or we can invest ourselves in the things of this world.

Will you regret not having done more for Christ?

Bible Reading
Leviticus 27 | Luke 11 | Psalm 29

Much More.

2 Chronicles 25:9
"And Amaziah said to the man of God, But what shall we do for the hundred talents which I have given to the army of Israel? And the man of God answered, The Lord is able to give thee much more than this."

What are you struggling with today?
What is it that you need?

Maybe only you and God know exactly what it is that you need in your life. Let our verse today encourage you that whatever the need, whatever the struggle, the Lord is able to give you much more than this.

Give it to the Lord today.

Place it in His hands. The hands that hold the world that He created. You don't have to carry those burdens anymore.
Jesus is waiting for you to give them to Him.

Maybe you've tried everything in your power to solve your problem? Let's face it, we've all been there. Have you done all that you can do? Give it to the Lord.

1 Corinthians 2:5
"That your faith should not stand in the wisdom of men, but in the power of God."

Moses saw the Red Sea parted through God's power. David slayed Goliath through God's power. Gideon defeated 120,000 soldiers with just 300 men through God's power. Samuel was given to Hannah through God's power. Elijah prayed the fire down from Heaven through God's power. Mary and Martha saw Lazarus raised from the dead through God's power. Esther saved her people through God's power. Peter walked on water through God's power. **What could you do through God's power?**

These and many others are examples for us of what is possible through God's power. What could He do for you? He is able to give you much more than this. **We need only to ask and have faith in Him.**

Bible Reading
Numbers 1-2 | Luke 12 | Psalm 30

Preserved.

Psalm 12:6-7

"The words of the LORD are pure words: as silver tried in a furnace of earth, purified seven times. Thou shalt keep them, O LORD, thou shalt preserve them from this generation for ever."

Praise the Lord for this promise that He will preserve His Word! Without this promise, we would not have the Word of God today. But thanks be to God that He has continued to preserve and protect the Scriptures so that we can have Them. Many people gave their lives so that we could have our Bible today.

What if you did not have a copy of God's Word?

There are many people across the world that do not have access to their own Bible. In America, we most likely have several Copies, and yet we forsake to open and read It every day. What a pity that is when millions of people are praying for their own copy of God's Word. As we pray for labourers, we should also pray for those who do not have a Bible to receive one.

With the promise that God has preserved His Word, we have even more evidence that there is only one True Word of God. As bookstores and websites contain countless versions, does this not lead to confusion when we seek to find God's preserved and inspired Word?

We find in 1 Corinthians 14:33, *"God is not the author of confusion…"* This tells us that the confusion in the world today over the correct Bible to use did not come from God. The god of this world has blinded the eyes and minds of those that may have a form of godliness, but deny the power thereof. When Satan approached Eve in the garden, his first subtle tactic was to question the very Word of God. He asked Eve, *"Yea, hath God said…"* From the Garden of Eden, the Truth of God's Word has been questioned.

Do you question the Word of God today? Within It's pages you will find the answer to every problem you face. **Seek the Lord through His Word, and thank Him for preserving It throughout the ages so that you could have your own Bible.**

Bible Reading
Numbers 3-4 | Luke 13 | Psalm 31 | 69

For Our Good.

Romans 8:28-31

"And we know that all things work together for good to them that love God, to them who are the called according to his purpose. For whom he did foreknow, he also did predestinate to be conformed to the image of his Son, that he might be the firstborn among many brethren. Moreover whom he did predestinate, them he also called: and whom he called, them he also justified: and whom he justified, them he also glorified. What shall we then say to these things? If God be for us, who can be against us?"

When in the middle of a trial or a period of tribulation, we often forget the truth of this passage of Scripture. **Whatever your struggle, your storm, your valley... God is working it together for your good, and ultimately for His glory.**

If you're focused on the wind and the waves of the storm you are enduring, remember Peter had the courage to walk on the water and he didn't start sinking until he took his eyes off the Master of the Sea. If you will focus your eyes on Him, then you, like Peter, can walk on the water.

Notice that after the Scripture encourages us *"that all things work together for good to them that love God"*, the Lord then reminds us of our progressive transformation through Christ Jesus. God first foreknew us before the foundation of the world. He predestinated us to be conformed to the image of His Son. He then called us to know and serve Him, while He also justified us in His sight. Notice the tense of this verse. We are called, justified, and glorified. In the past tense, this tells us that in the mind of God, He has already allowed those things to take place in us. As He sees us through the blood of His Son, Jesus Christ, we are called, justified, and glorified. Because we are called, justified, and glorified, what can we say?

"If God be for us, who can be against us?"

Remind yourself today that through Christ you are called, justified, and glorified by God. **Because we love God and are called according to his purpose, He is working all things together for our good and for His glory.**

Bible Reading
Numbers 5-6 | Luke 14 | Psalm 32

To Sustain Thee.

1 Kings 17:8-9
*"And the word of the Lord came unto him, saying, Arise, get thee
to Zarephath, which belongeth to Zidon, and dwell there: behold, I have
commanded a widow woman there to sustain thee."*

There were many widows in Israel in the days of Elijah, but unto none of them was he sent except into Zarephath where this simple widowed woman lived with her son. They did not have much. In fact, they had so little that because of the drought that was upon the land, they were down to their last meal. This woman went to gather sticks knowing that she and her son were about to starve to death after they ate their little cake. Yet, as she was gathering the sticks, she heard a man, asking her to fetch him a little water since he was thirsty. She had never met the man, but she kindly went to grant him his request. As she went, he spoke again asking for a morsel of bread in addition to the water. She then explained her situation.

Elijah was a man of such faith that he predicted the three-year drought in the land of Israel. This man would also pray fire and rain down from heaven. **Although he heard the woman's plea due to her situation, he knew that this was the woman that God said He would use to sustain him.** He asked for a cake first, and despite knowing the amount of her supply, the woman gave him a cake first. **God honored her sacrifice.** Throughout the rest of the drought, the woman's barrel of meal and cruse of oil never failed. She, her son, and Elijah were sustained because she did what the Lord asked of her. She did what she could.

What could God do through us if we would only do the simple things He asks us to do?

This widow was not only sustained by the Lord in her meals, but also after her son fell sick and there was no breath left in him. She witnessed a miracle. God used Elijah to heal and revive the child and restored her son unto her.

When we obey the Lord, we too can see Him work miracles in our lives. Whatever your need today, He can supply it. Whatever your hurt, He can heal it. Whatever your storm, He can speak peace in the midst of it.

He can sustain us today to press on through our trial, if only we would put Him first in our lives.

Bible Reading
Numbers 7-8 | Luke 15 | Psalm 33

Reciprocated.

Psalm 18:18-19
*"They prevented me in the day of my calamity:
but the LORD was my stay.
He brought me forth also into a large place;
he delivered me, because he delighted in me."*

Why did the Lord deliver David?
Because He delighted in David.

David didn't earn the Lord's delight by his merit; it was by God's grace. He was a man after God's own heart. He was seeking and delighting himself in the Lord, therefore the Lord delighted also in him.

David's delight was reciprocated.

Psalm 37:4
*"Delight thyself also in the LORD;
and he shall give thee the desires of thine heart."*

Like David, if we delight ourselves in Him,
He will be delighted in us.

Through God's unmerited favor, we can find Him delighting in us as we delight in Him. **Our Saviour reciprocates our delight.**

Delight in Him today,
and remind yourself that He delights in you too.

He will deliver us from the storms of our lives,
because of His delight in us.

Bible Reading
Numbers 9-10 | Luke 16 | Psalm 34

A Threefold Cord.

Ecclesiastes 4:12
*"And if one prevail against him, two shall withstand him;
and a threefold cord is not quickly broken."*

Threads are easily broken. When a thread stands alone, it is not nearly as strong as it can be when it is banded together with other threads to form a rope or cord.

The illustration that Solomon gives us in this chapter of Ecclesiastes shows us what type of relationships the Lord wants us to have. He wants us to have friendship and communion with different people along our journey. He wants us to choose fellowship over isolation. *"Two are better than one…"*

The Lord puts people in our life for a reason. It might be for a short season or a lifetime, but He brings us to certain people right when we need it the most…to fulfill His purpose. A family member, a friend, a coworker, a significant other, a spouse… with the mention of these, faces fill our minds of those that the Lord has brought across our path in one way or another.

In verse 12, we see the illustration for the foundation of any successful relationship: *"…a threefold cord is not quickly broken."* Picture an unbraided rope with three strands… one of the strands represents you; another represents someone that God has placed in your life… that family member, that friend, that significant other. The third strand, Christ, stays in the middle while the other two strands are braided around It. When completed, you would have a much stronger rope than you would if each of the three strands were on their own. **When we wrap our relationships with people around the Lord, we have a threefold cord that is not quickly broken.**

If we put Jesus Christ at the center of every relationship, we will find that our threefold cord is not quickly broken, and that it gives God the glory He deserves.

Bible Reading
Numbers 11-12 | Luke 17 | Psalm 35

The Big Picture.

Proverbs 16:9
"A man's heart deviseth his way:
but the LORD directeth his steps."

Isn't it funny how many times throughout our lives we think we have our life all figured out? The job we will have, the person we will marry, the kids we will raise, the house we will live in, and so on. Too often in our lives, we let our heart's desire guide our way without even consulting the Lord about what He would have us to do.

What does the Bible say about our heart?
Jeremiah 17:9
"The heart is deceitful above all things,
and desperately wicked: who can know it?"

Can you look back over your life and see how the Lord has directed your steps? That person you thought for sure you would marry…they are now off the deep end. That job you wanted…it would have prevented you from doing what God has called you to do. That disappointment you faced… turns out it prepared you for what the Lord knew you would need later in life. **Sometimes the Lord lets us look at our life from the Shepherd's point of view, and allows us to see the big picture that God saw from the beginning.**

What in your life has the Lord directed you away from?
What has He directed you to?

Our flesh often thinks that it knows what we need, and always leads us to destruction. However, if we follow the Lord and His direction for us, we cannot fail. **Resist the temptation to manipulate and plan for the future you think you want or need**. Seek the Lord, and His guidance, while placing your life into His hands. His ways are higher than our ways.

Bible Reading
Numbers 13-14 | Luke 18 | Psalm 36

When God Has Another Plan.

Isaiah 55:8-9

"For my thoughts are not your thoughts, neither are your ways my ways, saith the LORD. For as the heavens are higher than the earth, so are my ways higher than your ways, and my thoughts than your thoughts."

For those times in life when we don't understand why things happen the way they do, may we always remember that His ways and His thoughts are higher than ours.

When we focus on the disappointments, we forget that God is in control. Things may not work out how we had hoped, planned, or prayed for, but God is always working things for our good!

Imagine what Joseph must have thought when he was forsaken by his brothers and cast into a pit. He then ended up being sold, working for Potiphar, and then cast into a prison. Those dark times weren't what Joseph had planned, but God was working things for his good.

When God has another plan…
We can walk in faith, believing He knows what is best for us.
We can trust Him despite our confusion.
We can rest in His sufficient grace.
Amy Shellem, Daryl Williams

Our circumstances may be dark and lonely,
but God has another plan.

Like Joseph, God is using the difficulties we are facing today
to one day bring us to a palace of our own, whether here or in Heaven.

Trust the Lord today, and remember
that His ways and His thoughts are higher than ours.

Bible Reading
Numbers 15-16 | Luke 19 | Psalm 37 | 75

Comfort.

2 Corinthians 1:3-5
*"Blessed be God, even the Father of our Lord Jesus Christ,
the Father of mercies, and the God of all comfort; Who comforteth us
in all our tribulation, that we may be able to comfort them which are in any
trouble, by the comfort wherewith we ourselves are comforted of God.
For as the sufferings of Christ abound in us, so our consolation
also aboundeth by Christ."*

Are you hurting today?
We serve the God of all comfort.

Comfort: to give strength and hope; to ease the grief or trouble

Then if we serve the God of all comfort, and we do, this tells us that He is able to give us strength and hope when we need it the most. **He is able to ease our grief and make our troubles cease.**

Have you ever wrapped a comforter around you on a dark and cold night? The warmth and relaxation provided by that quilt as it wraps around you helps us forget how cold and dark it is outside. **When we allow God to comfort us, He will wrap His loving arms around us, providing strength to make it through the storms of life.**

No matter what you are dealing with today: confusion, sadness, persecution, oppression, trouble, etc. **God is willing and able to comfort you.** He allows us to suffer so that we may be partakers of Christ's sufferings, and comforts us so that we may have peace and comfort others.

John 16:33
*"These things I have spoken unto you,
that in me ye might have peace. In the world ye shall have tribulation:
but be of good cheer; I have overcome the world."*

Bible Reading
Numbers 17-18 | Luke 20 | Psalm 38

Temporary.

2 Corinthians 4:17-18
"For our light affliction, which is but for a moment, worketh for us a far more exceeding and eternal weight of glory; While we look not at the things which are seen, but at the things which are not seen: for the things which are seen are temporal; but the things which are not seen are eternal."

Though the weight you are carrying today may seem very heavy and nearly unmovable, the Apostle Paul describes our affliction as *"light"*. You may feel that the battle you are facing today is anything but light! The Lord understands that feeling, but thankfully the verse does not stop there.

The next phrase reminds us that though we are afflicted, it is *"but for a moment"*. **Our battle is temporary!** Not only is it temporary, but it is also promised to work *"for us a far more exceeding and eternal weight of glory".*

The load we carry in our daily lives cannot compare to the glory that it will bring Him in eternity. The circumstances we see around us are temporary, but thanks be to God that those unseen things He provides for us are eternal!

Be encouraged today
that no matter what you are facing,
it is temporary.

Our time is running short,
and our Lord will soon be coming for us in the air!

1 Corinthians 15:52
*"In a moment, in the twinkling of an eye, at the last trump:
for the trumpet shall sound, and the dead shall be raised incorruptible,
and we shall be changed."*

Bible Reading
Numbers 19-20 | Luke 21 | Psalm 39

Philippians 2:3
*"Let nothing be done through strife or vainglory;
but in lowliness of mind let each esteem other better than themselves."*

One of the most convicting verses in the Bible.

Though our thoughts become our actions towards others, **God knows our thoughts even if we do not put them into action.** His thoughts are certainly higher than ours, but how many of our thoughts are contrary to this verse? Convicting isn't it?

"lowliness of mind"
How lowly are your thoughts?

"let each esteem other better than themselves."
This does not mean to simply focus on our weaknesses and call ourselves "humble". Instead of focusing on our strengths & weaknesses, God wants us to realize other people's strengths. **True humility is not focusing on yourself at all, but rather in seeing other people's needs and experiences.**

As convicting as this verse can be, it can become overwhelming when we realize the context of this passage. The first four verses of this chapter set up the context, which is brought forth in verse 5: *"Let this mind be in you…"* Whose mind? *"…which was also in Christ Jesus:"*

May our thoughts and minds be more like Christ Jesus today.

An Alabaster Box.

Mark 14:8
*"She hath done what she could:
she is come aforehand to anoint my body to the burying."*

Have you ever met one of those women who may not have had much, but whatever she had she gave to the Lord for His glory?

I have been privileged to know several. One who always stands out was my grandmother. Nanny didn't have much, but **she did what she could.** She was a preacher's wife, a godly mother, and an active church member with a loving heart for people. **Everything she did pointed people to Jesus.**

She reminded me of Mary of Bethany, Lazarus' sister, who had an alabaster box of ointment. **She didn't have much, but she used what she had to honor and glorify the Lord.** Her sacrifice caught the attention of the people around her, many of whom murmured against her.

Can you relate with Mary today? Perhaps you have given what little you have to the Lord in His service only to have people murmur and complain about your sacrifice. Remember what Jesus said as He rebuked the complainers: *"Let her alone; why trouble ye her? she hath wrought a good work on me."*

If you are doing a good work for the Lord,
don't let the opinions, suggestions, and complaints of others stop you.

Continue to use your alabaster box for the Lord's glory.

Mark 14:9
"Verily I say unto you, Wheresoever this gospel shall be preached throughout the whole world, this also that she hath done shall be spoken of for a memorial of her."

Bible Reading
Numbers 23-24 | Luke 23 | Psalm 41 | 79

Remove The Wood.

Proverbs 26:20
"Where no wood is, there the fire goeth out:
so where there is no talebearer, the strife ceaseth."

Do you have a friend that you trust enough to tell them anything? They are rare. If you are blessed to have one or a few, be thankful for them today.

Trustworthiness in a friendship is irreplaceable and needful.
Praise the Lord for faithful friends!

A talebearer is one who bears tales. The word in the Hebrew means to cause to walk. So we can see that a talebearer causes the tales that they choose to bear to have feet and move about to anyone who is willing to listen.

The best motivation to not be a talebearer is to consider someone bearing your tales. You would want your friend to remove the wood from the fire so that it goes out. Following the golden rule then, **let's not add wood to the fires of the tongues of others**; instead, cause the fire and strife to cease by removing the wood.

We read in James *"the tongue is a fire, a world of iniquity".* When we run our mouths about the latest drama or let negativity fill our words, we add fuel to a fire the Lord is not pleased with. Someone must decide to stop the fire of our words. Be that person. Be a firefighter.

It's hard to control our tongues sometimes. isn't it? With the Lord's help we can achieve it. **Ask Him to help you today not only to control your tongue, but also to help remove the wood from the fires of the talebearers around you.**

Proverbs 11:13
"A talebearer revealeth secrets: but he that is
of a faithful spirit concealeth the matter."

Bible Reading
Numbers 25-26 | Luke 24 | Psalm 42

Rewarded.

Hebrews 11:6
*"But without faith it is impossible to please him:
for he that cometh to God must believe that he is,
and that he is a rewarder of them that diligently seek him."*

We all want to please God, and in order to please Him we must have faith.

Faith on the mountain and in the valley.
Faith in the middle of the storm and in the darkness of doubt.
Faith despite our fears.
Faith for His provision and protection.
Faith for His direction.
Faith.

At the beginning of Hebrews 11, we find that *"faith is the substance of things hoped for, the evidence of things not seen."* We are to have complete trust and confidence that despite our circumstances or desires, God will always do what is right according to His will for our lives.

When we have faith and are diligently seeking Him in all we do, He will reward us. The Creator of the Universe wants to reward you. The King of Kings and Lord of Lords wants to bless your life as you seek His direction.

How will the Lord reward us?
Psalm 103:4
John 14:1-3
James 1:12
1 Corinthians 3:13-14

The Lord has many rewards for us if we will only trust, seek and obey Him. These rewards are not for us to display inside our mansions, but rather for us to cast at our Saviour's feet. What a glorious day that will be, when our Jesus we shall see, and we look upon His face, the One who saved us by His grace!

Let us work for Him so that we may obtain our rewards to lay before His throne. He is worthy to receive glory, honour and power!

Bible Reading
Numbers 27-28 | Mark 1 | Psalm 43

Conditional Blessings.

Hebrews 10:35-36
"Cast not away therefore your confidence, which hath great recompence of reward. For ye have need of patience, that, after ye have done the will of God, ye might receive the promise."

God wants us to receive His promises. He is waiting with open arms to dispense the rewards He has for us, but oftentimes there are conditions to receiving them.

These conditional blessings are when the Lord promises us a blessing after a requirement is made. These conditions are not impossible standards, but rather simple steps of faith that unveil vast promises from God The Father. When God promises something, He always keeps His Word.

The Bible is full of conditional blessings.

Proverbs 3:6
Condition: *"In all thy ways acknowledge him..."*
Blessing: *"...and he shall direct thy paths."*

Acts 16:31
Condition: *"...Believe on the Lord Jesus Christ…"*
Blessing: *"...and thou shalt be saved..."*

Here in Hebrews we find that after we have done the will of God, we will receive the promise. Did you notice what God requires us to have before we do the will of God? We have need of patience.

Oftentimes, even when we are energetically impatient to do something for the Lord, He has us to wait. We may get anxious to serve Him, excited to make a difference. While this excitement is encouraging, **God sometimes uses the waiting periods of our lives to cause us to grow in the grace and knowledge of Him** in ways that we could not if it were not for the apparent "delay" in His will for our life. God is never late. **He is always on time.** We are the impatient ones, even when we are sensing God's leading and wanting to see the end result on our timetable.

If you are waiting for direction, keep seeking Him through His Word. The Bible will be a lamp unto your feet and a light unto your path. Acknowledge Him, and He will direct your paths today.

Search the Scriptures today for conditional blessings.
See what God has promised us if we will simply obey Him.

Bible Reading
Numbers 29-30 | Mark 2 | Psalm 44

Stand On His Promises.

Romans 4:20-21
"He staggered not at the promise of God through unbelief; but was strong in faith, giving glory to God; And being fully persuaded that, what he had promised, he was able also to perform."

Abraham, against hope, believed in hope. He staggered not. He considered not his own body, which was about an hundred years old. It did not matter to Abraham what his body was telling him; He believed God's promise. He did not consider the deadness of Sarah's womb. God had promised that he would be the father of many nations. He did not question God or His methods. He simply believed God at His Word.

Although He believed that God would do what He said He would, Abraham got ahead of God. He wanted God's promise to be fulfilled so much so that he took matters into his own hands. He thought he needed to help God carry out His plan. Can you relate to him today?

Have you ever gone ahead of the will of the Lord? You had good intentions, but in trying to fulfill God's plan you ended up making a mess of the situation. Thankfully, we can have hope because God didn't leave Abraham in his mess. He didn't even acknowledge his error. He recognized Isaac as Abraham's only son. God can look past your mistakes, and make a miracle out of your life.

What has God promised you?

"…the LORD thy God is with thee whithersoever thou goest." Joshua 1:9
"I will instruct thee and teach thee in the way which thou shalt go: I will guide thee with mine eye." Psalm 32:8
"Come unto me…and I will give you rest." Matthew 11:28
"…I will never leave thee, nor forsake thee." Hebrews 13:5

Be strong in faith today and take God at His Word.
Give Him the glory for what He has done, is doing, and what He will do!

Standing on His promises we cannot fall.
Stand on His promises today!

Bible Reading
Numbers 31-32 | Mark 3 | Psalm 45 | 83

Lost & Found.

Matthew 16:24-25
*"Then said Jesus unto his disciples, If any man will come after me,
let him deny himself, and take up his cross, and follow me.
For whosoever will save his life shall lose it: and whosoever
will lose his life for my sake shall find it."*

Remember Achan? He took of the accursed thing, and hid it in the earth within his tent. He thought that he could save his stolen treasure. The Lord made Achan's sin known among the people. Joshua's messengers took him, his treasure, his children, and his animals to the valley of Achor. Achan had troubled all the children of Israel by his hidden sin. He ended up being stoned by all of Israel, burned with fire, and then stoned again. **He lost his life because he tried to save it.**

By holding on to things or people in our life, we are saving them only to lose them. When we give the things we love the most to the Lord, He will work as only He can and lead us to His perfect will. What are you holding on to today? Let go of it! Let go of your relationships, your career, your children, your future, etc. **Let God have your life. You will not regret it.**

It is completely against our human nature to let go of our control on the situations of our life. It isn't easy, but when we give God our life He promises we shall find exactly what He desires for us.

True victory and success can only come from our submission to the Lord.

When we lose our life for Christ's sake, we find more than we ever had before. **A life worth living is only found through taking up our cross and following Jesus.** He can take your life and mold it into something new.

Bible Reading

Numbers 33-34 | Mark 4 | Psalm 46

The Plot.

Mark 14:1-2
"After two days was the feast of the passover, and of unleavened bread: and the chief priests and the scribes sought how they might take him by craft, and put him to death. But they said, Not on the feast day, lest there be an uproar of the people."

In the days before Easter, let us take the next few days to get a glimpse of some of the events that transpired before the Easter weekend that made it possible for our eternity to be changed.

Nearing the feast of the Passover, the religious leaders plotted and schemed of how they might kill the Lord Jesus Christ. This was right before Mary of Bethany worshipped her Lord by breaking her box and pouring the ointment of spikenard upon His head.

Possessed by Satan, Judas Iscariot seeks out the chief priests to betray Christ. He had followed Him, he had served along side of Him, and yet he traded his relationship with Jesus Christ Himself for 30 pieces of silver. He sold out. Judas had already talked with the priests before the Passover in the upper room. Christ sat down with His eleven disciples and the betrayer himself.

The world we live in today is similar to that of what Jesus and His disciples faced. **Religious oppression and persecution is becoming more rampant with each day that passes.** The Name of Jesus is not popular. What was once considered right is now considered wrong, and vice versa.

Isaiah 5:20
"Woe unto them that call evil good, and good evil; that put darkness for light, and light for darkness; that put bitter for sweet, and sweet for bitter!"

The devil uses many tactics to distract and deter from the truth. He wants to keep people in the dark. The world is getting used to the dark, and they like it. The Bible even warns us of their love of darkness, and their hate of the Light. The darkness of this world gives us, as Christians, the opportunity to let our lights shine for Jesus Christ so that others may see.

The darker it gets, the more effective a few lights can be!

Bible Reading
Numbers 35-36 | Mark 5 | Psalm 47 | 85

The Colt.

Luke 19:32-35
"And they that were sent went their way, and found even as he had said unto them. And as they were loosing the colt, the owners thereof said unto them, Why loose ye the colt? And they said, The Lord hath need of him. And they brought him to Jesus: and they cast their garments upon the colt, and they set Jesus thereon."

The Lord Jesus was near Bethany again at the Mount of Olives. He sent two of His disciples into the village to fetch a colt. He warned the disciples that people would question what they were doing, and even told them what to say in response. *"The Lord hath need of him."*

The disciples were not aware of why the Lord needed him. **They did not question the Lord or His methods… they simply obeyed.**

Matthew 21:6
"And the disciples went, and did as Jesus commanded them"

When they arrived in the village, they found the colt tied up exactly how Christ said. No one had ever sat upon that colt. It was preordained to be used for the triumphal entry of Christ into Jerusalem.

The Lord sends us on our way, searching for those in need of Him. Perhaps for those that have never heard of Jesus. The people around us may question us, but we should not let that stop us from our mission. Like the disciples brought the colt, we can bring people to Jesus by obeying the Lord's commands.

The phrase *"brought him to Jesus"* appears one other time in Scripture, referring to Andrew bringing his brother, Simon Peter, to the Saviour. Andrew was a soul winner. He brought people to Jesus.

Read His Word today and search for what He would have you to do.
Then simply obey and you can bring people to Jesus!

Bible Reading
Deuteronomy 1-2 | Mark 6 | Psalm 48

The Triumphal Entry.

John 12:12-13

"On the next day much people that were come to the feast, when they heard that Jesus was coming to Jerusalem, Took branches of palm trees, and went forth to meet him, and cried, Hosanna: Blessed is the King of Israel that cometh in the name of the Lord."

The Lord Jesus sat upon the colt that the disciples had fetched Him, and began to ride toward Jerusalem. As He came near the city, can you imagine what He saw?

A multitude of people had created a path. The people's clothes were on the ground and palm tree branches were being waved. The people shouted *"Hosanna to the son of David: Blessed is he that cometh in the name of the Lord; Hosanna in the highest."*

The crowd shouted in an exclamation of adoration.
They prepared a parade for His entry into Jerusalem.

They had much respect for the Messiah.

What about us today?
Do we shout in adoration to Him?
Do we prepare for His arrival in our church services?
Do we prepare for Him to move in our lives?
Do we respect the Saviour as the people did that day?

**Take some extra time to remember what
this coming Easter week means to you.**

Easter is not about the hiding of eggs or the receiving of candy.
Teach your children the real reason for Easter.
For Christ is the Reason for the Season.

Bible Reading
Deuteronomy 3-4 | Mark 7 | Psalm 49

The Rejection.

Isaiah 53:3-4

"He is despised and rejected of men; a man of sorrows, and acquainted with grief: and we hid as it were our faces from him; he was despised, and we esteemed him not. Surely he hath borne our griefs, and carried our sorrows: yet we did esteem him stricken, smitten of God, and afflicted."

In Isaiah 53, we find the Gospel of Christ prophesied in the Old Testament. What better time to read and study this chapter than the beginning of the Easter week.

Christ was despised and rejected of men, a Man of sorrows.
Jesus was acquainted with grief.

It was our sin that caused Him to be despised and rejected.
Our sin gave Him sorrow upon sorrows.
Our sin caused Him to be acquainted with grief.
Our sin.

Yet today, people still reject Him and hide their faces from Him. The lost hide from Him. The convicted reject Him. Even the Christian has a tendency to hide from Him when they sense He is asking them to do something.

Are you hiding today?
What has He given you to do for Him?
Are you rejecting His leading?

He bore our griefs and carried our sorrows. He did this so that we could have eternal life with Him in Heaven. Isaiah 53 paints a picture of the enormity of the crucifixion and the display of God's love for us. Read it today, and remind yourself what Christ suffered on the cross for your sin. Begin this week leading up to Easter with the mindset of remembering His sacrifice for us.

**If the Lord has burdened your heart toward serving Him,
take up your cross and follow Him today.**

Bible Reading
Deuteronomy 5-6 | Mark 8 | Psalm 50

The Iniquity.

Isaiah 53:5-6
*"But he was wounded for our transgressions,
he was bruised for our iniquities: the chastisement of our peace was
upon him; and with his stripes we are healed. All we like sheep have gone
astray; we have turned every one to his own way;
and the LORD hath laid on him the iniquity of us all."*

His wounds, His bruises, His stripes.
Our transgressions, our iniquities.
Our sin made the crown of thorns.
Our sin caused the scourging.
Our sin drove the nails in His hands and feet.
Our sin caused the spear to pierce His side.

Our sin.
But because of His stripes we are healed.

His suffering was sacrificial and substitutionary.
He gave Himself as the sacrifice. He took our place.

The reason we can have peace today is because the penalty of our sin was purged that day on the cross of Calvary. The weight of our sin was upon Jesus Christ. He bore our judgment. He paid our debt. We can be healed from our sin by believing in the payment He made on the cross outside the gate of Jerusalem at the Place of the Skull. If you travel to Jerusalem today, you can still see the skull face within that hillside.

Reflect today on His wounds, His bruises, and His stripes
that He endured because of our iniquity.

We put Him there, but the amazing thing about it all is that He willingly took our place. He did not have to die for us, but He knew it was the only way to save us.

If you are a sheep that has gone astray, come back to Him today. He is waiting for you with His arms wide open just like they were when He died on Calvary. **Run to Him today.**

Bible Reading
Deuteronomy 7-8 | Mark 9 | Psalm 51

The Submission.

Luke 22:42-44

"Saying, Father, if thou be willing, remove this cup from me: nevertheless not my will, but thine, be done. And there appeared an angel unto him from heaven, strengthening him. And being in an agony he prayed more earnestly: and his sweat was as it were great drops of blood falling down to the ground."

Have you ever asked God to remove something? Most likely we all have. Did you ask Him to do so only if it was His will? When we are in pain, whether physical, emotional, or spiritual, our flesh wants it to end.

The Lord Jesus Christ felt the same way.

He asked God the Father, if He was willing, to remove Him from the suffering. He could have stopped there. He could have decided not to go any further in His mission…but He did not. Look at the next word… *"nevertheless".*

What an example the Saviour sets for us… Jesus dismissed His own will.
"nevertheless not my will, but thine, be done."

It's interesting to see that after the Saviour once again submits to the will of the Father, an angel comes to strengthen Him. God gave Him the strength to fulfill the will of God. **When we submit our own will to God's will, He will strengthen us!**

Christ then proceeded to pray earnestly in the Garden of Gethsemane. He prayed and agonized so much so that He began to sweat drops of blood. This is a very rare medical condition called hematohidrosis. The capillary blood vessels that fed Jesus' sweat glands ruptured. This caused His blood to exude out of His pores. This condition only occurs under conditions of extreme physical or emotional stress. That is how fervently and earnestly Jesus Christ prayed for us before He gave His life for our sins on the Cross of Calvary. Most likely none of us have ever prayed so hard that we sweat blood. But Jesus loved us so much that He prayed to His Father, and our Father, with extreme focus. **No matter what you are facing today, Jesus shows us what it means to submit to the will of God.**

Ask the Lord today to remove and resolve your situation IF it is His will to do so. Then follow Jesus Christ's example…*"nevertheless not my will, but thine, be done."*

Bible Reading
Deuteronomy 9-10 | Mark 10 | Psalm 52

The Cross.

Luke 23:33-34

"And when they were come to the place, which is called Calvary, there they crucified him, and the malefactors, one on the right hand, and the other on the left. Then said Jesus, Father, forgive them; for they know not what they do. And they parted his raiment, and cast lots."

We read in Genesis that God created the earth in six days. God created every ocean, every river, every mountain, and every hill.

Just outside the gate of Jerusalem there is a hillside. On the side of that hill, even today, there is a visible face of a skull. God created that hill, just like any other hill across the entire earth. Yet God, in His foreknowledge, knew that this hill, Golgotha, was unlike any other hill He ever created. This was Calvary, the hill that He would see His only begotten Son give His life on. **Jesus Christ freely gave His life on the cross so that we could receive the free gift of salvation through faith in His blood.**

The cross that Jesus was lifted up on stood between two thieves. Of the three men on Calvary that day, only two were guilty. Each of the guilty malefactors went in separate directions after their death on their crosses. The world today is full of guilty sinners that have to make the same choice those two thieves made… whether to believe in who Jesus was and what Jesus did, or pay the debt themselves.

Jesus looked down on those that surrounded His cross and He did not condemn them… He prayed for them. *"Father, forgive them; for they know not what they do."* Jesus had compassion even on those who took part in His crucifixion. However the acts of the chief priests, Pharisees, and soldiers that were there that day did not place Jesus on the cross. **Our sin placed Him there.** Our sin was placed upon Him, and because our sin was purged that day through His blood, we can have peace with God if we will only believe.

Take a moment today and reflect on Calvary, the cross, and the crucified Saviour that took our place. **Thank Him for His sacrifice and for making it possible for us to spend eternity in Heaven with Him.**

Bible Reading
Deuteronomy 11-12 | Mark 11 | Psalm 53

The Substitution.

John 19:30
"When Jesus therefore had received the vinegar, he said, It is finished: and he bowed his head, and gave up the ghost."

It was finished. Jesus Christ the Lamb of God had given His life for the sins of the world. They did not take His life; He gave it. It is important to remember that. He was the Word made flesh with a free will just like us. He made the choice to be born to die. **He took our place.**

2 Corinthians 5:21
"For he hath made him to be sin for us, who knew no sin; that we might be made the righteousness of God in him."

1 Peter 3:18
"For Christ also hath once suffered for sins, the just for the unjust, that he might bring us to God, being put to death in the flesh, but quickened by the Spirit:"

Christ's death on the cross was the substitutionary atonement for our sin. He paid the price that we can only pay ourselves by spending eternity in Hell, separated from Him forever. Either we accept Christ's payment, and believe in what He did for us, or we accept our punishment in the Lake of Fire. It's a choice that every person must make - to receive Him or reject Him. **Have you made that choice?** If not, please read about the Free Gift that is waiting for you.

If you have received the Free Gift of salvation…take a moment today and every day to thank the Lord Jesus Christ for dying on the cross for our sins.

Thank God for the sending His Son to take our place.

I should have been crucified,
I should have suffered and died.
I should have hung on the cross in disgrace,
But Jesus, God's Son, took my place.
Gordon Jensen - "I Should Have Been Crucified"

Bible Reading
Deuteronomy 13-14 | Mark 12 | Psalm 54

The Napkin.

John 20:7
"And the napkin, that was about his head, not lying with the linen clothes, but wrapped together in a place by itself."

This napkin was placed upon the face of the Lord Jesus Christ after He had given up the ghost on the cross, and His body was placed in the new tomb of Joseph of Arimathaea.

When Mary Magdalene, Peter, and John each arrived at the sepulchre, they each saw the empty grave where Jesus had been for three days. The men ran toward the tomb and, before going in, John stooped down outside the grave. Can you imagine how overwhelmed he was? Known as the disciple whom Jesus loved, John had a very close relationship with Christ. He was the one the Lord trusted enough to give the responsibility of caring for His mother, Mary.

Peter ran in and saw the linen clothes; the ones that had been wrapped around Jesus' body, both at His birth and His death. The swaddling clothes He was wrapped in as a baby signified the purpose for which He came…to give His life as a ransom for many.

Set apart from the linen clothes lied a napkin folded nice and neat. What did this signify? **He was not finished!**

The price paid for the sin of the world was finished, Jesus had completed His purpose that God had ordained before the foundation of the world. He had given His life, and raised victoriously three days later defeating death, hell and the grave! But He left His napkin folded neatly in His tomb to show that He is coming back! Very soon He will return and meet His bride, the church, in the air…*"and so shall we ever be with the Lord."*

He is coming back… are you ready?

The Empty Tomb.

Matthew 28:6
*"He is not here: for he is risen, as he said.
Come, see the place where the Lord lay."*

Outside the city walls of Jerusalem, near a hill called Calvary, there is a garden. In the depths of that garden there is a tomb. This tomb was hewn out in a rock, and never had a body ever decayed within its walls.

Joseph of Arimathaea begged Pilate for the body of Jesus and wrapped it in linen clothes before placing Him within his new tomb. Did he believe that Jesus would rise again as He said He would? He was a disciple of Jesus, but the Scripture is silent of his thoughts about Jesus after he placed His body in the tomb. Christ, Himself, told how He would be placed in the tomb for three days in Matthew 12:40.

**Not only did Jesus foretell of His death and burial,
He prophesied of His resurrection.**

Matthew 20:17-19
"And Jesus going up to Jerusalem took the twelve disciples apart in the way, and said unto them, Behold, we go up to Jerusalem; and the Son of man shall be betrayed unto the chief priests and unto the scribes, and they shall condemn him to death, And shall deliver him to the Gentiles to mock, and to scourge, and to crucify him: and the third day he shall rise again."

Praise God that Jesus was Who He said He was! He died for our sins, spent three days and three nights in the tomb, and then raised victoriously on the third day defeating death, hell, and the grave. **His resurrection made the Gospel possible!** Without the resurrection, our faith would be in vain. His resurrection provided us the free gift of salvation, if we would only believe.

Crowds of people gather daily at the Garden Tomb outside of Jerusalem, longing to see the fact that Christ is not in that grave. Some come searching for answers to believe, but many come already knowing the answer, *"He is not here: for he is risen".*

We set aside a weekend every year to celebrate His sacrifice and resurrection, and we should, but the truth is…the Monday after Easter, He is STILL our Risen Saviour!

Every day is Easter.
Hallelujah for our Risen Saviour!

Bible Reading
Deuteronomy 17-18 | Mark 14 | Psalm 56

The Commission.

Mark 16:15
*"And he said unto them, Go ye into all the world,
and preach the gospel to every creature."*

The 7 Sectors of the Great Commission:

Go. A verb. A verb requires action to take place. Go simply means to move from one place to another, to leave, to travel. **Who should go?**

Ye. Who was He talking to? His followers. Are you a follower of Christ today? Do you profess to be a Christian - a follower of Christ? Then this applies to you just as much as it did to those who heard the words from the very lips of the risen Saviour. **How are you involved in the Great Commission?**

Into. A preposition, meaning to express movement or action with the result that someone or something becomes enclosed or surrounded by something else. **What or where does Christ tell us to go into?**

All the world. He wants us to go into all the world. Not only in your Jerusalem; not just in your Judaea; not just in your Samaria, but also unto the uttermost part of the earth. We are to go out into the highways and the hedges and compel them! **Where do you share what Christ has done for you?**

Preach. How are we supposed to relay the Message? We are to preach… to publicly proclaim or teach; to earnestly advocate our belief. This is not limited to those called men of God who are preachers. This is to every Christian. **What are you to proclaim?**

The Gospel. The death, burial, and resurrection of Jesus Christ…plus nothing, minus nothing. We cannot earn our way to Heaven. It is only by our belief and acceptance of how Jesus paid the price for our sin and rose victoriously from the grave on the third day. **Who are you to share the Gospel with today?**

To every creature. He did not exclude anyone. There is not a person on the planet that does not need the Gospel. We have the Good News, and yet we routinely keep it to ourselves. Who can you tell? **Who is waiting for you to tell them?**

"The Gospel is only good news if It gets there in time."
Carl Henry

Bible Reading
Deuteronomy 19-20 | Mark 15 | Psalm 57 | 95

It All Starts With Him.

Genesis 1:1
"In the beginning God created the heaven and the earth."

The first verse in the Bible is very well known,
even by those that do not profess to be Christians.

There are no coincidences within God's Word, so it was not by chance that the very first four words are *"In the beginning God"*.

It all starts with Him!

Everything we do must begin with God.
Until we ask for His permission and His help,
we have not truly begun.

Have you ever set out to do something, yet failed to ask God for permission first, much less for His help to accomplish the task? If we are honest, we've all been guilty of it. Maybe we finished the job, maybe we were unable to, but how much better would it have been if we had the Creator of the universe to support us in our endeavor? He is willing and waiting, yet so often we forget, or do not even bother, to ask.

**Our creative process is in vain
if we do not yield ourselves to Him Who created us.**

Seek God's face for His direction before putting thought into action.
The results are sure to be far better than if we were to do it on our own.

For without Him, we are nothing.

Purified By Truth.

John 17:17
"Sanctify them through thy truth: thy word is truth."

Jesus Christ and His disciples had recently had the Passover meal where He taught them what we know now as the Lord's Supper, a memorial of what Christ did for us on Calvary. After instructing them about the meal, He served them by washing their feet. **What an example Christ sets for us as a servant to others.** Their Master, their Lord, was on His hands and knees taking a towel to wash the dirt off their feet. **Jesus was the Ultimate Servant.**

Afterwards He spent some time instructing the disciples about the days to follow. Many of the disciples were confused and posed questions to Christ about what He was saying. Here we find such great passages written in red in our Bibles.

John 14:1
"Let not your heart be troubled: ye believe in God, believe also in me."

John 14:14
"If ye shall ask any thing in my name, I will do it."

John 16:33
*"These things I have spoken unto you, that in me ye might have peace.
In the world ye shall have tribulation: but be of good cheer;
I have overcome the world."*

Jesus Christ spoke these words to His disciples, and under the inspiration of the Holy Spirit the Apostle John pinned them into Scripture. However, in chapter 17, Christ shifts His words from His earthly followers to His Father in Heaven. He is praying not for Himself, but for His followers…His disciples then, and now. **He prayed for us!**

John 17:9
*"I pray for them: I pray not for the world,
but for them which thou hast given me; for they are thine."*

As He continues to pray to the Father, we find our text verse today in verse 17, *"Sanctify them through thy truth:"*. **Christ asks God the Father to purify us and consecrate us by the truth.** What is the truth? The verse goes on to tell us, *"thy word is truth."* He has given us the Truth for us to read and live by each day. He asked the Father to use His Word to cleanse us from all unrighteousness. **We are purified by the Truth!**

Bible Reading
Deuteronomy 23-24 | Acts 1 | Psalm 59

Be Ready To Answer.

1 Peter 3:15

"But sanctify the Lord God in your hearts: and be ready always to give an answer to every man that asketh you a reason of the hope that is in you with meekness and fear:"

Here we find the word sanctify again, but with a different meaning. We have no need to try and purify the Lord God, for He is already pure!

Sanctify: to render or acknowledge; to separate from profane things and dedicate to God; to consecrate things to God; to purify.

God wants us to separate our hearts to Him so that we are ready to be a witness for Him when we are asked. Have you ever had someone ask, "Hey, you're a Christian. Can I ask you a Biblical question?" Maybe you knew the answer, but maybe you were caught off guard, not sure what to say.

Christ wants us to be ready to give an answer!
We have a reason of hope that this world does not have.
This makes us a peculiar people. God wants us to be different!

When we have a close relationship with our Lord, we will stick out like a sore thumb in this dark and wicked world. The Light within us should shine for others to see without us having to tell people how we shine. D.L. Moody had a great way of putting this truth. He said, "We are told to let our light shine, and if it does, we won't need to tell anybody it does. Lighthouses don't fire cannons to call attention to their shining – they just shine."

The Lord wants us to be ready to answer, but not to be belligerent and unruly about our knowledge. At the end of our text today, we see that we should be filled with *"meekness and fear"*. A mild and gentle disposition coupled with a godly fear is pleasing to the Lord. **Be ready, Christian, for you know not when someone will ask you the reason for your hope in the Lord.** It could be today. It could be tomorrow.

**Ask the Lord to help you be ready
to give an answer that would be pleasing to Him.**

Bible Reading
Deuteronomy 25-26 | Acts 2 | Psalm 60

How Much Does It Cost?

Isaiah 55:1
"Ho, every one that thirsteth, come ye to the waters, and he that hath no money; come ye, buy, and eat; yea, come, buy wine and milk without money and without price."

We find in our verse today an invitation to *"come ye, buy, and eat; yea, come, buy wine and milk without money and without price."* Those that were invited to the waters didn't have any money, yet they were able to both buy and eat. How can a person buy and eat without paying a set price with money? The context of our passage today is that of salvation. Our verse today is an invitation to come and partake of the benefit of the Gospel of grace. What provision the grace of God is! Grace is unmerited favor. Within our verse, the wine and milk was unearned. The partaker did not pay for it, but rather the Provider had paid the price. Food costs money, and it only satisfies for a short period of time. But thanks be to God who offers us free nourishment for more than just our physical bodies, He nourishes our soul!

How much does it cost to be a Christian?
It cost God His only begotten Son. It cost Jesus Christ His life.
It is a gift to us.

Romans 6:23
*"For the wages of sin is death; but **the gift of God** is eternal life through Jesus Christ our Lord."*

Gifts are given voluntarily, without payment in return, or the need to be earned. **God gave His Son, Jesus Christ. He paid the debt we owed.**

Ephesians 2:8-9
*"For by grace are ye saved through faith; and that not of yourselves: **it is the gift of God**: Not of works, lest any man should boast."*

God offers us salvation freely, but in order to have eternal life we must receive it. A gift is of no use unless it is received, and it cannot be given unless it's already been paid for. Have you received this gift? If so, then why keep it to yourself? The gift of salvation is inexhaustible; it will never be out of stock. That family member or friend needs to hear about the free gift that is waiting for them to receive. They may not know it is available, or they may need to hear the Truth once again. Share the Gift with someone today.

This Gift can change their life.

Bible Reading
Deuteronomy 27-28 | Acts 3 | Psalm 61

Follow His Steps.

1 Peter 2:21
"For even hereunto were ye called: because Christ also suffered for us, leaving us an example, that ye should follow his steps:"

Where are we called? We are called to suffer.

1 Peter 2:19-20
"For this is thankworthy, if a man for conscience toward God endure grief, suffering wrongfully. For what glory is it, if, when ye be buffeted for your faults, ye shall take it patiently? but if, when ye do well, and suffer for it, ye take it patiently, this is acceptable with God."

Christ suffered for us, and He left us an example to follow.

1 Peter 2:22-23
"Who did no sin, neither was guile found in his mouth: Who, when he was reviled, reviled not again; when he suffered, he threatened not; but committed himself to him that judgeth righteously:"

He suffered wrongfully. And if we are to be like Him, we too shall suffer unjustly. You might not get that promotion you think you deserve, but God is keeping you at your desk for a reason. Maybe your co-worker needs the Gospel. Your spouse may make some choices that the family will reap the consequences of, but God is giving you an opportunity to trust Him to bring you through it. Are you suffering wrongfully today? God has a reason.

Follow Christ's example. **Follow His steps.** No deceit was found in his mouth. He did not condemn His enemies. He did not threaten to get even. He simply committed Himself to the One Who judges righteously, God The Father. **What can we do when we suffer wrongfully?** We can wait patiently on the Lord with courage that He will give us the strength we need to endure the trial.

Psalm 27:14
"Wait on the LORD: be of good courage, and he shall strengthen thine heart: wait, I say on the LORD."

Christ bare His body on the tree of Calvary so that we who were dead in our sins could live unto righteousness. Every day that we breathe we are given a choice of whether or not we will die to ourselves and let the Lord guide us through our day. Follow the example Christ set for us. **Take up your cross and follow His steps today.**

Bible Reading
Deuteronomy 29-30 | Acts 4 | Psalm 62

Toward Them.

1 Thessalonians 4:11-12
"And that ye study to be quiet, and to do your own business, and to work with your own hands, as we commanded you; That ye may walk honestly toward them that are without, and that ye may have lack of nothing."

Have you ever met someone who seemed liked they studied just so they could tell everyone everything they know? It's distracting from the purpose at hand, isn't it? As we study the Scriptures, we find that God wants us to study to be quiet, to be peaceable and gentle in our speech.

Have you ever met someone who paid attention just to know your business? Or someone who put their hands on a project where they did not belong? Our text today shows us that we are to work with our own hands while doing our own business. The meddlers of this world must not have read this passage! It is a great reminder to those of us serving in the ministry that we have a purpose. We have a calling that should be our focus; we should let others focus on their own ministries.

Why is this important? So *"That ye may walk honestly toward them that are without"*. **It is important for us to focus on our purpose & calling so that we can take the Gospel to those who are without it.** We are to walk honestly toward them. The lost are waiting with empty hearts whether they realize it or not. Only the Gospel of Jesus Christ can fill the emptiness of their hearts and hands. **We have been entrusted with the Gospel, and it is our commission to share it with others.**

What does the verse say will happen when we do this? *"that ye may have lack of nothing."* God has promised us that He will supply all of our needs, IF we will trust Him and carry the Gospel to this lost and dying world.

Colossians 4:5
"Walk in wisdom toward them that are without, redeeming the time."

How are you carrying the Gospel today?

How are you redeeming the time
that God has given you to reach the lost?

Bible Reading
Deuteronomy 31-32 | Acts 5 | Psalm 63

Start Where You Are.

Luke 24:46-47
"And said unto them, Thus it is written, and thus it behoved Christ to suffer, and to rise from the dead the third day: And that repentance and remission of sins should be preached in his name among all nations, beginning at Jerusalem."

Christ was behoved both to suffer and to rise from the dead so that repentance and remission of sins should be preached in His name among all nations!

Matthew 9:13
"…for I am not come to call the righteous, but sinners to repentance."

We know that this was Jesus' purpose when He left His throne in Heaven; He was made flesh and dwelt among His creation. Although the Gospel of repentance should be preached in His Name to all nations, notice where it is to start, *"beginning at Jerusalem."*

When Christ gave the Great Commission before He ascended to Heaven after His resurrection, He told how the Gospel was to be spread.

Acts 1:8
"But ye shall receive power, after that the Holy Ghost is come upon you: and ye shall be witnesses unto me both in Jerusalem, and in all Judaea, and in Samaria, and unto the uttermost part of the earth."

Applying that to the world we live in today:
"in Jerusalem" – Your City or Town
"in all Judaea" – Your State
"in Samaria" – Your Country
"the uttermost part of the earth." – The World

Start where you are. Your community is your Jerusalem. We can't expect to make a difference in the world if we aren't making a difference at home. Not sure how to start? **Read your Bible.** God will help prepare you through His Word. **Pray and ask God to direct your path.** If you ask Him to give you an opportunity to share the Gospel with someone, He is sure to open the door. **Talk to your Pastor.** Ask Him to guide you in what ministry you can help with in your local church. **Give a Gospel tract to someone.** God has used Gospel tracts in many many ways to make a difference in people's lives, and prepare their hearts for the Seed of the Gospel of Jesus Christ. Contact us if you would like to receive some Gospel tracts to distribute.

Bible Reading
Deuteronomy 33-34 | Acts 6 | Psalm 64

Point To Him.

John 3:30
"He must increase, but I must decrease."

In one of his last testimonies before being sent to prison by Herod, John the Baptist spoke these words as his disciples are celebrating his ministry and how he foretold of Christ's ministry.

John 3:27
"John answered and said, A man can receive nothing, except it be given him from heaven."

John knew that he was just a friend of the bridegroom. He knew that Jesus had received His power from His Father, and he goes on to explain why Christ must increase and his own notoriety must decrease. **He wanted his followers to see Christ and not himself.** This is the motive of a true follower, a real Christian.

What would the world be today if we as Christians truly let Jesus increase and ourselves decrease? **Instead of pointing to ourselves, we need to acknowledge that everything we are able to accomplish comes from Him!** John the Baptist knew that, and he made sure to convey that message to his followers.

In a world where self-promotion and self-centeredness are rampant, this Biblical principle is hardly anywhere to be found, even in the church. We need more Christians like John the Baptist, who instead of allowing others to point to them, will point to the One from whom all things are received!

He > I

When we get the equation backwards we are asking for trouble. If we try to let others see us instead of Him, we have our reward. Seek to hide yourself behind the cross today. **If others point to you, point them to Him!**

If we were more like John,
we would make it our life's goal to proclaim the Gospel.

John 3:36
"He that believeth on the Son hath everlasting life: and he that believeth not the Son shall not see life; but the wrath of God abideth on him."

Point to Him today!

Bible Reading
Joshua 1-2 | Acts 7 | Psalm 65

Look Up.

Colossians 3:1
"If ye then be risen with Christ, seek those things which are above, where Christ sitteth on the right hand of God."

If you are saved, this verse is speaking directly to you!

On those days when your mind is spinning, and you don't know which way to turn, this is a great verse to help reset your perspective. **Look up! When we seek those things which are above, our outlook changes to what really matters.**

It is so easy to get weighed down with the cares of this world. Whether great or small, our enemy the devil knows just what buttons to push to get us distracted and deter us from our purpose. On those days when nothing seems to go right and you feel like a failure (let's face it, we've all been there), remind him of his future!

Our verse today tells us where our Saviour currently resides, seated on the right hand of God. He is sitting because His work is finished. But one day, very soon, He will once again leave His heavenly throne. Only this time, He will meet us, His bride, in the air and will escort us into the place He went to prepare for us.

Satan is having a hay day right now, as he knows his time is running out. He knows he has only a little while longer to continue his reign as the god of this world. Don't focus on him and his friends. That's exactly what he wants. He wins when we let down our guard and allow him to change our focus from what God would have us to do. Sometimes he uses people, even Christians, to distract us. Don't let him get the victory.

Look up today, Christian!
Our redemption draweth nigh!

Remind yourself of your home in Heaven that Christ has prepared for you. Remind Satan of his future and tell him to leave you alone. You are not his; **you are a child of the King of Kings!**

Bible Reading
Joshua 3-4 | Acts 8 | Psalm 66

From Prayer To Praise.

Psalm 57:7-11

*"My heart is fixed, O God, my heart is fixed: I will sing and give praise.
Awake up, my glory; awake, psaltery and harp: I myself will awake early.
I will praise thee, O Lord, among the people: I will sing unto thee among
the nations. For thy mercy is great unto the heavens, and thy truth unto the
clouds. Be thou exalted, O God, above the heavens:
let thy glory be above all the earth."*

David is in distress. In the context of this chapter, David was running for his life. Saul, the king of Israel, was so jealous of David that he wanted him dead.

Maybe you can relate with him. Have you ever felt like someone was out to get you? They may not be physically threatening, but their malicious intent is obviously pointed in your direction. It's not fun, and can make you want to get even or settle the score.

Instead of getting even, **David first prayed about his situation.** The first six verses of the chapter, he lays out his plea for mercy and displays his trust in God to deliver him.

Psalm 57:1

"Be merciful unto me, O God, be merciful unto me: for my soul trusteth in thee: yea, in the shadow of thy wings will I make my refuge, until these calamities be overpast."

After pleading for help, David then begins to praise God despite his circumstances. He is expecting God to give the mercy he requested, and therefore he praises God because he knows He is sure to answer.

Psalm 57:7

*"My heart is fixed, O God, my heart is fixed:
I will sing and give praise."*

When you feel like you're in a cave hiding from your enemies, ask the Lord for mercy and praise Him for what He will do.

Today turn your problems into praise.

Bible Reading
Joshua 5-6 | Acts 9 | Psalm 67 | 105

Support His Work.

Philippians 4:19
"But my God shall supply all your need
according to his riches in glory by Christ Jesus."

This verse is often used for all sorts of situations. When studying the Scriptures, the most essential element is context. God can supply what you need. He is willing and able to do so; but the context of Philippians 4 is giving to the Lord's work, missions. The church at Philippi understood the concept of missions. They were birthed from Paul's Macedonian mission in Acts 16. We learn that Lydia, the seller of purple, was fruit of that trip as she was saved down by the river. Paul sent his letter to the Philippians, writing of his thankfulness for their sacrificial giving toward the work of the ministry. The people of Philippi were very poor, yet they gave anyway. They were a church on a mission field that was giving so that other churches could be planted. **This is the Lord's pattern for missions.** We also see why Paul desired their support.

Philippians 4:17
"Not because I desire a gift: but I desire fruit
that may abound to your account."

It was not because he wanted a gift or money, but because he desired fruit. Fruit that would abound to the church's account. Fruit that would remain. **When we support the Lord's work, God promises that He will supply our need!** His riches are inexhaustible. They never run dry. His glory will never diminish. Christ Jesus is the Giver of all our spiritual blessings. He gives us exactly what we need, when we need it! **Let us be faithful to give to the work of the Lord so that others may come to know Him!** In doing so, we can claim the promise that:
"But my God" - He is a personal God.
"shall supply" - Give to His work, and He will supply for you.
"all your need" - He knows what you need, even before you ask.
"according to His riches" - The measure of His supply available to us.
"in glory" - He blesses us so that He can receive the glory He deserves.
"by Christ Jesus." - When we give to Him we are investing in eternity.

Consider what Christ could do through you and for you if you would give. **When we give, we are obeying His Word by supporting His Work.**

Bible Reading
Joshua 7-8 | Acts 10 | Psalm 68

Transformed.

Romans 12:2
*"And be not conformed to this world: but be ye transformed
by the renewing of your mind, that ye may prove what is that good,
and acceptable, and perfect, will of God."*

God wants to transform us.

He has made us new creatures in Him, and it is because of that transformation that He wants us to continually be shaped according to His will. We must make renewing our minds a daily priority. Renewal comes from the time we spend with Him in prayer and reading God's Word. As we receive the Words He has given us, He renews us and directs us in the way He would have us to go and what He would have us to do.

We cannot be transformed or renewed if we are conformed to the world around us. We must separate ourselves from worldly pleasures. Ask God to reveal to you what things are hindering your walk with Him. Once He shows you, ask Him to help you remove them from your life. Sin is always camouflaged in everything we have ever wanted. Our fleshly desires are hard to defeat, but *"greater is he that is in you, than he that is in the world."* Though we are new creatures in Christ, we still have our flesh to contend with each day that we live and breathe.

Ephesians 4:22-24
*"That ye put off concerning the former conversation the old man, which
is corrupt according to the deceitful lusts; And be renewed in the spirit of
your mind; And that ye put on the new man, which after God is created in
righteousness and true holiness."*

In order to put on the new man each day we must separate ourselves from the world, and strengthen ourselves by renewing of our minds through Christ Jesus our Lord. Pray. Read. For then you will find the strength you need to fight against the wiles of the devil and against the lusts of the flesh. Romans 12 is filled with clear instruction for following God's direction. Take the time to read the chapter today and see what passages God uses to shine the Light on areas of your life that need to be transformed in order to find the *"good, and acceptable, and perfect, will of God"* for your life.

Bible Reading
Joshua 9-10 | Acts 11 | Psalm 69

Understanding.

Proverbs 2:6
*"For the LORD giveth wisdom: out of his mouth
cometh knowledge and understanding."*

Before we can begin to understand the Word of God, there are some things required of us.

1 Corinthians 2:14
"But the natural man receiveth not the things of the Spirit of God: for they are foolishness unto him: neither can he know them, because they are spiritually discerned."

We must be saved. We receive the Holy Spirit the moment we place our faith in Jesus Christ. Without the Holy Spirit residing within us, we are just an empty vessel, unable to discern the Truth of the Scriptures.

John 17:17
"Sanctify them through thy truth: thy word is truth."

We must believe the Bible to be the Truth. Jesus prayed these words for us just before Judas betrayed Him and He began His journey to Calvary. He believed that God's Word was true. Do you?

Psalm 119:18
"Open thou mine eyes, that I may behold wondrous things out of thy law."

We must ask God to help us. In order to understand the Bible, we must pray for God to reveal Himself to us through the Scriptures. Ask God to prepare your heart for understanding the Scriptures.

Psalm 119:47
"And I will delight myself in thy commandments, which I have loved."

We must love our Bible. The Bible is not just any other book, it is the very Words of God Almighty in written form. It is inspired, preserved, and inerrant. The Bible is the only Book ever written whose Author is always present. This should allow us to develop a love for our Bible.

John 5:39
"Search the scriptures; for in them ye think ye have eternal life: and they are they which testify of me."

We must be willing to do more than read. Jesus Christ tells us that there is more than just reading our Bibles. He said we should search the Scriptures for understanding.

Bible Reading
Joshua 11-12 | Acts 12 | Psalm 70

His Goodness.

Psalm 107:8
*"Oh that men would praise the LORD for his goodness,
and for his wonderful works to the children of men!"*

This verse is repeated four times in Psalm 107 in verses 8, 15, 21 and 31. Four times God used these Words to plead that people would see the enormity of His goodness and His wonderful works. Every Word of God is important. God only has to say something once to make it True; but the passages that God inspired to be pinned more than once should make us take more time to study them and apply them to our lives.

Where would we be without the goodness of God?

His goodness led us to see ourselves as sinners in need of a Saviour.
Romans 2:4
*"Or despisest thou the riches of his goodness and
forbearance and longsuffering; not knowing that
the goodness of God leadeth thee to repentance?"*

His goodness fills our hungry souls.
Psalm 107:9
*"For he satisfieth the longing soul, and filleth the hungry
soul with goodness."*

His goodness gives us strength.
Psalm 27:13
*"I had fainted, unless I had believed to see the
goodness of the LORD in the land of the living."*

His goodness endures forever.
Psalm 52:1
*"Why boastest thou thyself in mischief, O mighty man?
the goodness of God endureth continually."*

His goodness allows us to see all of the wonderful works
that He has done in our lives.

Take some time today to focus on how good He has been to you.

As you do, He will reveal more of how His goodness
has changed your life.

Bible Reading
Joshua 13-14 | Acts 13 | Psalm 71

A Call From Somebody.

Acts 16:9-10
"And a vision appeared to Paul in the night; There stood a man of Macedonia, and prayed him, saying, Come over into Macedonia, and help us. And after he had seen the vision, immediately we endeavoured to go into Macedonia, assuredly gathering that the Lord had called us for to preach the gospel unto them."

It is because of Paul's obedience to the Holy Spirit that we in America have the Gospel. What if Paul had disobeyed?

The Scripture tells us that Paul went immediately.
He didn't run the other way like Jonah…he endeavoured to go.

Where is the Lord calling you?

The Lord had called Paul to preach the Gospel unto the Macedonians.
Who has He called you to give the Gospel to?

There is somebody out there that needs you to share the Gospel with them. It's up to you to reach them.
Somebody is waiting.
Somebody is calling.

Will you answer the call? Or will you disobey?
Will you endeavor to go to them? Or will you sit in the pew?

Will you go immediately?
Or will you make excuses and head another direction?

What if the person who shared the Gospel with you
had not answered the call to do so? Think about it.

Endeavor to go to someone today.
A family member. A friend. A co-worker. A stranger.
God has called us to proclaim the Gospel to those who are without.

Will you answer that call today?

Bibel Reading
Joshua 15-16 | Acts 14 | Psalm 72

Do Good & Communicate.

Hebrews 13:15-16
"By him therefore let us offer the sacrifice of praise to God continually, that is, the fruit of our lips giving thanks to his name. But to do good and to communicate forget not: for with such sacrifices God is well pleased."

How often should we praise God?
Continually.

Much like we are to pray without ceasing, we are to praise Him continually. Our lips are to give thanks to His Name. When we thank God, we praise Him. **The objective of our entire lives should be to please God.** In this passage He shows us some ways in which we can please Him.

God wants us to share what we have with others.

Benevolence and communication are the foundation of friendship, finding common ground with others. We cannot find that common ground if we are not doing good unto them and communicating. **When we share what we have, not only are we blessing the recipient, but also we ourselves also receive a blessing, and God is pleased.** He wants us to yield ourselves to Him so that He may use us to bless others. In his letter to the Philippians, Paul writes of how he was blessed by them and their giving.

Philippians 4:18
"But I have all, and abound: I am full, having received of Epaphroditus the things which were sent from you, an odour of a sweet smell, a sacrifice acceptable, wellpleasing to God."

Remember the context…missions giving. The church of Philippi had given sacrificially to Paul's ministry because they desired for him to bear fruit. He reminded them that God would supply all their need because of their gift of love and their desire for fruit as well. **Paul's friends provided for him so that he could serve where God had sent him.**

God wants us to do more than praise Him with our lips. **He tells us that we should not forget to do good and communicate with others.** We please the Lord when we sacrifice our time and service to bless those around us.

If you have godly friends in your life, praise the Lord for them today.
He has crossed your paths so that you may be a blessing to each other.

Bible Reading
Joshua 17-18 | Acts 15 | Psalm 73

He Sees Tomorrow.

Isaiah 57:15
"For thus saith the high and lofty One that inhabiteth eternity, whose name is Holy; I dwell in the high and holy place, with him also that is of a contrite and humble spirit, to revive the spirit of the humble, and to revive the heart of the contrite ones."

Our God is high and lofty. There is no creature like Him. No one can even be compared to Him. He even tells us this repeatedly in Isaiah.

Isaiah 45:5-6
"I am the LORD, and there is none else, there is no God beside me…there is none beside me. I am the LORD, and there is none else."

Isaiah 46:9-10
"Remember the former things of old: for I am God, and there is none else; I am God, and there is none like me, Declaring the end from the beginning, and from ancient times the things that are not yet done, saying, My counsel shall stand, and I will do all my pleasure:"

He declares the end from the beginning.
He inhabits eternity. **He sees tomorrow.**

When we don't know what tomorrow holds, we can rest in knowing the One Who holds tomorrow…and the next day, and the day after that. **God does not view time like we do, for there is none like Him.**

Since He dwells in eternity…
When He was with David as he slew Goliath, He saw you.
When He was with Daniel in the lion's den, He saw you.
When He was with Ruth as she gleaned from Boaz's field, He saw you.
When He was with Elijah as he prayed fire down from Heaven, He saw you.
When He was with Esther as she risked her life for her people, He saw you.
When He was with Peter walking on the water, He saw you.
When He was with Paul on his missionary journeys, He saw you.
When He was hanging on the cross at Calvary, He saw you.

As He dwells in His high and lofty place, He sees those that are of a contrite and humble spirit. He wants to revive our hearts today, if only we will humble ourselves and be of a contrite spirit.

Our God sees your today, and He sees your tomorrow.

Bible Reading
Joshua 19-20 | Acts 16 | Psalm 74

Sow & Reap.

2 Corinthians 9:6
"But this I say, He which soweth sparingly shall reap also sparingly; and he which soweth bountifully shall reap also bountifully."

In the spring, many people prepare gardens in hopes of yielding great fruit when the harvest comes. If the gardener seeks to have a great bounty, they must plan and plant accordingly. If only a few seeds are planted, only a little fruit will be produced, and the planter is sure to be disappointed.

As Christians, we can learn from these principles. If we plant the Seed of the Word of God sparingly, we will reap little. And likewise, if we sow bountifully to our flesh, we will reap corruption.

Galatians 6:7-9
"Be not deceived; God is not mocked: for whatsoever a man soweth, that shall he also reap. For he that soweth to his flesh shall of the flesh reap corruption; but he that soweth to the Spirit shall of the Spirit reap life everlasting. And let us not be weary in well doing: for in due season we shall reap, if we faint not."

The activity in which we sow resolves what we shall reap.
The approach in which we sow determines how we will reap.
The amount in which we sow is proportionate to that which we will reap.
If we desire to reap more, we must sow more.

**Sow the Word today,
and tomorrow reap the fruit that remains.**

Bible Reading
Joshua 21-22 | Acts 17 | Psalm 75

Search Me.

Psalm 139:23-24
*"Search me, O God, and know my heart: try me,
and know my thoughts: And see if there be any wicked way in me,
and lead me in the way everlasting."*

If we want the Lord to lead us in the way everlasting, we must first ask Him to search our hearts and our thoughts. We must cleanse out the wickedness that lives within us. Our hearts are deceitful and desperately wicked. And if we are honest with ourselves, we know that it is true.

The Lord is willing and able to lead us.
Be thankful for this promise.

The Psalmist, David, knowing the condition of his wicked heart, asks the Lord to find any wicked way in him. He wanted the Lord to purge out even the sin that was unbeknownst to David. What would God do in our lives if we prayed this prayer and followed the Lord's leading in removing the iniquity from our hearts?

Proverbs 4:23
"Keep thy heart with all diligence; for out of it are the issues of life."

We must guard our hearts. We must watch over everything we allow in our hearts. **Our actions come from our hearts.** We must keep our eyes, our ears, our mouths, our hands and our feet, but above all, we must keep our hearts.

Ask the Lord to search your heart today.
Ask Him to try your thoughts.

He will reveal things you have forgotten about, or maybe even never considered to be a problem. That's how the Lord works.

He knows everything about us, and yet…He still loves us.
Isn't that amazing?

Bible Reading
Joshua 23-24 | Acts 18 | Psalm 76

The Abundance Of The Heart.

Luke 6:45
*"A good man out of the good treasure of his heart bringeth forth
that which is good; and an evil man out of the evil treasure of
his heart bringeth forth that which is evil:
for of the abundance of the heart his mouth speaketh."*

Matthew 12:33-35
*"Either make the tree good, and his fruit good; or else make the tree
corrupt, and his fruit corrupt: for the tree is known by his fruit.
O generation of vipers, how can ye, being evil, speak good things?
for out of the abundance of the heart the mouth speaketh. A good man
out of the good treasure of the heart bringeth forth good things: and an
evil man out of the evil treasure bringeth forth evil things."*

Not only do our actions come from our hearts, but our heart determines our words as well. If our hearts are filled with good things, we display good treasure. If we fill our hearts with that which is evil, we will not have a good testimony for our Saviour.

What is your heart saying today?

The issues of our life are determined by the condition of our hearts. That's why we would consciously guard our hearts from anything that displeases our Lord. We are known by the fruit we produce. **If there is no fruit, we have our answer as to the condition of our hearts.** A corrupt heart cannot bring forth fruit. This fruit is not produced by planting a tree or a garden, but by the example we allow our lives to set. Are you producing fruit today?

Are you reaching others with the Gospel?
Are you supporting others in their endeavor to proclaim the Gospel?
Are you shining your Light in the darkness of this world?
Are you teaching and training others to spread the Word?
Are you living a righteous example for others to follow?

If we are not doing these things, we are not producing the fruit that the Lord desires. Examine your life today and see if you are a fruit bearer.

**Dig in the Word and see how you can bare fruit
that will remain to give our Saviour the glory He deserves.**

Bible Reading
Judges 1-2 | Acts 19 | Psalm 77

Stand Sure.

2 Timothy 2:19
*"Nevertheless the foundation of God standeth sure, having this seal,
The Lord knoweth them that are his. And, Let every one that nameth the
name of Christ depart from iniquity."*

Despite the unbelief, the persecution, and the turmoil we face in this world, if our foundation is built upon the Lord Jesus Christ, we cannot fail.

Christian, be encouraged today that you stand upon the Rock of Ages!
Our foundation in Him will always keep us safe
regardless of our circumstances.

Though some may choose not to believe in the Truth of God's Word, their unbelief does not make the Scriptures untrue. God does not need the approval of men. Jesus said He is the Way, the Truth, and the Life. He is THE TRUTH regardless if men choose to believe in Him or not.

The context of our text today deals with facing situations where those around us question our faith or they may not believe at all. Look at the first word of our verse, *"Nevertheless"*. **God wants us to press on despite the opinions and disbelief of those around us.**

We are sealed through the power of the Holy Spirit. Why is that? Because we trusted in Jesus, and He knows our name! The Good Shepherd knows His sheep, and He calls us by name.

Sometimes our faith may waver, but the foundation of God standeth sure!
Our feet are on the Solid Rock, and because we rest ourselves in Him we can stand sure that He will always do what is best for us.

Stand sure today regardless of the storm. God has you right where you are for a reason. He knows the strength of the winds that are raging and the waves that are tossing you to and fro. He is able to speak peace to the storm you are facing. **Trust Him today. Stand sure in the foundation that He does all things well for our good and His glory!**

Bible Reading
Judges 3-4 | Acts 20 | Psalm 78

He Is Faithful.

1 Thessalonians 5:24
"Faithful is he that calleth you, who also will do it."

Do you ever doubt what God's purpose is for your life? Being unsure of what God wants is the perfect condition for God to do something miraculous in your life. If you find yourself unsure where to go or what to do next, stand still. Ask the Lord to guide you. Acknowledge Him and ask Him to direct your paths. Then…wait. **Wait on Him to make a way where right now you see no way.**

When God orchestrates something, He will bring it to pass. When He calls someone, He will equip them to carry out the task. God doesn't call the qualified. He qualifies the called. **He wants us to depend on Him to carry us through whatever He has called us to do so that we can give Him the glory He deserves, because He is Faithful.**

1 Corinthians 1:9
*"God is faithful, by whom ye were called unto
the fellowship of his Son Jesus Christ our Lord."*

He has called you for a purpose.

Romans 8:28
*"And we know that all things work together for good to them that love
God, to them who are the called according to his purpose."*

He will enable you to fulfill your calling, because He is Faithful.

2 Timothy 1:9
*"Who hath saved us, and called us with an holy calling, not according to
our works, but according to his own purpose and grace, which was given
us in Christ Jesus before the world began,"*

If the Lord is directing you toward something that seems impossible and overwhelming, remind yourself today that He is Faithful. When He calls you to do something, He will make a way when there is no way. The Lord does not want our ability. He wants our availability. Make yourself available to be used by Him, and watch Him use you in ways you never thought possible.

Where He guides, He provides.
Where He leads, He precedes.
Where He directs, He protects.

Bible Reading
Judges 5-6 | Acts 21 | Psalm 79

Times Of Waiting.

1 Samuel 1:27-2:2

"For this child I prayed; and the LORD hath given me my petition which I asked of him: Therefore also I have lent him to the LORD; as long as he liveth he shall be lent to the LORD. And he worshipped the LORD there. And Hannah prayed, and said, My heart rejoiceth in the LORD, mine horn is exalted in the LORD: my mouth is enlarged over mine enemies; because I rejoice in thy salvation. There is none holy as the LORD: for there is none beside thee: neither is there any rock like our God."

Hannah sets an example for us in our prayer lives. She had a situation that she knew only God could resolve. She asked, she pleaded, and then she promised that if God would give her a son she would give him back to the Lord.

Have you ever prayed for something for a long time and seemed to never get an answer? Maybe you even questioned if God heard your request at all. Hannah most likely felt this way; but she never complained. She just took the matter to the One that she knew could help her. She petitioned the Lord for her need, and the Lord granted her request.

The Lord always answers our prayers. Sometimes the answer is a direct yes or no, and sometimes He allows us to wait. The waiting period can be some of the most trying, most difficult times of our lives, but **God allows us to wait so that we may learn to trust Him.**

All of us have experienced a waiting period in our life. For Hannah, it was a child. For others it might be a job, a spouse, a clear direction of God's will, a specific need, a love one's salvation, a healing, or maybe all of the above. **God knows your need today. He knows what you've asked for and that you are waiting for the clarity of His will to unfold.**

Keep asking for God's direction and His provision in your need today. He will answer in His timing, and in a way that will make the waiting period worth the pain and struggle.

Don't doubt God in the times of waiting.

He wants to use this time to strengthen you and to prepare you for what He has in store. Let Him mold you into a vessel of honor that can be used for His service.

Bible Reading

Judges 7-8 | Acts 22 | Psalm 80

Come Boldly.

Hebrews 4:16
"Let us therefore come boldly unto the throne of grace,
that we may obtain mercy, and find grace to help in time of need."

In today's passage we find the explanation for why we can bring our petitions to the Lord. We have a Great High Priest that is sitting on the right hand of the Father. Jesus Christ, the only begotten Son of God, was touched with the feelings of our infirmities. He was tempted in all points just as we are today; yet He did not sin. It is because of His sinless sacrifice that we can come boldly to the throne of grace. It is there that we can obtain mercy when we confess our sins, and it is there that we can find grace to help us in our time of need. We have access to the throne of grace continually. The Father's ears are always open to our cry.

Psalm 34:15
"The eyes of the Lord are upon the righteous,
and his ears are open unto their cry."

He is always waiting to hear from us. Have you ever wished that a friend would call you, yet the call never came? Imagine how God feels when we do not acknowledge, much less use, our privilege of access to His throne room. When we call upon Him, we never have to leave a voicemail.

Jeremiah 33:3
"Call unto me, and I will answer thee,
and shew thee great and mighty things, which thou knowest not."

Just as the relationship between you and your best friend is strengthened by communication, our walk and relationship with the Lord is strengthened when we call upon Him. Our love grows as we call out to Him.

Psalm 116:1-2
"I love the Lord, because he hath heard my voice and my supplications.
Because he hath inclined his ear unto me,
therefore will I call upon him as long as I live."

Need mercy? You can obtain it at the throne of grace.
Need help in your time of need? You can find it at the throne of grace.

Take time today to come boldly before the throne of grace.

Bible Reading
Judges 9-10 | Acts 23 | Psalm 81 | 119

Resist The Adversary.

1 Peter 5:8-9
"Be sober, be vigilant; because your adversary the devil, as a roaring lion, walketh about, seeking whom he may devour: Whom resist stedfast in the faith, knowing that the same afflictions are accomplished in your brethren that are in the world."

There is someone who wants to keep us from coming boldly to the throne of grace...our adversary the devil. **The god of this world wants to do anything within his power to distract us and delay us from accessing the throne room.** He knows that it is there that we obtain mercy and there that we find grace to help us in our times of need.

Peter warns us that our enemy walketh about. He is still walking and roaring around us today just as he did with Peter and the disciples. He wants to devour us. He wants to defeat us before he is defeated.

We must resist our adversary. How can we do this? By our faith in Christ! We must be stedfast, unmoveable and always abound in the work of our Lord, for our labour is not in vain! Our afflictions are for His glory. Satan cannot attack us without the Lord's permission. Remember Job? Satan went to ask God before he could touch him. Despite Job's circumstances, he remained faithful; and because of his stedfast faithfulness, God rewarded his efforts by restoring his health and his household. If you feel like Job today, God can do the same thing for you. The afflictions that we face in this life are for our good and for His glory.

Resist the enemy's attack on your mind, your body, and your soul.

James 4:7
"Submit yourselves therefore to God. Resist the devil, and he will flee from you."

He cannot win because we have Jesus Christ on our side!

Bible Reading
Judges 11-12 | Acts 24 | Psalm 82

Count It All.

James 1:2-3
*"My brethren, count it all joy when ye fall into divers temptations;
Knowing this, that the trying of your faith worketh patience."*

For those times when it seems like our adversary is working overtime on us, James tells us that we should *"count it all joy"*. Easier said than done, right?

When our faith is tried, it gives us patience. We've all heard not to pray for patience, because God is sure to bring something into our lives to teach us to be patient as we wait. This is one lesson that is very hard for our flesh to learn.

There are no coincidences within the Word of God, so it's interesting to find that there are three words to describe how much of our temptations and trials we should turn to joy… **Count. It. All.** Not just a few of our trials or some of them, we are to count them ALL.

1 Thessalonians 5:18
"In every thing give thanks:"

As hard as it is sometimes, we can find the good whether we can see it or not. **Look for the bright side of your situation.** The rainbow in the midst of the storm. Ask God to show you His purpose. Ask Him to help you learn from the circumstances and allow you to grow in His grace.

Not only are there three words to describe how much, there are three letters to describe what to turn our trials into… J-O-Y. Wondering how to find real joy? **Put Jesus first in your life, others second, and yourself last.**

Jesus
Others
You
J-O-Y

When you find yourself struggling to find the good, wondering what purpose God could possibility have in the midst of your surroundings…
Count to three. 1-2-3.

Where can you be reminded of this Truth? James 1:2-3
1-2-3. Count it ALL J-O-Y today.

Bible Reading
Judges 13-14 | Acts 25 | Psalm 83

The Lord Is On My Side.

Psalm 118:6
"The LORD is on my side; I will not fear: what can man do unto me?"

What comforting words to read from the Word of God! When we live by this principle, we can obtain fearlessness to the things of this world and those around us. We can be fearless because we have the Lord on our side.

David was a man after God's heart. When he was down and discouraged, he did not look around to find help, he looked up! After his wives were taken captive, he did not look to his friends for help and encouragement.

1 Samuel 30:6
"And David was greatly distressed; for the people spake of stoning him, because the soul of all the people was grieved, every man for his sons and for his daughters: but David encouraged himself in the Lord his God."

David encouraged himself by seeking the Lord his God.
We can do the same by daily seeking encouragement from God's Word.

David knew that he had enemies. He was reminded of that quite often. If you've ever tried to do something for the Lord, you can relate with David. Whenever we strive to make a difference and reach people with the Gospel, we find out who our friends are. Most of the conflicts in the ministry do not come from outside the church, but within. It's a sad thought, but it's often the truth. Praise God that no matter where our conflict comes from, we can press on because the Lord is on our side!

Psalm 56:11
*"In God have I put my trust:
I will not be afraid what man can do unto me."*

When you get fearful say, *"The LORD is on my side."*
When you are doubtful say, *"The LORD is on my side."*
When you feel surrounded by your enemies say,
"The LORD is on my side."

Romans 8:31
*"What shall we then say to these things?
If God be for us, who can be against us?"*

Bible Reading
Judges 15-16 | Acts 26 | Psalm 84

The Lord's Side.

Exodus 32:26
"Then Moses stood in the gate of the camp, and said, Who is on the LORD's side? let him come unto me. And all the sons of Levi gathered themselves together unto him."

It is an amazing thing to realize that the Lord is on our side, but we should ask ourselves, **"Are we on God's side?"**

Moses asked the children of Israel the question, *"Who is on the LORD's side?"* after he had been up on the mount for an extended period of time, spending time with God face-to-face. The Lord had given the two tables of testimony, and Moses was to carry them back down to the people. While Moses and Joshua were gone, Aaron took matters into his own hands and told the people to bring him golden earrings from which he crafted a molten calf for the people to worship as their god.

Needless to say, God was angry. Moses was also angry. The people had corrupted themselves. They chose to create a false idol instead of worshipping the One True God. The God Who had sent the 10 plagues unto Egypt, brought them across the Red Sea, provided food for them in the wilderness, and had performed miracles before their very eyes...yet they chose to disobey.

After Moses rebuked them, he asked, **"Who is on the LORD's side?"** It was obvious not many were at this point. The children of Levi were the only ones that came forward. They wanted to serve the One True God.

If a modern day Moses was to ask the same question today to the people of America, how many would come forward? Considering the state of our country today, there would most likely be very few modern day Levites among us.

President Abraham Lincoln knew that as great as it is to have the Lord on our side, it is more important to make sure that we are on God's side. He is known for saying, "Sir, my concern is not whether God is on our side; my greatest concern is to be on God's side, for God is always right."

Are you on the LORD's side today?

Bible Reading
Judges 17-18 | Acts 27 | Psalm 85 | 123

The Results Of Delight.

Isaiah 58:14
"Then shalt thou delight thyself in the Lord; and I will cause thee to ride upon the high places of the earth, and feed thee with the heritage of Jacob thy father: for the mouth of the Lord hath spoken it."

When we delight ourselves in the Lord, only He knows what can take place as we yield ourselves to Him.

Is the Lord the delightful subject of your thoughts today?

Psalm 94:19
"In the multitude of my thoughts within me thy comforts delight my soul."

**Allow the Lord to delight your soul today
through the comfort that only He can give.**

2 Corinthians 1:3-4
"Blessed be God, even the Father of our Lord Jesus Christ, the Father of mercies, and the God of all comfort; Who comforteth us in all our tribulation, that we may be able to comfort them which are in any trouble, by the comfort wherewith we ourselves are comforted of God."

Delighting in the Lord gives us strength to climb the mountain and reach the high places that God has prepared for us.

Habakkuk 3:19
"The LORD God is my strength, and he will make my feet like hinds' feet, and he will make me to walk upon mine high places."

As we delight in the Lord, He feeds us through His Word. When Jesus was tempted by Satan to make the stones bread, Jesus rebuked him.

Matthew 4:4
"But he answered and said, It is written, Man shall not live by bread alone, but by every word that proceedeth out of the mouth of God."

Delight in His Word.
Be hungry for the Word of God. Savor the Scriptures.

Where could the Lord lead you if you will simply delight in Him?
The only way to find out is to step out in faith, and daily seek His direction.
Let Him guide you to the high places.

Bible Reading
Judges 19-20 | Acts 28 | Psalm 86

If Ye Have Faith.

Matthew 17:20
"And Jesus said unto them, Because of your unbelief: for verily I say unto you, If ye have faith as a grain of mustard seed, ye shall say unto this mountain, Remove hence to yonder place; and it shall remove; and nothing shall be impossible unto you.

The disciples were confused. They were unable to cure the lunatick son, and were reproved by Jesus, being called a faithless generation. They came to Him privately and asked, "Why could not we cast him out?" Jesus answered them with our text verse today.

How many times in our life have we been confused, wondering why God has not allowed us to do something within our lives? We've all been there. But the disciples' problem is the same one we deal with on a daily basis. *"Because of your unbelief…"*

We say we believe that God can do all things, yet when it comes down to it our flesh doubts.

We doubt every day. Sometimes we are conscious of it, and sometimes we just doubt to be doubting. Our flesh wants us to focus on the negative. To never believe or to believe that it will never happen. **How many times does our flesh get the victory?**

Jesus gives us the solution to our problem of unbelief.
"…If ye have faith…"

He doesn't require much faith or great faith, but just the faith of a grain of mustard seed. Why did Christ choose the mustard seed for His example? The mustard seed is one of the tiniest seeds found in the Middle East. This implies that the amount of faith needed to do great things is very small. A black mustard plant grows to be over nine feet tall…yet it starts as just a tiny seed.

If we will have just a bit of true faith in God, we can see that nothing is impossible with Him…Little is much when God is in it!

Bible Reading
Judges 21 | Romans 1 | Psalm 87

He Knows The End.

Isaiah 46:9-10

"Remember the former things of old: for I am God, and there is none else; I am God, and there is none like me, Declaring the end from the beginning, and from ancient times the things that are not yet done, saying, My counsel shall stand, and I will do all my pleasure:"

Just like He told the children of Israel, God wants us to remember where He has brought us from. We made it safe thus far because He is God, and there is none like Him. We will make it safely through each day, because He knows the end from the beginning. **In the every day things, and in the entire life things, He knows the end from the beginning.**

The day conviction fell upon our hearts and we realized our need for a Saviour, He knew when we would accept Him, and how He would use our lives for His glory.

The morning we received the unpleasant news, He knew how the day would end, and how He would use it for our good.

He knows the end before the phone call.
He knows the end before the diagnosis.
He knows the end before the proposal.
He knows the end before the _____.

Regardless of your situation today,
He knows the end from the beginning.

Trust Him to carry you through.
Rest in His strength.
Delight in Him.

Bible Reading
Ruth 1 | Romans 2 | Psalm 88

Friends.

Proverbs 27:17
*"Iron sharpeneth iron;
so a man sharpeneth the countenance of his friend."*

The Lord places people in our lives for a reason. Some are only there for a short time, some stay forever. Some have been there for a long time, some come right when you need them. If God has crossed your path with a friend that walks alongside of you in your walk with the Lord, thank the Lord for them today.

Thank the Lord today for a friend that laughs with you.
Proverbs 17:22
*"A merry heart doeth good like a medicine:
but a broken spirit drieth the bones."*

Thank the Lord today for a friend that rebukes you.
Proverbs 27:5-6
"Open rebuke is better than secret love. Faithful are the wounds of a friend; but the kisses of an enemy are deceitful."

Thank the Lord today for a friend that encourages you.
Ecclesiastes 4:9-10
"Two are better than one; because they have a good reward for their labour. For if they fall, the one will lift up his fellow…"

Thank the Lord today for a friend that counsels you.
Proverbs 27:9
*"Ointment and perfume rejoice the heart:
so doth the sweetness of a man's friend by hearty counsel."*

Thank the Lord today for a friend that prays for you.
James 5:16
"Confess your faults one to another, and pray one for another, that ye may be healed. The effectual fervent prayer of a righteous man availeth much."

Thank the Lord today for the godly friends He has placed in your life, and for the Friend that sticks closer than a brother.
Proverbs 18:24
*"A man that hath friends must shew himself friendly:
and there is a friend that sticketh closer than a brother."*

Bible Reading
Ruth 2 | Romans 3 | Psalm 89 | 127

Encouragement.

Ecclesiastes 4:9-10
"Two are better than one; because they have a good reward for their labour. For if they fall, the one will lift up his fellow: but woe to him that is alone when he falleth; for he hath not another to help him up."

We often don't realize the drastic need to encourage others until we find ourselves in need of encouragement.

The best way to encourage others is with the Word of God.

After a tough day, we need encouraged to *"not be weary in well doing: for in due season we shall reap, if we faint not."* Galatians 6:9

During a long night with a sick child, we need encouraged that *"joy cometh in the morning."* Psalm 30:5

Before a big event, we need encouraged that we *"can do all things through Christ which strengtheneth"* us. Philippians 4:13

When we feel weak, we need encouraged that His *"grace is sufficient"*, for His *"strength is made perfect in weakness."* 2 Corinthians 12:9

In times of persecution, we need encouraged that *"the sufferings of this present time are not worthy to be compared with the glory which shall be revealed in us."* Romans 8:18

When we feel unsure about what the future holds, we need encouraged to *"lean not unto thine own understanding"*, but to *"acknowledge him, and he shall direct thy paths."* Proverbs 3:5-6

We want our friends and family to remind us of these and the many more Truths that can encourage us, but we should want to be the one to encourage others even more. **Would someone call you an encourager?**

May we all strive to be an encouragement to others in their time of need, so that when our time comes around, the Lord will send an encourager to our side.

When we feel like we are alone and need encouraged, let us follow David's example…*"David encouraged himself in the Lord his God."* 1 Samuel 30:6

Bible Reading

Ruth 3 | Romans 4 | Psalm 90

He Knows.

Matthew 6:8
"Be not ye therefore like unto them:
for your Father knoweth what things ye have need of,
before ye ask him."

Before you kneel, bow your head, or even close your eyes…**God knows what you need.** Before you ask, He knows what you need for your situation.

In the context of our verse today, Jesus is warning His disciples and followers that they should not use vain repetitions when they pray.

Do you find yourself praying the same prayer out of habit? Especially when it comes to praying before a meal, this is easy to do…but Jesus tells us not to pray with vain repetitions like the heathen do. **He already knows what we need, and He wants us to sincerely ask Him for His will in our situation.**

How does God know what we need before we ask? Because He is God, and there is no one else like Him! Since He inhabits eternity, He is already in our tomorrow, and He is aware of what needs will arise. Not only is He aware, but He cares for us to provide for us and supply our needs!

How amazing is it to know that our Heavenly Father watches over us today, and is already preparing us for tomorrow?

In times of doubt or despair, trust Him because He does all things well. **He is in control of everything.** He knows your name, and the number of hairs on your head. He knows everything about you, and yet He still loves you.

He loved us enough to give His only begotten Son to die for our sins and paid the debt that we could not pay.

You trusted Him with your eternity; trust Him for your tomorrow.

He knows who you need, what you need, when you need it, where you need it, and how you need it.

He knows.

Bible Reading
Ruth 4 | Romans 5 | Psalm 91 | 129

Stand In Liberty.

Galatians 5:1
"Stand fast therefore in the liberty wherewith Christ hath made us free, and be not entangled again with the yoke of bondage."

In New York Harbor on Liberty Island stands our nation's iconic symbol of the freedom that America has to offer, the Statue of Liberty. She is often referred to as Lady Liberty, holding tall a torch with broken chains at her feet. As immigrants came over from foreign lands seeking freedom, she was a welcoming sight. If you have ever visited New York City and caught a glimpse of her radiance, she beams with patriotism; especially from Liberty Island beneath her as she towers above thousands of tourists each day.

As much as she stands as a symbol of the freedom we have in our country, she is also a great reminder of the liberty we have in Christ Jesus.

The Apostle Paul knew what the liberty found in Christ can do for a person. When he met Jesus on the road to Damascus, he was set free from the bondage of his sinful life. He went on to preach of that same liberty all across Asia and Europe and pinned countless examples of that liberty under the inspiration of the Holy Spirit throughout the pages of the Bible.

John 8:32,36
"And ye shall know the truth, and the truth shall make you free…If the Son therefore shall make you free, ye shall be free indeed."

God wants to set us free through Jesus Christ in salvation, but He also provides us freedom to serve Him by loving those around us. He has called us into liberty!

Today seek to stand in the liberty that is found in the Lord.

Allow Him to guide you and give you boldness
to stand and shine your Light for His glory.

2 Corinthians 3:17
*"Now the Lord is that Spirit:
and where the Spirit of the Lord is,
there is liberty."*

Bible Reading
1 Samuel 1-2 | Romans 6 | Psalm 92

The Lord Alone.

Deuteronomy 32:12
*"So the LORD alone did lead him,
and there was no strange god with him."*

Israel did not lead themselves out of Egypt, nor sustain themselves in the midst of the wilderness. The Lord God, Jehovah, led and sustained them. It was by God's power, and His alone, that they were brought out of Egypt. Remember the ten plagues? Only God could have done each of them. He showed His mighty power by creating plague after plague in order to get Pharaoh's attention. Remember the Red Sea? The Lord parted the waters and made a way for them to cross over on dry ground. It was also by God's power, and His alone, that they were sustained for 40 years in the midst of the wilderness. Remember the manna He sent each day? Miraculously, their clothes and shoes never wore out. He led them in a Pillar of Cloud by day and a Pillar of Fire by night.

Deuteronomy 2:7
"For the LORD thy God hath blessed thee in all the works of thy hand: he knoweth thy walking through this great wilderness: these forty years the LORD thy God hath been with thee; thou hast lacked nothing."

Just as the Lord led them, provided for them, and sustained them through the wilderness…He wants to lead us, provide for us, and sustain us through the wildernesses of our lives. He is willing and able to do all of this and more for us…*"exceeding abundantly above all that we ask or think"* Ephesians 3:20. Yet, we continually choose to allow other things to take His rightful place in our lives. We often get our mind and focus on the things of this world, and what our flesh desires, that we make strange gods out of every day things. What might God do if every Christian yielded themselves to be led by the Lord alone? We would see revival like never before.

If you feel like you are at the banks of the Red Sea with no where to turn, God can make a way for you where there is no way. Allow Him to part the waters of your situation, and praise Him as you walk across on dry ground.

May we take time today to refocus our hearts and minds on Him alone, and allow Him to lead and guide us, while providing for us. May we remove the strange gods from our lives, and begin *"Looking unto Jesus…"* Hebrews 12:2. **Look unto Him today...The Lord alone!**

Bible Reading
1 Samuel 3-4 | Romans 7 | Psalm 93 | 131

The Worth Of A Soul.

Matthew 16:26
*"For what is a man profited, if he shall gain the whole world,
and lose his own soul? or what shall a man give in exchange for his soul?"*

Christ gave His life on Calvary in order to save the souls of men. He did not hold anything back. He gave it all in order to save us from spending eternity in the Lake of Fire.

How much would you give to win a soul to Christ?
We can give our time, our talent, our treasure.

What would those that are in hell right now say? If they doubted it before they experienced it, they now know what lies ahead for those who reject Christ. They are right now facing the punishment for their sin. They did not accept Christ's payment and chose to pay the debt themselves. How much would they give to have another chance to trust Christ?

The greatest love we can share to those around us is to share the Gospel with them. We can do all the good things we can, but if we do not share the love of Christ by telling what He did for them, we have failed miserably.

Where are our tears for the lost?
We must weep over those that do not know Christ.

Psalm 126:5-6
*"They that sow in tears shall reap in joy.
He that goeth forth and weepeth, bearing precious seed,
shall doubtless come again with rejoicing,
bringing his sheaves with him."*

We must endeavor to reach the lost before it's eternally too late. We must share the Good News of the Gospel with those who have not heard. Those that have heard, we must warn again.

We must weep. We must sow the Seed of the Gospel. We must give our lives so that others may know Christ. If we don't, who will?

How much is a soul worth to you?

Bible Reading
1 Samuel 5-6 | Romans 8 | Psalm 94

Exhausted.

Galatians 6:9
*"And let us not be weary in well doing:
for in due season we shall reap, if we faint not."*

Have you ever been exhausted, not just physically but mentally, emotionally and maybe even spiritually exhausted? The word weary in our text today literally means to be utterly spiritless, or exhausted. **The Lord knew that through our journey we would find ourselves at times to be utterly exhausted in every aspect of our lives.** He led the Apostle Paul to pin these words of warning to us so that we could guard ourselves against becoming weary or exhausted.

The latter part of the verse gives us a great reason to not grow exhausted in the fight... *"for in due season we shall reap"*. He tells us that eventually the well doing will pay off, and we will reap what we have sowed. But we will only get to reap those rewards if we do not faint along the way. Our reward may seem to be delayed, maybe even until we get to Heaven, but God promises us that He will bless us for our good works.

Don't quit today, Christian! Guard your heart. Stand against the wiles of the devil no matter what he throws your way. Look to the Lord for the strength to press on and pursue the victory.

**We can have victory by renewing ourselves
through God's Word everyday.**

2 Corinthians 4:16
*"For which cause we faint not; but though our outward man perish,
yet the inward man is renewed day by day."*

We can have victory by constantly asking the Lord for help.

Luke 18:1
*"And he spake a parable unto them to this end,
that men ought always to pray, and not to faint;"*

If you are exhausted, seek the victory today.

Bible Reading
1 Samuel 7-8 | Romans 9 | Psalm 95 | 133

Overwhelmed.

Luke 10:40-41
"But Martha was cumbered about much serving, and came to him, and said, Lord, dost thou not care that my sister hath left me to serve alone? bid her therefore that she help me. And Jesus answered and said unto her, Martha, Martha, thou art careful and troubled about many things:"

Martha was overwhelmed by her misplaced priorities. She had lost her joy in serving by being distracted by the demands she put on herself. Maybe you can relate with her.

In our fast paced, on the go, busy society we tend to get wrapped up in the details that don't really matter instead of focusing on what is most important, or slowing down to spend time with those we love.

Martha loved Jesus and wanted to serve Him, yet her focus was on the particulars instead of His presence.

How often do we set aside time to spend with the Lord only to find ourselves busy and troubled about other things instead? Or maybe we are so busy that we do not even set time aside to spend with Him.

Jesus told Martha, *"But one thing is needful…"*

Every thing else in life is not needed outside of His presence. When will we realize that when we leave Him out, we are the ones who are left without? **We are nothing without Him, and in order to walk with Him and shine our lights for Him, we must spend time in His presence.**

In John 12:1-2, we find Martha still serving, but yet she was seated at the table with Christ, along side her sister and brother. Martha had learned to be always abounding in the work of the Lord without forgetting about the Lord of the work.

Be busy working for the Lord, but be careful not to be so busy that you neglect to spend time with Him. **We will render ourselves ineffective if we allow ourselves to be serving without sitting at His table.**

Let us learn from Martha's example,
and remind ourselves daily the words of Christ to her,
"But one thing is needful…"

Bible Reading

1 Samuel 9-10 | Romans 10 | Psalm 96

Honour Your Parents.

Ephesians 6:1-2
*"Children, obey your parents in the Lord: for this is right.
Honour thy father and mother;
(which is the first commandment with promise;)."*

God points out to us through the Scripture that this is not only one of the commandments, but if we follow and obey this commandment we receive something in return…

Ephesians 6:3
"That it may be well with thee, and thou mayest live long on the earth."

We find that these verses refer back to the Old Testament
when God gave Moses the Law.

Exodus 20:12
"Honour thy father and thy mother: that thy days may be long upon the land which the LORD thy God giveth thee."

It appears that of the Ten Commandments, this is the only one that has a conditional blessing attached. If we will honour our parents, God will not only make things to be well with us, but He will also increase the days of our life.

May we all honour and bless our parents while we have them in our lives. Far too often we see those who have lost their parents wishing they had done more for them, spent more time with them, and showed how much they loved them.

As Mother's Day approaches, take the time to love on those around you. Honour them. Bless them. **God promises to bless us as we bless them.**

A Virtuous Woman.

Proverbs 31:10
"Who can find a virtuous woman? for her price is far above rubies."

Virtuous women are a rare find. **If God brings someone's name to mind, praise God for them and their presence in your life.** Learn from them. Glean their wisdom. God has given them to you for a reason.

A virtuous woman willingly serves wherever she is needed. - v.13

A virtuous woman will go wherever she is required. - v.14

A virtuous woman provides for her family and those she serves with. - v.15

A virtuous woman is careful to consider the Lord's guidance. - v.16

A virtuous woman asks the Lord to strengthen her for His glory. - v.17

A virtuous woman takes a Godly pride in what God has given her. - v.18

A virtuous woman endures the work regardless of the repercussions. - v.19

A virtuous woman allows others to see her worth. - v.25

A virtuous woman allows God to guide her thoughts and words. - v.26

A virtuous woman redeems the time God has given her. - v.27

A virtuous woman is praised by her family for the testimony she has. - v.28

A virtuous woman sticks out of the crowd. Her life speaks for itself. - v.29

When King Solomon pinned these Words under the inspiration of the Holy Spirit, he was referring to his mother...Bathsheba. What an example of the forgiveness that can be found from God if we will simply confess our sin! When Bathsheba's name is mentioned, what is the first thing you think of? Most likely David. This was the woman whom David looked upon with lust from his rooftop. That lust brought forth sin. That sin when it was finished brought forth death. But God forgave David when he confessed his sin and asked the Lord to cleanse him. Bathsheba's repentance is not documented in Scripture, yet in Proverbs 31 we find these principles that she taught to King Solomon. **She is a picture that God can bring you out of any circumstance and use you for His glory!** She raised her son Solomon, teaching him and admonishing him and God used him as the King of Israel.

Your greatest contribution to the Kingdom of God may not be something you achieve, but someone you raise.

Bible Reading

1 Samuel 13-14 | Romans 12 | Psalm 98

Praise Her.

Proverbs 31:30-31
"Favour is deceitful, and beauty is vain: but a woman that feareth the LORD, she shall be praised. Give her of the fruit of her hands; and let her own works praise her in the gates."

We live in a world where people are consumed with their outside appearance and their reputation, while unconcerned with the condition of their heart. Most people desire to be seen and known for their looks and their worth. Women today are surrounded by pressure to wear the latest style and put on the newest makeup brand. Fashion magazines fly off the shelves as women seek to find out what the new trend will be this season, and they prepare accordingly.

A virtuous woman does not focus on the trends of fashion or beauty. *"Strength and honour are her clothing."* Though she wants to look her best for her husband, and the Lord, she does not desire to be noticed for her looks. **God does not look on the outward appearance. He looketh on the heart.** He tells us that these virtuous women are hard to find, and their value is worth more than precious rubies.

Since virtuous women are a rare find, God tells us that we should praise them. Yet, the virtuous woman does not seek, request, or expect to be praised. She works out of love for her family, and allows the fruit of her labor to earn any praise she receives. She simply serves without expectation, knowing that the results are left up to the Lord which blessed her with the opportunity.

A virtuous woman's beauty shines from the inside out. If you are blessed to have a virtuous woman in your life, tell her how you notice her service. Show her how much she means to you. Actions speak louder than words.

Seek to be a virtuous woman today. Serve the Lord with gladness as you take care of the family He has blessed you with. Labor with strength and honour in the ministry He has given you. Allow the results of your labor to speak for you. All that we accomplish in this life is because He has enabled us.

Bible Reading
1 Samuel 15 | Romans 13 | Psalm 99

Tell Your Story.

Ephesians 2:8-9
"For by grace are ye saved through faith; and that not of yourselves: it is the gift of God: Not of works, lest any man should boast."

These verses are often used in soul winning or witnessing situations. They simplify salvation, help us display to others that God's grace can save them by placing their faith in what He did for them, and realizing that there is nothing they can do on their own to get to Heaven. What Truth that is!

How often when we use these verses in times of witnessing do we forget that the Truth here applies to us just as much as the person we are trying to win to the Lord?

God saved us by His grace.

There is nothing that we can do on our own to get to Heaven.
God saved us through our faith in what He did for us.

There is no amount of works we can do.
Salvation was a Gift to us!

Remind yourself today of the grace that God gave you that day you trusted in Him. Remember the faith that you placed in Him alone that day. Recognize again that you could never earn it on your own. Realize that you still possess the Gift you received that day, and nothing can take it away from you.

Restore the joy of your salvation today. **If we will daily remind ourselves of our salvation experience, it will encourage us to share our story with others.** The greatest witnessing tool that we have in our possession is the fact of what Jesus did for us!

Tell your story to someone today.

Bible Reading
1 Samuel 16 | Romans 14 | Psalm 100

A Name Above All Names.

Philippians 2:9-11
*"Wherefore God also hath highly exalted him, and given him a name
which is above every name: That at the name of Jesus every knee should
bow, of things in heaven, and things in earth, and things under the earth;
And that every tongue should confess
that Jesus Christ is Lord, to the glory of God the Father."*

Philippians 2 shows us the Ultimate Example of the life God desires us to live. **Jesus made Himself of no reputation and took upon Him the form of a servant.** Would others describe us as a servant today?

Because Jesus humbled Himself being found in fashion as a man and was obedient even unto the death of the cross, God exalted Him.

Luke 14:11
"For whosoever exalteth himself shall be abased; and he that humbleth himself shall be exalted."

God The Father chose to honor and exalt His Son by giving Him a Name that is above every other name. He chose the Name of Jesus for a reason. **The very Name of Jesus describes the reason why He came...Jehovah Is Salvation.**

Acts 4:12
"Neither is there salvation in any other: for there is none other name under heaven given among men, whereby we must be saved."

John 20:31
"But these are written, that ye might believe that Jesus is the Christ, the Son of God; and that believing ye might have life through his name."

In the world today the Name of Jesus is being pushed out of everything. Though the world may want to avoid Him, they will not get to Heaven without Him. He is the Way, the Only Way. He is the Truth. He is the Life. No one comes unto the Father, but by Him. But when Jesus is received and welcomed in, anything is possible.

Find rest in His Name today. Find boldness in His Name today. Find peace in His Name today. Proclaim His Name today.

There is just something about His Name!

Bible Reading
1 Samuel 17 | Romans 15 | Psalm 101 | 139

By The Book Success.

Joshua 1:8
"This book of the law shall not depart out of thy mouth; but thou shalt meditate therein day and night, that thou mayest observe to do according to all that is written therein: for then thou shalt make thy way prosperous, and then thou shalt have good success."

We all want to succeed in life. Success is not found in attending the right school, securing the right career, or marrying the right spouse. Even being a member of the right church will not make you successful. **Real success is found by developing Biblical principles in your life.** In our verse today, we find a Biblical equation for success. Moses had just died, and the Lord is speaking to Joshua, the new leader of the children of Israel.

Reflect On The Book.
"...but thou shalt meditate therein day and night..."
Sometimes the Lord may lay a verse on your heart that seems to stick with you all day. The more you ponder over it, the more God reveals the Truth of His Word. When you go to study out the verse, you then find more verses that go right along with the thought and context of the Scripture. This is meditating on The Word. Simply reflecting on the Truth of God's Word, and then beginning to attempt to apply it to your life. The more we reflect on God's Word, the more prosperous we will be and the more direction we will find.

Obey The Book.
"...that thou mayest observe to do according to all that is written therein..."
Once we observe a Truth within the Word of God, we must apply it to our lives by simply obeying. There are conditional promises all throughout Scripture that guarantee us something from the Lord, if we will simply obey the condition. **When we observe and obey what God has given us in the Scripture, we will find good success.**

Joshua's life serves as an example of this Truth for us. He obeyed what the Lord told him to do, and He achieved success as he led the children of Israel. It was Joshua who led the Battle of Jericho. It was Joshua who led Israel into the Promised Land. He observed the Lord's commands and was successful because of his obedience.

What could God do in our lives
if we will simply observe His commands and be obedient?

Bible Reading
1 Samuel 18-19 | Romans 16 | Psalm 102

Effectually & Fervently.

James 5:16
"Confess your faults one to another, and pray one for another, that he may be healed. The effectual fervent prayer of a righteous man availeth much."

The words *"effectual fervent"* are translated from the Greek word, *energeō*, which means to be at work, to put forth power, or to display one's activity. The word itself sounds like energy, doesn't it? **God wants us to put energy into our prayers!** He wants us to pray with power without wavering in our belief that our God can supply whatever the need!

James 1:6
"But let him ask in faith, nothing wavering. For he that wavereth is like a wave of the sea driven with the wind and tossed."

When the righteous actively pray, God promises that much can happen.
We just need to believe that He will accomplish that which He pleases.

Mark 11:22-24
*"And Jesus answering saith unto them, Have faith in God.
For verily I say unto you, That whosoever shall say unto this mountain,
Be thou removed, and be thou cast into the sea; and shall not doubt in his heart, but shall believe that those things which he saith shall come to pass;
he shall have whatsoever he saith. Therefore I say unto you,
What things soever ye desire, when ye pray,
believe that ye receive them, and ye shall have them."*

In order to pray effectually and fervently, we must first believe that God is Able. He is Able to heal the sick. He is Able to supply the need. He is Able to direct our paths. He is Able to save that soul. He is Able!

Before we even bow our head, or utter the first word of our prayer, **we must believe in the God Who answers prayer, and His ability to provide for us.** His ears are open to our cry. He knows our need before we even ask. Believe in His provision. Believe in His unfailing ability to do exceeding abundantly above all that we ask or think.

Endeavor today to pray effectually and fervently.
Put energy behind your prayers,
and patiently wait for God to move in your situation!

Bible Reading
1 Samuel 20-21 | 1 Corinthians 1 | Psalm 103 | 141

Pray Believing.

Matthew 21:22
*"And all things, whatsoever ye shall ask in prayer,
believing, ye shall receive."*

Why must we believe when we pray? **Believing takes the emphasis off of ourselves and off of the prayer we offer, and places the focus on the One Who is Able to answer.** We must believe in Him, and then believe that He is Able to provide whatever the need. That belief must first be expressed in faith within our heart and then expressed within the prayer we pray to our Heavenly Father.

We see this Truth described in Romans in reference to salvation.

Romans 10:10
*"For with the heart man believeth unto righteousness;
and with the mouth confession is made unto salvation."*

In salvation it is not the prayer that saves you, but your belief (faith) in that Who you are asking is able to accomplish the request. If someone asks the Lord to save them from their sins without believing that He alone can save them, the prayer is in vain.

The same Truth applies to every prayer we pray. **If we do not pray believing that God can and will deliver our plea if it is His Will to do so, we pray in vain.** The words are just words, but when those same words are combined with faith that God is Able anything is possible!

Luke 18:27
*"And he said, The things which are impossible with men
are possible with God."*

Pray believing.
Pray expecting.

God will meet you at your expectation!

Bible Reading
1 Samuel 22-23 | 1 Corinthians 2 | Psalm 104

25 Words.

John 3:16
"For God so loved the world, that he gave his only begotten Son, that whosoever believeth in him should not perish, but have everlasting life."

25 words. So much Truth. God in His foreknowledge knew the moment He breathed life into Adam that one day He would give His Son in order to have a relationship with him. He knew that because of one man's sin, One Man would have to die to save the entire world. Within the 25 words of the most well known verse of the Bible lies the Truth of God's eternal plan of salvation.

"For God so loved…"
God loved His creation so much that He gave us Himself wrapped in human flesh. The Word dwelt among us so that we could dwell with Him.

"…the world,…"
God did not and does not select a few or some to be His elect. Today's version of Calvinism wants us to believe that He loves all of us, but He only died for those He chose to be with Him. John 3:16 tells us the Truth. God so loved the world. He died for every single person that has ever been and will ever be born… because He loves us.

"…that he gave his only begotten Son,…"
God gave us everything in His Son. Jesus Christ willingly left His throne in Heaven to be made flesh and dwell among His creation. God in the flesh lived a sinless life and walked willingly to Calvary to be crucified. God gave His Son. Jesus gave His life.

"…that whosoever believeth in him…"
God reiterates that He so loved the world that whosoever believeth in His only begotten Son could be saved. Whosoever. Anyone, no matter who, if they believe in Jesus Christ as their only means of salvation can be saved.

"…should not perish, but have everlasting life."
Our sin separates us from God, but the moment we believe in Jesus Christ and place our faith in Him alone to save us, we obtain everlasting life. This removes the penalty of perishing and provides the Way for us to spend eternity in the presence of our Saviour. Everlasting life is made possible through Jesus Christ, God's only begotten Son.

Share the Truth of these 25 words with someone today.

Bible Reading
1 Samuel 24-25 | 1 Corinthians 3 | Psalm 105 | 143

Communicate Effectively.

Philemon 6
"That the communication of thy faith may become effectual by the acknowledging of every good thing which is in you in Christ Jesus."

How are you communicating your faith?
Is the communication of your faith effectual?
Are you seeing fruit?
When we ask ourselves these questions, we begin to take a look at our effectiveness as disciples for Christ.

How can we make our communication of our faith effective?
We must acknowledge that every good thing we have,
every good thing that is in us, is all because of Jesus Christ.

It is Him Who works in us for His good pleasure.

Philippians 2:13
*"For it is God which worketh in you both
to will and to do of his good pleasure."*

It is Him Who works through us.

Galatians 2:20
"I am crucified with Christ: nevertheless I live; yet not I, but Christ liveth in me: and the life which I now live in the flesh I live by the faith of the Son of God, who loved me, and gave himself for me."

It is Him Who gives the increase of the fruit we that we bare.

1 Corinthians 3:6
"I have planted, Apollos watered; but God gave the increase."

Communicate your faith today.
Acknowledge that everything is because of Him.

Bible Reading
1 Samuel 26-27 | 1 Corinthians 4 | Psalm 106

An Open Door.

1 Corinthians 16:9
*"For a great door and effectual is opened unto me,
and there are many adversaries."*

The Lord had opened a door for Paul
to preach the Gospel to the Gentiles.

Acts 14:27
*"And when they were come, and had gathered the church together, they
rehearsed all that God had done with them, and how he had opened the
door of faith unto the Gentiles."*

The Lord has also opened a door unto us. His last words before He
ascended up into Heaven were the Great Commission.

Matthew 28:19-20
*"Go ye therefore, and teach all nations, baptizing them in the name of the
Father, and of the Son, and of the Holy Ghost: Teaching them to observe
all things whatsoever I have commanded you: and, lo, I am with you alway,
even unto the end of the world. Amen."*

What are we doing with the door that has been opened unto us? Are we
sitting back and letting others carry out the Great Commission? Christ did
not exclude any of us from His command. He promises to equip us with the
power to be witnesses of the Gospel.

Acts 1:8
*"But ye shall receive power, after that the Holy Ghost is come upon you:
and ye shall be witnesses unto me both in Jerusalem, and in all Judaea,
and in Samaria, and unto the uttermost part of the earth."*

Start in your Jerusalem, wherever that may be.

There will be persecution. The adversaries will come, some even
camouflaged as Christians. Our enemy walketh about like a roaring lion,
seeking whom he may devour. Resist him, and he will flee. *"...be strong in
the Lord, and in the power of his might."* Ephesians 6:10

Stand today with the whole armour of God.
We have an open door.
Be bold, and use your time wisely.

Bible Reading
1 Samuel 28-29 | 1 Corinthians 5 | Psalm 107 | 145

No Turning Back.

Romans 11:29
"For the gifts and calling of God are without repentance."

God does not repent, or change His mind, in His gifts and calling. They are irrevocable. What He purposes, He accomplishes. What He promises, He delivers. When He enters into a covenant, He does not regret it.

Those who come to Him for salvation, He will not turn away. He is not willing that any should perish. His gifts of grace, of salvation, of adoption, of justification, of eternal life, etc. are forever.

We as followers of God should develop this attribute in our walk with Him. Once we place our faith and trust in Jesus Christ as our Saviour, we begin our walk with and for God. **Regardless of the persecution we face or the suffering we endure, we must press on in our work with Him.**

Colossians 1:22-23
"…to present you holy and unblameable and unreproveable in his sight: If ye continue in the faith grounded and settled, and be not moved away from the hope of the gospel, which ye have heard…"

Continue. Ground and settle yourself in your faith. Be unmoveable, always abounding in the work of the Lord. **Don't turn around.** Endeavor to daily die to yourself, pick up your cross, and follow Him.

Matthew 16:24
"Then said Jesus unto his disciples, If any man will come after me, let him deny himself, and take up his cross, and follow me."

I have decided to follow Jesus;
no turning back, no turning back.

Though none go with me, still I will follow;
no turning back, no turning back.

My cross I'll carry, till I see Jesus;
no turning back, no turning back.

The world behind me, the cross before me;
no turning back, no turning back.
Anonymous

Bible Reading

1 Samuel 30-31 | 1 Corinthians 6 | Psalm 108

His Grace Is Sufficient.

2 Corinthians 12:8-9

"For this thing I besought the Lord thrice, that it might depart from me. And he said unto me, My grace is sufficient for thee: for my strength is made perfect in weakness. Most gladly therefore will I rather glory in my infirmities, that the power of Christ may rest upon me."

Aren't you glad that God's grace is sufficient? Often this verse is interpreted that God's grace is enough (and it is!), but more often than not the Scripture has hidden treasures that the Lord wants us to search to find.

Paul had prayed three times asking God to remove his thorn in the flesh, yet God answered in a different way than Paul wanted or expected. His thorn was never removed. Instead, Jesus Christ told Paul that **His grace was more than enough.** The word sufficient here means to suffice, but it also means to be content, to be made strong, to be possessed of unfailing strength.

Hebrews 13:5

"Let your conversation be without covetousness; and be content with such things as ye have: for he hath said, I will never leave thee, nor forsake thee."

Philippians 4:13

"I can do all things through Christ which strengtheneth me."

Although God chose not to remove the thorn, **Paul decided to glory in his physical infirmity because it made him rely on Christ's grace and strength.** It was a daily battle for Paul to serve and minister to the people he was sent to. The word glory here means to rejoice or find joy within. Paul did not focus on the negative aspects of his thorn or what it hindered him from accomplishing. He instead found joy in the fact that his thorn caused him to rely not on his own strength but in Christ's.

God may choose not to remove your thorn. But rest assured that if you choose to rejoice despite the struggle, despite the pain, God's grace will give you an unfailing strength to endure. **Allow His strength to make you strong today.** Your thorn may not be a physical ailment. His grace is sufficient for every trial, every storm, every difficulty, every circumstance, every problem. His grace is sufficient for every day. The good days, the bad days, the in-between days, the chaotic days, the uneventful days, the days when you face the unknown of the future… **His grace is sufficient.**

Bible Reading
2 Samuel 1-2 | 1 Corinthians 7 | Psalm 109 | 147

Spiritually Minded.

Colossians 3:2
"Set your affection on things above, not on things on the earth."

God wants us to focus our minds on heavenly eternal things instead of the temporal every day things. Take an account today of what has your focus.

Are you constantly looking at material things, maybe having a "keeping up with the Joneses" mentality? Are you career driven, wanting to climb the corporate ladder? There is nothing wrong with having nice things or desiring a successful career. **The trouble comes when your attention or motivation is consumed with the secular things.**

Romans 8:6
"For to be carnally minded is death;
but to be spiritually minded is life and peace."

To be carnally minded refers to pursuing fleshly things. The lust of the flesh, the lust of the eyes, and the pride of life are all things that the Lord warns us about throughout Scripture. Are you pursuing fleshly things?

God desires for us to be spiritually minded.
Are you focusing on eternity?

Paul contrasts the carnal mind with the spiritual mind. Note the disparity of death and life. Romans 8 is focused on spiritual life or death and the love of God that we cannot be separated from once we receive Him.

Being spiritually minded comes from having eternal life. Once we are in Christ, and we become new creatures, our desire should be to share with others what He has done for us. To keep the Gospel to ourselves is selfish. Share your faith with others. Allow God to change their life too.

If you have lost your focus on eternity, refocus today. Ask God to help you seek to invest in eternity by supporting and contributing to the spreading of the Gospel of Jesus Christ.

Those who invest in eternity with not be empty handed when they reach their heavenly home. **Be spiritually minded today, and every day.**

Bible Reading
2 Samuel 3-4 | 1 Corinthians 8 | Psalm 110

Pride & Humility.

Matthew 23:12
*"And whosoever shall exalt himself shall be abased;
and he that shall humble himself shall be exalted."*

Here we see a contrast between pride and humility. The Lord Jesus Christ spoke these Words as an example for us to learn from. He promises that not only is there a punishment that comes from exalting ourselves, but there is also a reward for humbling ourselves. We find these principles and promises throughout Scripture.

The Punishment – Proverbs 16:5,18-19
"Every one that is proud in heart is an abomination to the Lord: though hand join in hand, he shall not be unpunished…Pride goeth before destruction, and an haughty spirit before a fall. Better it is to be of an humble spirit with the lowly, than to divide the spoil with the proud."

The Reward - I Peter 5:6
"Humble yourselves therefore under the mighty hand of God, that he may exalt you in due time."

Our passage today also displays a unique Truth in relation to salvation. Those who come to God submitting the works that they have done in order to be worthy of Heaven are exalting themselves. When we rely on our works, we exalt ourselves because of our pride. God promises that there is a punishment…*"For the wages of sin is death…"*

God has already paid the price; He gives us the free gift of salvation through His Son, Jesus Christ, *"…but the gift of God is eternal life through Jesus Christ our Lord."* In order to come to God and receive that Free Gift, we must humble ourselves. **When we come to God with a humble heart admitting ourselves as a sinner, placing our faith and trust in Jesus Christ alone for salvation, we are exalted to become the Sons of God.**

James 4:10
"Humble yourselves in the sight of the Lord, and he shall lift you up."

Bible Reading
2 Samuel 5-6 | 1 Corinthians 9 | Psalm 111

Rise Up & Build.

Nehemiah 2:18
"Then I told them of the hand of my God which was upon me; as also the king's words that he had spoken unto me. And they said, Let us rise up and build. So they strengthened their hands for this good work."

Nehemiah had confidence. Not in himself, but confidence that God would use him to do a work among His people. You can be confident in God's ability to work through you without exalting yourself.

When we follow God's leading, we cannot go wrong. If God has ordained it, it cannot fail. **Where God guides, He provides.** Where He leads, He precedes. Where He directs, He protects.

We can follow Nehemiah's example. He told of his God-given vision, and was bold to proclaim what God had shown him. Through his leadership, God allowed the wall to be built by the people in a cooperative team effort. God knew their heart, and He blessed their efforts.

What vision has God given you?
What does He want you to rise up and build?

Proverbs 29:18
*"Where there is no vision, the people perish:
but he that keepeth the law, happy is he."*

**Develop a God-given confidence
by relying on Him to work through you.**
Be bold as He strengthens your hands for His work.

Rise up. Build.
Let God enable you in all that you do today.

Bible Reading
2 Samuel 7-8 | 1 Corinthians 10 | Psalm 112

Ecclesiastes 5:1-2
"Keep thy foot when thou goest to the house of God, and be more ready to hear, than to give the sacrifice of fools: for they consider not that they do evil. Be not rash with thy mouth, and let not thine heart be hasty to utter any thing before God: for God is in heaven, and thou upon earth: therefore let thy words be few."

God has a reason for everything. He gave us two ears and one mouth. Perhaps it is because we should listen twice as much as we speak. Our passage today refers to listening and speaking within the house of God and within His presence.

As he writes of the vanities he learned within his aged years, Solomon exhorts us to be aware that before we enter the church house we should prepare our hearts and ears to listen to what God has for us to hear. We are to *"be more ready to hear"*; he knew that listening was important.

How often are we too distracted by our murmurings and disputings to really hear the message that God has given the preacher?

In a high technological society, our cell phones often distract us during a service. Text messages and social media notifications do not stop when we enter the sanctuary. We sit in the pew "ready" to worship our Lord and tend to be more in tune with the notifications than we are with what God has for us during the service. **Does God need to send us a text message to get our attention?**

Many times we are more concerned about what we "have to say" than what we need to hear. God wants us to listen. God wants us to hear Him.

James 1:19
"Wherefore, my beloved brethren, let every man be swift to hear, slow to speak, slow to wrath:"

Take note of the ratio of how much you hear and how much you say today. **Ask God to help you realize when you need to listen.**

Bible Reading
2 Samuel 9-10 | 1 Corinthians 11 | Psalm 113

Go To Church.

Hebrews 10:23-25
"Let us hold fast the profession of our faith without wavering; (for he is faithful that promised;) And let us consider one another to provoke unto love and to good works: Not forsaking the assembling of ourselves together, as the manner of some is; but exhorting one another: and so much the more, as ye see the day approaching."

How can we continue to hold fast our profession of faith?
How can we provoke one another unto love and to good works?
By not *"forsaking the assembling of ourselves together"*.

Under the inspiration of the Holy Spirit, the writer of Hebrews acknowledges that there were some that were not faithful… *"as the manner of some is"*. This Truth still applies today and perhaps on an even greater level. We have seen a trend in recent days of churches going away from their "traditional" schedules due to lack of attendance in the evening and midweek services. Churches try to appeal to their targeted demographics, while compromising on what has worked in the past… Biblical principles. While some may believe that an evening service on Sundays only stems from tradition, its foundation lies within the pages of Scripture.

John 20:18-19
"Mary Magdalene came and told the disciples that she had seen the Lord, and that he had spoken these things unto her. Then the same day at evening, being the first day of the week, when the doors were shut where the disciples were assembled for fear of the Jews…"

The disciples assembled together on Sunday evening. So should we. Instead of making only Sunday morning a priority, we should make church a priority every time the doors are open, *"Not forsaking the assembling of ourselves together, as the manner of some is…"* Hebrews 10:25

Why is church attendance so important?

Matthew 18:20
"For where two or three are gathered together in my name, there am I in the midst of them."

Bible Reading
2 Samuel 11-12 | 1 Corinthians 12 | Psalm 114

Opportunity.

Galatians 6:10
"As we have therefore opportunity, let us do good unto all men, especially unto them who are of the household of faith."

Opportunity: an amount of time or a situation in which something can be done; a set of circumstances that makes it possible to do something.

We as Christians have an unknown amount of time left on this earth to do something for the cause of Christ. **We need to redeem the time that we have while we have it.** What are we doing with our opportunity?

The Apostle Paul pinned these words under the inspiration of the Holy Spirit to encourage the people of Galatia to do good unto all men but especially to those who were a part of their church.

Are we doing good unto all men? Are we doing good to our church family and the ministry that God has allowed us to be a part of? We have been given an opportunity to make a difference.

Opportunities do not last forever. What opportunity have you let pass you by? Was it forgetting to invite the cashier at Walmart to church? Was it the lady you passed on the street that you didn't give a Gospel tract to?

We must use every opportunity we are given.
Our life is like a vapor, it will soon vanish away.

James 4:14-15
"Whereas ye know not what shall be on the morrow. For what is your life? It is even a vapour, that appeareth for a little time, and then vanisheth away. For that ye ought to say, If the Lord will, we shall live, and do this, or that."

Don't let an opportunity past you by.

Bible Reading
2 Samuel 13-14 | 1 Corinthians 13 | Psalm 115

He Sees The Rainbow.

Ezekiel 1:28
"As the appearance of the bow that is in the cloud in the day of rain, so was the appearance of the brightness round about. This was the appearance of the likeness of the glory of the LORD. And when I saw it, I fell upon my face, and I heard a voice of one that spake."

The prophet Ezekiel knew the Lord was in the rainbow. He remembered the promise God had made and symbolized by the bow in the cloud. The rainbow in Ezekiel's vision was around a throne. Upon that throne sat a Man, the Man Christ Jesus. This passage is reminiscent to Revelation 4, where we see another glimpse of Christ's throne and a description of the worthiness of the One Who occupies the throne.

Revelation 4:11
"Thou art worthy, O Lord, to receive glory and honour and power: for thou hast created all things, and for thy pleasure they are and were created."

After a summer rain, sometimes the majesty of a beautiful rainbow fills the sky opposite the sun. The peacefulness from the calm of the storm eases the havoc that the storm caused. Isn't that just like our lives as Christians? After the Lord speaks *"Peace, be still"* to our storm, He sometimes sends us a rainbow of provision to remind us that He is in control, and He is working things for our good.

Oftentimes when we are focused on the storms of our lives, we forget that God already sees the rainbow that awaits us once the storm is over. He sees the end from the beginning. **He sees the rainbow when we only see clouds.**

The same One that Ezekiel saw is the Lord you serve today. The same One Who sits on the throne of Heaven, Who is worthy to receive glory and honour and power, is the One Who is waiting to hear your cry today. He is *"the same, yesterday, and to day, and for ever."*

God knows what rainbow you need in your life.
Seek Him today.

Bible Reading
2 Samuel 15-16 | 1 Corinthians 14 | Psalm 116

The Right Hand.

Isaiah 41:10,13
*"Fear thou not; for I am with thee: be not dismayed; for I am thy God:
I will strengthen thee; yea, I will help thee; yea, I will uphold thee with
the right hand of my righteousness…For I the Lord thy God will hold
thy right hand, saying unto thee, Fear not; I will help thee."*

Earlier this year, we visited this chapter in Isaiah. We discussed the Truths of verses 8-10, which remind us that we are chosen, called, and comforted.

Praise God for the times when He comforts us!

We find the reason for that comfort in the latter part of verse 10. **God upholds us by the Right Hand of His righteousness.** Who sits at the right hand of God the Father? His Son, Jesus Christ! It is through Him that we are upheld and comforted when we are fearful and dismayed. It is by Him that we are strengthened and helped.

He reminds us of this Truth again in verse 13.
"Fear not; I will help thee."

What is happening when He speaks these Words and reminds us of the comfort He brings? He is holding our right hand!

Have you ever been in the middle of despair and confusion only to seek the Lord and be overcome with the peace that passes all understanding? It is at that moment that the Lord holds our right hand and comforts us like only He can. **Allow the Lord to take you by the right hand today and help guide you through the battle you are facing.** Maybe it seems that no one understands, maybe no one even knows about it…but God does. He is working everything for your good. **You only need to be still, and allow Him to help you in your time of need.**

Praise the Lord that His hand is never too busy to hold the hands of His children! Reach out to Him today. He will meet you right where you are. **Because the Lord our God holds our right hand by His Right Hand, we can turn our fear into faith!**

Bible Reading
2 Samuel 17-18 | 1 Corinthians 15 | Psalm 117 | 155

Poured Out.

1 Samuel 1:15
*"And Hannah answered and said, No, my lord, I am a woman
of a sorrowful spirit: I have drunk neither wine nor strong drink,
but have poured out my soul before the Lord."*

Hannah had run out of words to describe her need, so she poured out her soul before the Lord. He heard the wordless petition that Hannah offered. He knew her heart.

In those times of our lives where we are so overwhelmed by the effects of our circumstance that we do not even have the words to form a prayer, **God hears our heart.** The Holy Spirit intercedes on our behalf when we are unable to pray.

Romans 8:26-27
"Likewise the Spirit also helpeth our infirmities: for we know not what we should pray for as we ought: but the Spirit itself maketh intercession for us with groanings which cannot be uttered. And he that searcheth the hearts knoweth what is the mind of the Spirit, because he maketh intercession for the saints according to the will of God."

Isn't it encouraging that when we don't even know what to pray, God hears our hearts?

Hannah poured herself out much like the drink offering that Jacob poured upon the altar he had built in the place where God talked with him. This was a sacrifice of dedication to the Lord. The drink offering is symbolic of the ultimate pouring out of sacrifice… Jesus' blood on the cross.

Have you poured yourself out to the Lord?

When there are no words to convey how you feel to the Lord, pour yourself out to Him. **Plead your situation to Him through tears and wordless prayers. He will hear you.**

Psalm 62:8
"Trust in him at all times; ye people, pour out your heart before him: God is a refuge for us. Selah."

Pour yourself out to the Lord today. Empty yourself of yourself so that the Lord can have full reign to work within you and your situation. It is only when we empty ourselves of ourselves that we can truly see God move as only He can.

Bible Reading
2 Samuel 19-20 | 1 Corinthians 16 | Psalm 118

The Word of God Is Not Bound.

2 Timothy 2:9
"Wherein I suffer trouble, as an evil doer, even unto bonds;
but the word of God is not bound."

Regardless of the persecution aimed at us as Christians today, we can be encouraged just as Paul was…*"but the word of God is not bound."* The Apostle Paul knew that despite the powers that tried to silence him and the disciples, God's Word will still work, it will still operate in the hearts of men.

Although this world may try to bind the hands of those proclaiming the Gospel of Christ, the Word of God can never be bound.

Psalm 119 is the longest chapter in the Bible which further explains just how much of a priority the Word of God should be in our lives.

The "Word of God Chapter of the Bible"…176 verses…giving us at least as many principles to live by. In nearly every verse there is at least one Word that refers to the Word of God.

Words referencing the Word of God:

Law of the Lord	Commandments
Testimonies	Judgments
Ways	Word
Precepts	Faithfulness
Statutes	Ordinances

When reading through the chapter, make an effort to find the specific Word within the verse that references the Word of God. Among the references are Truths about the Scripture that we can apply to our lives and allow It to encourage us in our walk with the Lord. **The Word of God magnifies Itself.** Later on in the Book of Psalms, the Scripture tells us that the Lord magnifies His Word even above His Name.

Psalm 138:2
"I will worship toward thy holy temple, and praise thy name
for thy lovingkindness and for thy truth:
for thou hast magnified thy word above all thy name."

Allow Psalm 119 to broaden your love for the Word.
Delight in Him today.

Bible Reading
Psalm 119

Freedom By Love.

John 15:13
*"Greater love hath no man than this,
that a man lay down his life for his friends."*

"Only two defining forces have ever offered to die for you.
Jesus Christ and an American Soldier. One died for your freedom,
the Other died for your soul."
Unknown

Remembering our freedom should be more than just a yearly holiday and excuse to have a 3-day weekend. Were it not for the soldiers who have sacrificed their lives for our country, we could not enjoy the freedoms that America has to offer to its residents and citizens. The men and women who defend our country and our flag do so out of duty but more so out of love. They must love the country they represent in order to be willing to lay down their life while protecting it. Let us not take for granted the freedom we possess that comes at the hands of American soldiers.

Our soldiers provide us the freedom to worship and serve the Ultimate Soldier. **Jesus Christ is our ultimate Example of the cost of freedom.** He laid down His life willingly so that He could have a relationship with us.

He made the sacrifice because He loved us.

Romans 5:6-8
"For when we were yet without strength, in due time Christ died for the ungodly. For scarcely for a righteous man will one die: yet peradventure for a good man some would even dare to die. But God commendeth his love toward us, in that, while we were yet sinners, Christ died for us."

While we remember our earthly freedoms, let us not forget the freedom that Christ provides for us every day, and for eternity. We are no longer in bondage of eternal death for His blood paid the debt we could not pay.

Galatians 5:1
"Stand fast therefore in the liberty wherewith Christ hath made us free…"

John 8:36
"If the Son therefore shall make you free, ye shall be free indeed."

Bible Reading
2 Samuel 21-22 | 2 Corinthians 1 | Psalm 120

Take A Stand.

Jeremiah 32:33
*"And they have turned unto me the back, and not the face:
though I taught them, rising up early and teaching them,
yet they have not harkened to receive instruction."*

How sad it is to see people who have been privileged to grow up in church turn their back on the Truth they have been taught. It may start with a change in the music they listen to, then dabbling in multiple versions of the Bible, and then a change in their entire belief in God and the Biblical Truths they had been taught since a child. It is heart wrenching to see such blatant choices to dismiss the doctrines they once believed in. But how much more must God's heart be grieved? Within the context of our text today that God was not pleased with the people of Jeremiah's day. They turned their backs on the Truths they had been taught. We must take a stand for the Truth.

Stand for the Scriptures. Whether it is realized at the time or not, a change in Bibles is a change in doctrine. When modern versions change or remove verses from God's Word, fundamental beliefs are changed or removed.

Acts 8:37
"And Philip said, If thou believest with all thine heart, thou mayest. And he answered and said, I believe that Jesus Christ is the Son of God."

In the previous verse, the eunuch asks Philip what hinders him from being baptized. Most of the modern versions today remove this verse stating that it was not in "most of the original manuscripts." Yet this verse is within the canon of Scripture within the King James Bible. Removing this verse from the text removes the need for believing in Christ for salvation.

Stand for Separation. Today e are seeing an ecumenical movement of epic proportions among today's "Christians". The church is becoming more like the world everyday. God tells us to separate ourselves from the world. When we are friends with the world, we make ourselves God's enemy.

James 4:4
"…know ye not that friendship of the world is enmity with God? whosoever therefore will be a friend of the world is the enemy of God."

A wise man once said, "If you don't stand for something, you'll fall for anything." **Take a stand today for Biblical Truth.**

Bible Reading
2 Samuel 23-24 | 2 Corinthians 2 | Psalm 121 | 159

For His Name's Sake.

Psalm 31:3
*"For thou art my rock and my fortress;
therefore for thy name's sake lead me, and guide me."*

David acknowledges many times that God is his Rock, his Refuge, and his Fortress. He had to seek safety sheltered in the arms of God numerous times throughout his life. Can you relate with David?

Psalm 18:2-3,6
"The Lord is my rock, and my fortress, and my deliverer; my God, my strength, in whom I will trust; my buckler, and the horn of my salvation, and my high tower. I will call upon the Lord, who is worthy to be praised: so shall I be saved from mine enemies…In my distress I called upon the Lord, and cried unto my God: he heard my voice out of his temple, and my cry came before him, even into his ears."

He knew that the ears of the Lord were ready and willing to hear his cry, and constantly asked the Lord for help. In this text, he spends the beginning of the chapter acknowledging Who God Is, and the mentions *"for thy name's sake"* within his prayer. **God does not deliver us, protect us, or lead us because we deserve it, but because of Who He Is.**

He is Righteous.
Psalm 23:3
"He restoreth my soul: he leadeth me in the paths of righteousness for his name's sake."

He is the Pardoner of sin.
Psalm 25:11
"For thy name's sake, O Lord, pardon mine iniquity; for it is great."

He is Powerful to save.
Psalm 106:8
"Nevertheless he saved them for his name's sake, that he might make his mighty power to be known."

God's attributes describe not only Who He Is, but also what He offers to us. We have mercy because God is Merciful. We have love because God is Love. What could the Lord do for you *"for his name's sake"*? **Focus on the attributes of God today, and discover more of the Truth of Who God is.**

Bible Reading
1 Kings 1-2 | 2 Corinthians 3 | Psalm 122

Divine Direction.

Psalm 32:8
*"I will instruct thee and teach thee in the way which thou shalt go:
I will guide thee with mine eye."*

God promises to instruct us, teach us, and guide us.
We can receive Divine Direction, if we will seek to find it.
When faced with a difficult decision, God's Word has the answer.

He Instructs Us Through His Word.
Psalm 19:8
*"The statutes of the Lord are right, rejoicing the heart:
the commandment of the Lord is pure, enlightening the eyes."*

He Teaches Us Through The Counsel Of Others.
Proverbs 11:14
*"Where no counsel is, the people fall:
but in the multitude of counsellors there is safety."*

He Guides Us Through The Holy Spirit.
John 16:13-14
*"Howbeit when he, the Spirit of truth, is come, he will guide you into all
truth: for he shall not speak of himself; but whatsoever he shall hear, that
shall he speak: and he will shew you things to come. He shall glorify me:
for he shall receive of mine, and shall shew it unto you."*

How has the Lord shown you Divine Direction? Ask Him to remind you
today of how He has directed you through difficult decisions before, and
rejoice in the fact that if He did it then, He can do it now…for He never
changes!

Seek the Lord today for the wisdom to make the right decision.

Bible Reading
1 Kings 3-4 | 2 Corinthians 4 | Psalm 123 | 161

Divine Guidance & Provision.

Isaiah 58:9-11
*"Then shalt thou call, and the Lord shall answer; thou shalt cry,
and he shall say, Here I am. If thou take away from the midst of thee the
yoke, the putting forth of the finger, and speaking vanity; And if thou draw
out thy soul to the hungry, and satisfy the afflicted soul; then shall thy light
rise in obscurity, and thy darkness be as the noon day;
And the Lord shall guide thee continually, and satisfy thy soul in drought,
and make fat thy bones: and thou shalt be like a watered garden, and like
a spring of water, whose waters fail not."*

Aren't you glad that the Lord is always there when we cry out to Him? Have you ever felt like He said "Here I am" to you just when you needed Him? How encouraging it is to know that our Heavenly Father has His ears open to us. What a privilege!

**When we earnestly come to the Lord in prayer,
and seek His face for help,
we will never leave disappointed.**

The Lord wants to guide us to exactly what we need.
He will continually guide us, if we will continually seek Him.

When our souls are dry and in need of a drink, the Water of Life is always there to satisfy our longing as only He can. Not only will He quench our thirst, the Bread of Life will make fat our bones. He wants to feed and strengthen us when we are hungry. Like the miracle of the multiplication, there is always more Bread than the need demands.

He is more than enough!

Bible Reading
1 Kings 5-6 | 2 Corinthians 5 | Psalm 124

What Do You Glory In?

Jeremiah 9:23-24
"Thus saith the LORD, Let not the wise man glory in his wisdom, neither let the mighty man glory in his might, let not the rich man glory in his riches: But let him that glorieth glory in this, that he understandeth and knoweth me, that I am the LORD which exercise lovingkindness, judgment, and righteousness, in the earth: for in these things I delight, saith the LORD."

What do you glory in?
Some glory in their knowledge, some in their strength, some in their wealth, (and some in all of the above); yet the Lord says that we should not glory in any of these things. **We are to glory in the fact that we know Him!**

We know His Lovingkindness.
Psalm 143:8
*"Cause me to hear thy lovingkindness in the morning;
for in thee do I trust: cause me to know the way wherein I should walk;
for I lift up my soul unto thee."*

We know His Judgment.
Psalm 119:75
*"I know, O Lord, that thy judgments are right,
and that thou in faithfulness hast afflicted me."*

We know His Righteousness.
Psalm 71:19
*"Thy righteousness also, O God, is very high,
who hast done great things: O God, who is like unto thee!"*

**Since our Lord delights in these things,
should we not as His children seek to exercise them in our lives?**

Micah 6:8
*"He hath shewed thee, O man, what is good;
and what doth the LORD require of thee, but to do justly,
and to love mercy, and to walk humbly with thy God?"*

Bible Reading
1 Kings 7-8 | 2 Corinthians 6 | Psalm 125 | 163

Be An Example.

1 Timothy 4:12
"Let no man despise thy youth; but be thou an example of the believers, in word, in conversation, in charity, in spirit, in faith, in purity."

No matter what your age, you can make a difference for Christ! **Whether young or getting older, there is still something for you to do for the Lord.**

The context of our text today is the Apostle Paul admonishing Timothy, his son in the faith. Timothy was younger than Paul, who had trained and discipled him to carry the mantle.

Maybe you're a Paul, maybe you are a Timothy; but regardless, God still has a plan and purpose for your life. **If you do not have a Paul or Timothy in your life, seek to find one…and be one.**

We see clearly in our verse today several ways we can serve the Lord:

Be An Example In Word.
Colossians 4:6
"Let your speech be always with grace, seasoned with salt, that ye may know how ye ought to answer every man."

Be An Example In Charity.
1 Corinthians 16:13-14
"Watch ye, stand fast in the faith, quit you like men, be strong. Let all your things be done with charity."

Be An Example In Faith.
Romans 4:20
"He staggered not at the promise of God through unbelief; but was strong in faith, giving glory to God; And being fully persuaded that, what he had promised, he was able also to perform."

Be An Example In Purity.
1 Timothy 5:21-22
"I charge thee before God, and the Lord Jesus Christ, and the elect angels, that thou observe these things without preferring one before another, doing nothing by partiality. Lay hands suddenly on no man, neither be partaker of other men's sins: keep thyself pure."

If we would all follow the charge that Paul gave to Timothy we would all be better Christians for the cause of Christ. **Let us therefore strive to be examples to those around us so that they may see Christ in us.**

Bible Reading
1 Kings 9-10 | 2 Corinthians 7 | Psalm 126

Shine.

Matthew 5:16
*"Let your light so shine before men,
that they may see your good works,
and glorify your Father which is in heaven."*

**The best example we can be is to
shine our light for Christ so that others can see Him!**

We are the light of the world!

As Christians, it is our duty to let our light shine, but it is also a privilege and an honor. **If we do not do our part to shine our light for Christ, who will?** In the darkness of this world, we must shine so that others can see the Light.

Notice how Jesus describes shining our light:
Matthew 5:14-15
*"Ye are the light of the world. A city that is set on a hill cannot be hid.
Neither do men light a candle, and put it under a bushel,
but on a candlestick; and it giveth light unto all that are in the house."*

Not everyone shines their light in the same way, each of us are different. We each have a unique purpose that God has planned for our lives, but we can all shine our light with our actions and words.

Let your light shine for Him!
How are you shining your light?
Are you hiding it under a bushel ashamed for others to see?

**Make your life a candlestick!
Let it shine, let it shine, let it shine!**

Bible Reading
1 Kings 11-12 | 2 Corinthians 8 | Psalm 127 | 165

A Holding Pattern.

Psalm 25:4-5
*"Shew me thy ways, O LORD; teach me thy paths.
Lead me in thy truth, and teach me: for thou art the God of my salvation;
on thee do I wait all the day."*

Have you ever been on an airplane that had to delay its landing for whatever reason? It may have been due to weather, air traffic, or some unforeseen circumstance at the final destination. When the pilot circles the runway it is called a holding pattern. **Though it may be inconvenient, there is a reason for the delay in reaching the ground.**

David knew what it was like to be in a holding pattern. Many times throughout his life he had to wait on God to deliver him from his circumstances. He had learned from experience that **it is better to wait on God to work rather than force the means of an apparent solution.** Notice the three things that David asks the Lord to do: *"Shew me…teach me… Lead me…"*

When God makes us wait it may be inconvenient, but it is for our benefit.

Romans 8:28
"And we know that all things work together for good to them that love God, to them who are the called according to his purpose."

While we wait…
We Can Rest. - Psalm 37:7

We Can Refocus. - Proverbs 16:3

We Can Refire. - 2 Timothy 1:6

When something does not happen when or as fast as we think it should, God always has a reason.

Isaiah 55:8-9
"For my thoughts are not your thoughts, neither are your ways my ways, saith the LORD. For as the heavens are higher than the earth, so are my ways higher than your ways, and my thoughts than your thoughts."

If we compare our position to others, we will only end up discouraged or defeated. Rest while you wait. **Allow God to deliver you from your holding pattern.**

Bible Reading
1 Kings 13-14 | 2 Corinthians 9 | Psalm 128

The Gift Of Grace.

James 4:6
"But he giveth more grace. Wherefore he saith,
God resisteth the proud, but giveth grace unto the humble."

Notice the contrast that we see here…the proud & the humble. God takes a specific action with each of these. He resists the proud, but He gives to the humble. **He will not give to those who think they deserve something.** But those that acknowledge that they do not deserve anything, it is to them that the Lord gives.

Not only does He give to the humble, notice the significance of the gift… His grace. The same grace that bringeth salvation and appeared to all men. The same grace by which we are saved. This grace is a Gift. We must acknowledge that we cannot save ourselves, and we are totally dependent on the finished work of Christ. **There is no salvation without humility.**

When we clothe ourselves in humility, God will bless us.
He promises to give to those that are humble.

1 Peter 5:5
"Likewise, ye younger, submit yourselves unto the elder. Yea, all of you be
subject one to another, and be clothed with humility: for God resisteth
the proud, and giveth grace to the humble. Humble yourselves therefore
under the mighty hand of God, that he may exalt you in due time:"

Humble yourself and wait.
God will give you grace.

See your need for this gift of grace.
Pray for it, and be thankful when God gives you what you need.

Bible Reading
1 Kings 15-16 | 2 Corinthians 10 | Psalm 129 | 167

Call Unto Him.

Jeremiah 33:3
*"Call unto me, and I will answer thee,
and shew thee great and mighty things, which thou knowest not."*

The greatest privilege ever given to humanity, yet the least taken advantage of, is prayer. We are able to call upon the God of the Universe, and if that is not astounding enough, His ears are open to our cry. He is waiting to hear from us!

God makes a simple request.
"Call unto me..."

God guarantees a sure response.
"...and I will answer thee..."

How much have we missed by simply not calling on God? **There are great and mighty things that we are missing out on when we do not pray.** What a convicting thought. We go about our daily lives in need of Him, yet we are more concerned with our news feed and what our so called friends on social media have to say, or better yet what we have to share with them.

How often do we allow distractions to keep our focus away from pausing to bow our head and ask God to help us? We are quick to pick up our phone and text or call our best friend, yet we don't bother to bring our need to the Friend that sticketh closer than a brother.

God has given us a simple command that when obeyed brings forth exceeding abundantly above all that we could ask or think. Great and mighty things that before we ask we have no knowledge that they exist, yet the our Creator, our Heavenly Father wants to show them to us.

Call unto Him today. Ask Him. Seek Him. Knock on the door of heaven. He promises that we shall receive, that we shall find, and that it shall be opened unto us…if only we will call unto Him.

Bible Reading
1 Kings 17-18 | 2 Corinthians 11 | Psalm 130

Tunnel Vision.

Hebrews 12:1-2

"Wherefore seeing we also are compassed about with so great a cloud of witnesses, let us lay aside every weight, and the sin which doth so easily beset us, and let us run with patience the race that is set before us, Looking unto Jesus the author and finisher of our faith; who for the joy that was set before him endured the cross, despising the shame, and is set down at the right hand of the throne of God."

When we see a *"wherefore"* in the Bible, the passage is always referring to the previous verses. In today's text we notice that the *"Wherefore"* here is the first word of Chapter 12, so we must look back at Chapter 11 to see the context of this verse.

Chapter 11 of Hebrews is quite often called the "Hall of Fame of Faith" or "The Faith Chapter". It is here where we find faith defined and explained by example. The *"cloud of witnesses"* of our verse today refers back to those heroes of our faith that are mentioned in Chapter 11. These were pillars of example that we can glean so much Truth from their faithful lives to their Faithful God.

Because of their examples of faith, we are admonished here to *"lay aside every weight, and the sin which doth so easily beset us"*. **We are to disregard the hindrances that are placed upon our lives to distract us from God's plan and purpose.** It is so easy to be blinded by sin until we become immune to the effect that is having on us. Sin weighs us down little by little until we are so consumed by it, we cannot walk with the Lord.

We must have tunnel vision!

When you travel through a tunnel, you can no longer see and experience your surroundings. You are forced to look ahead. When you nearly reach the other side of the tunnel, the light begins to appear first, then gradually gets larger until you emerge out of the tunnel on the other side to find your surroundings completely different. **The tunnel has a purpose.** It was taking you through something that you could not pass through easily had it not been there.

We must develop tunnel vision as Christians as we run the race that is set before us. As we enter the tunnel of faith we are no longer blinded by the sin of the world around us, and we are forced to look ahead. *"Looking unto Jesus the author and finisher of our faith..."*

Bible Reading
1 Kings 19-20 | 2 Corinthians 12 | Psalm 131 | 169

Invest.

Romans 12:1
*"I beseech you therefore, brethren, by the mercies of God,
that ye present your bodies a living sacrifice, holy, acceptable unto God,
which is your reasonable service."*

When the fears and doubts of life assail, it is time to reevaluate what we investing in. How do we spend our time and energy?

Invest By Sacrificing.
When we present our bodies as a living sacrifice, we must be yielded. A living sacrifice has the ability to get up off of the altar, and lets face it…we have all been there. We yield ourselves to the will of God only to pick our will back up off of the altar as we get up off our knees. Instead, **we must invest ourselves in finding God's will for our lives by spending time in prayer and reading our Bible.** The Scripture we read and the supplications we plead will help us to live holy lives that are acceptable to God.

Invest By Serving.
As we sacrifice our own will, God will then give us the desires of our heart that line up with His will for our lives. As He directs us, He will provide for us. Within this provision we will find opportunities to serve. **We can serve Him by serving others and showing Christ's love for them by shining our light.** He may give us opportunities to do great things for Him, but often before the "big" things come, He will allow "little" occasions to see if we mean business. Are we willing to sweep the floors of the church without an audience? Clean the bathrooms? Take out the trash? Open a door for someone? Give an offering to the missionary that presented their work? Let someone else have "our seat"? It is as much our reasonable service to do these things as it is to sing in the choir, go soul-winning, pass out a tract, or do a devotion. **God desires us to be willing to serve when no one else is watching and when no one else shows up.** It is reasonable for God to ask us to do anything for His glory. He willingly chose to leave His throne in Heaven to come and die for our sin. Can we not do our reasonable service for Him?

Take account today of how you are investing.
How are you sacrificing? How are you serving?
Remember your reasonable service.

Bible Reading
1 Kings 21-22 | 2 Corinthians 13 | Psalm 132

Into His Ears.

Psalm 18:6
*"In my distress I called upon the Lord, and cried unto my God:
he heard my voice out of his temple, and my cry came before him,
even into his ears."*

David knew what he needed to do amidst the sorrow and distress he was facing. He knew that he could call upon the Lord. David cried out in faith, knowing that God was going to hear not only his voice, but also his cry for help. The very ears of Almighty God heard each word that David spoke to Him.

It is a comforting reminder that, just like God heard David's prayers, He hears ours. **We need only to call upon Him and cry out to the God Who hears and answers prayers.**

Psalm 130:1-2
*"Out of the depths have I cried unto thee, O LORD.
Lord, hear my voice:
let thine ears be attentive to the voice of my supplications."*

In James 4:2 we find the Truth, *"ye have not, because ye ask not".* The same is true in times of distress and sorrow. **We cannot be rescued if we do not ask for help.** The Lord's ears are open to our cry; we need only to stop and simply ask Him to intervene.

Bring your supplications to Him today.

Philippians 4:6
*"Be careful for nothing; but in every thing by prayer and supplication
with thanksgiving let your requests be made known unto God."*

Bible Reading
2 Kings 1-2 | Galatians 1 | Psalm 133

Pace Yourself.

Isaiah 40:31
*"But they that wait upon the Lord shall renew their strength;
they shall mount up with wings as eagles; they shall run,
and not be weary; and they shall walk, and not faint."*

When a runner sets out to run a marathon, they do not sprint off the starting line. They get a good place in line and then they set a pace in order to finish. They have trained themselves to run with patience the long race that is set before them. If they do not train ahead of time, they will not be able to run for long before they have to walk or stop before they faint.

Have you ever been weary in the race?
Do you feel as if you are about to faint?

We see in our text today an order of effectiveness to our service to the Lord. In those times when we feel as if we are about to faint, we must slow down and walk with the Lord, developing an endurance for the race that is set before us. We must build up our strength in Him in order to run this race.

We can renew our strength by waiting on Him. In those times when we want to do things by the way of our flesh, we need to stop and wait for His direction. We must stand still and let Him be God. While we wait we can develop strength to endure within the race.

Psalm 27:13-14
"I had fainted, unless I had believed to see the goodness of the LORD in the land of the living. Wait on the LORD: be of good courage, and he shall strengthen thine heart: wait, I say, on the LORD."

Have courage today.
We cannot see His goodness until we believe.
We cannot receive strength until we wait on the Lord.

Walk with the Lord.
Don't faint in the middle of the race. Build up your strength and endurance so that you can run and not be weary.

Wait on the Lord.
He will give us the strength
we need to continue to serve Him.

Bible Reading
2 Kings 3-4 | Galatians 2 | Psalm 134

Purpose.

Philippians 2:16
"Holding forth the word of life; that I may rejoice in the day of Christ, that I have not run in vain, neither labored in vain."

Why should we pace ourselves? **We have the privilege and duty to hold forth the Word of Life to this lost and dying world.** If we do not shine forth the Light of the glorious Gospel of Jesus Christ, who will? There is someone that only you can reach. There is a song that only you can sing. There is a purpose that only you can fulfill.

Run With Purpose
I Corinthians 9:22-27
"To the weak became I as weak, that I might gain the weak: I am made all things to all men, that I might by all means save some. And this I do for the gospel's sake, that I might be partaker thereof with you. Know ye not that they which run in a race run all, but one receiveth the prize? So run, that ye may obtain. And every man that striveth for the mastery is temperate in all things. Now they do it to obtain a corruptible crown; but we an incorruptible. I therefore so run, not as uncertainly; so fight I, not as one that beateth the air: But I keep under my body, and bring it into subjection: lest that by any means, when I have preached to others, I myself should be a castaway."

Labour With Purpose
I Corinthians 15:58
"Therefore, my beloved brethren, be ye stedfast, unmoveable, always abounding in the work of the Lord, forasmuch as ye know that your labour is not in vain in the Lord."

God will enable us to run this race that is set before us with patience; so that, in the day of Christ, we can rejoice that we have done all we can for Him. **Run and labour with purpose today in order to finish well.**

Bible Reading
2 Kings 5-6 | Galatians 3 | Psalm 135

Godly Friends.

Colossians 3:16
"Let the word of Christ dwell in you richly in all wisdom; teaching and admonishing one another in psalms and hymns and spiritual songs, singing with grace in your hearts to the Lord."

The Apostle Paul instructs us by the inspiration of the Holy Spirit that we should allow the Word of God to influence everything we do. As the Word begins to influence us, we should also allow it to inhabit us…to *"dwell"* in us.

God wants us to make His Word the central point of our lives, and that within us the Truth of the Scriptures would abound in such a way that it is overflowing from our lips…*"richly in all wisdom".*

When we allow our lives to be saturated with Biblical Truths, we can then begin to *"admonishing one another"*…to warn and exhort because of our love and care for each other. **A godly friend will counsel you if they are led by God to do so.** There will not be a critical spirit involved, but God can use a loving, concerned friend to help you.

Proverbs 27:6
*"Faithful are the wounds of a friend;
but the kisses of an enemy are deceitful."*

Proverbs 18:24
*"A man that hath friends must shew himself friendly:
and there is a friend that sticketh closer than a brother."*

We must be willing to be a friend to someone because we need someone to be our friend. **Allow God to use the godly friends that He has placed in our life to help you.** Show yourself friendly. You never know when someone will need a friendly word or deed to brighten their day. God may just use that word or deed to begin a friendship that you need for your current season of life.

**Take the time to admonish someone
through the Truth of the Word of Christ today.**

Bible Reading
2 Kings 7-8 | Galatians 4 | Psalm 136

Ask In Jesus' Name.

John 16:23-24
"...Verily, verily, I say unto you, Whatsoever ye shall ask the Father in my name, he will give it you. Hitherto have ye asked nothing in my name: ask, and ye shall receive, that your joy may be full."

What a privilege it is that the God of the universe wants us to pray to Him. He desires to hear from us. How amazing is that?

Jesus tells us that if we will simply pray in His Name, according to the Father's will, we will receive.

John 14:13-14
"And whatsoever ye shall ask in my name, that will I do, that the Father may be glorified in the Son. If ye shall ask any thing in my name, I will do it."

We are not told to pray in the Name of the Father or in the Name of the Holy Ghost, but in the Name of Jesus, God's Son. Why is that? Because His Name is above all names! There is just something about the Name of Jesus!

John 15:16
"Ye have not chosen me, but I have chosen you, and ordained you, that ye should go and bring forth fruit, and that your fruit should remain: that whatsoever ye shall ask of the Father in my name, he may give it you."

He chose us, and He chooses to have us ask Him for what we need. He knows what we need before we even ask, yet in His love He desires to hear from us. His ears are always open to our cry, our pleading, our asking, our seeking, our knocking, our supplications. He is always there.

Whatever your need, call on Him today.

Bible Reading
2 Kings 9-10 | Galatians 5 | Psalm 137 | 175

Search The Scriptures.

John 5:39
*"Search the scriptures; for in them ye think ye have eternal life:
and they are they which testify of me."*

The Preacher of all preachers uses the Jews of our text as an example for all of us today. They had witnessed the healing of the lame man at the Pool of Bethesda, and then rebuked him for carrying his bed on the Sabbath. They persecuted both the healed and the Healer. We read of Jesus telling them that the privilege of searching the Holy Scriptures is not limited to just one group or a few people. He tells these Jews who did not believe John the Baptist's message that the Scriptures tell of how to obtain eternal life. **These people had boasted of reading the Scriptures daily, yet they missed the message.**

There were men like this during the days that Christ walked on this earth, and there are still likeminded people within our churches today. They read, study and search the Word for their own glory – to prove how much they know. They glorify themselves instead of the only One worthy of glory, honour, and praise. Let us allow this group to be an example to us of what to avoid in our walk with the Lord.

James 1:22-26
*"But be ye doers of the word, and not hearers only,
deceiving your own selves."*

1 Corinthians 2:9-10,14
"But as it is written, Eye hath not seen, nor ear heard, neither have entered into the heart of man, the things which God hath prepared for them that love him. But God hath revealed them unto us by his Spirit: for the Spirit searcheth all things, yea, the deep things of God…But the natural man receiveth not the things of the Spirit of God: for they are foolishness unto him: neither can he know them, because they are spiritually discerned."

**We can experience the power and influence of the Word of God
through yielding to the Holy Spirit
as we read, study, and search the Scriptures.**

Bible Reading
2 Kings 11-12 | Galatians 6 | Psalm 138

Ready To Receive.

Acts 17:11
*"These were more noble than those in Thessalonica,
in that they received the word with all readiness of mind,
and searched the scriptures daily, whether those things were so."*

Paul and Silas had left Thessalonica and arrived in Berea. The Berean people greeted them differently than the Jews of Thessalonia. Rather than set an uproar amongst the city, many of the Bereans chose to receive the Truth of the Gospel and many of them believed. Some believed in Thessalonica, but many believed in Berea.

We sit under the sound of the preaching of the Word of God, and many of us believe the Truths of the messages our pastors faithfully preach to us. However, some choose not to believe and receive. Many stop their walk with the Lord just past their salvation experience. Yes, they are saved and on their way to Heaven, but they choose to not receive the Word and apply it to their lives.

As we enter the doors of the sanctuary and sit down in our seats, are we ready to receive the Word? Or do we only come out of obligation or the desire to be seen? We've all seen churchgoers who sit in a pew physically, yet their attention is elsewhere…the cares of life get in the way of their focus or the entertainment of their news feed seems to win their concentration. Perhaps we've all been there before too.

When you open the door to the church house, ask yourself…
When you open your Bible, ask yourself…
Am I ready to receive the Word?
We must open our hearts and minds to receive the Word of God.

If we are ready to receive the Word, God will bless our efforts. He will speak to our hearts with just what we need at that exact moment in our lives. Expect to hear from God, and He will answer. **Be ready to receive so that you can give.** God loveth a cheerful giver, and what better gift than the Truth of the Word?

1 Peter 3:15
"But sanctify the Lord God in your hearts: and be ready always to give an answer to every man that asketh you a reason of the hope that is in you with meekness and fear:"

Bible Reading
2 Kings 13-14 | Ephesians 1 | Psalm 139 | 177

His Words.

John 15:7
*"If ye abide in me, and my words abide in you,
ye shall ask what ye will, and it shall be done unto you."*

Jesus speaks of His Words in each of the Gospel accounts.
Matthew 24:35
"Heaven and earth shall pass away, but my words shall not pass away."

The Lord doesn't have to repeat Himself to make something true, yet we find this same Truth pinned in three of the Gospel accounts. Those that do not believe in the preservation of the Scripture must not have these verses in whatever version they have chosen to read. When you change your Bible, you change your doctrine. **Praise the Lord for how He has preserved His Word to all generations so that we can have the Word of God today!**

He goes on in the Gospel of John to bring to light the Truth that the Jews had the writings of Moses, who wrote of Christ's coming, yet they chose not to believe that He was the Messiah.

John 5:46-47
"For had ye believed Moses, ye would have believed me; for he wrote of me. But if ye believe not his writings, how shall ye believe my words?"

How many Bibles sit in homes within the freedoms of America,
yet they are never opened to be read?

God's Word cannot abide in us if we do not read it.
We must not only read. We must study. We must search.

Read. - Joshua 1:8
Study. - 2 Timothy 2:15
Search. - Acts 17:11

Let His Words abide in your heart today and every day.

Bible Reading
2 Kings 15-16 | Ephesians 2 | Psalm 140

His Word Will Stand.

Isaiah 40:6-8
*"The voice said, Cry. And he said, What shall I cry?
All flesh is grass, and all the goodliness thereof is as the flower of the
field: The grass withereth, the flower fadeth: because the spirit of the Lord
bloweth upon it: surely the people is grass. The grass withereth, the flower
fadeth: but the word of our God shall stand for ever."*

When everything else around us is withering and fading away, the Word
of God will stand. What a comforting thought that can bring us a godly
confidence as we walk with the Lord. **Regardless of our circumstances, we
can rest in the Truth of God's Word, for It will never fail us.**

The Apostle Peter took from this passage in Isaiah during his discourse of
the Word of God at the beginning of his first epistle.

1 Peter 1:25
*"Being born again, not of corruptible seed, but of incorruptible, by the
word of God, which liveth and abideth for ever. For all flesh is as grass,
and all the glory of man as the flower of grass. The grass withereth, and
the flower thereof falleth away: But the word of the Lord endureth for ever.
And this is the word which by the gospel is preached unto you."*

Peter understood that **even in the midst of the trial of your faith we can
rest in the fact that God's Word will endure forever** and when we have a
desire for the Truth we can grow through the trials.

Lamp & Light.

Psalm 119:105
"Thy word is a lamp unto my feet, and a light unto my path."

This familiar verse gives us hope and direction. In this one verse, we have a promise that His Word provides both present and future direction.

His Word Is Our Lamp
"...a lamp unto my feet..."
We can have present direction because we have been given a Lamp that we can hold in our hands to shine in the darkness, and allow us to see where to take the next step in our walk with the Lord. **He wants us to have the faith to trust Him each step of the way.** He doesn't show us the big picture of His will all at once, but through the Lamp we can develop faith that He will guide us through every step. In order to shine, a Lamp must have oil. The Oil of the Holy Spirit provides us the understanding to discern the Truths of the Scripture.

His Word Is Our Light
"...a light unto my path."
His Word shines Light ahead providing us direction as to which path to continue to take, or allows us to see that we are heading down the wrong one. Praise God for the times in our lives that we have been redirected by the Scripture and applied the changes that were needed in order to regain our fellowship with the Lord. **When we allow the Light of the Scripture to direct our lives, we cannot be led astray.** When we don't know which way to turn, the Light of the Word provides understanding.

Psalm 119:130
"The entrance of thy words giveth light;
it giveth understanding unto the simple."

God has given us exactly what we need. Direction for today, and for tomorrow. **He instructs us through each phase and journey of life through His Word**, if only we would take the time to read and apply His Truth to our life. **Delight in both the Lamp and the Light today.**

Proverbs 6:23
"For the commandment is a lamp; and the law is light;
and reproofs of instruction are the way of life:"

Bible Reading
2 Kings 19-20 | Ephesians 4 | Psalm 142

The Living Sword.

Hebrews 4:12
"For the word of God is quick, and powerful, and sharper than any twoedged sword, piercing even to the dividing asunder of soul and spirit, and of the joints and marrow, and is a discerner of the thoughts and intents of the heart."

When the circumstances of life get us down, it becomes a struggle to make it through the day. Sometimes it is hard to find the energy to continue to do even routine tasks due to the weight of the burdens upon us. It is in those times that we should stop, and turn to the Word of God for It is quick to bring us the help we need. The word *"quick"* in our verse today refers to the act of giving life, or making something alive.

John 6:63
"…the words that I speak unto you, they are spirit, and they are life."

We see several references within today's verse to the characteristics of a sword. The Sword of the Spirit is *"sharper than any twoedged sword"* so that It can cut us to our core and correct us when we go astray. **The Word of God can pierce through the hardest heart and bring conviction to both the sinner's heart and the backslidden Christian.**

Ephesians 6:17
"And take the helmet of salvation, and the sword of the Spirit, which is the word of God:"

When we put on the whole armour of God, there are many defensive tools, yet only One offensive. **The Word of God is the only offensive weapon that we need in order to be able to stand against the wiles of the devil.** Jesus Christ proved this Truth when Satan came to Him and tempted Him. Each time Satan offered the Lord Jesus something, how did Christ respond? *"For it is written…"* This should encourage us to fill our hearts and minds with Scripture so that we can fight against the fiery darts of the wicked.

The Living Sword brings life to our weary souls, provides power to continue to work for the Lord, cuts us to the core when we need corrected, heals our wounded hearts, and defeats our enemy's spiritual attacks.

**Take your Sword with you today,
and allow the Truths of God's Word to bring life to your soul.**

Bible Reading
2 Kings 21-22 | Ephesians 5 | Psalm 143

John 1:1-5

"In the beginning was the Word, and the Word was with God, and the Word was God. The same was in the beginning with God. All things were made by him; and without him was not any thing made that was made. In him was life; and the life was the light of men. And the light shineth in darkness; and the darkness comprehended it not."

Throughout our study over the past several days on the Word of God, we have focused on several different aspects of the Truth of God's Word. **Within the Scriptures about the Word of God we can learn more about our Lord and Saviour, Jesus Christ.**

We find here in the first five verses of the Gospel of John that Jesus is The Word. Not only was He with God, He was God and He is God. *"He came unto His own, and His own received Him not."* They denied Him as God, and they rejected Him as their Messiah and Saviour.

He was present at creation in the very Words that God the Father said as He spoke this world into existence. All things were made by The Word, and there was nothing made without Him. Including us.

We find life within The Word. When God breathed into the dust of the ground and man became a living soul, He gave us life through The Word. Then when Adam and Eve fell in sin, Jesus Christ was the Lamb slain before the foundation of the world. He provided us the means of eternal life by willingly offering Himself on the Cross of Calvary for our sin.

The Word still shines Light today through the darkness, and yet the darkness still doesn't comprehend the Truth. Instead, this dark world continues to push out the Light of the Son and the Light of the Scripture.

We have the Light within us,
and can hold the Light in our hands.

Shine the Light of the Word through you today.

Bible Reading
2 Kings 23-25 | Ephesians 6 | Psalm 144

One Way.

Galatians 1:6-8

"I marvel that ye are so soon removed from him that called you into the grace of Christ unto another gospel: Which is not another; but there be some that trouble you, and would pervert the gospel of Christ. But though we, or an angel from heaven, preach any other gospel unto you than that which we have preached unto you, let him be accursed."

When we take grace out of salvation, or mix grace with works, it is *"another gospel: Which is not another"*. **Salvation apart from the grace of Christ's sacrifice, or adding to the grace of His substitutionary death, is not the Gospel at all.**

Acts 4:12

"Neither is there salvation in any other: for there is none other name under heaven given among men, whereby we must be saved."

Peter understood that there was only One Way, and that not only those who he was preaching to, but he as well can only be saved through Jesus Christ alone. The same Truth still applies today. **Regardless of religious or denominational affiliation, there is only One Way to Heaven.**

"Any faith that rests short of the Cross is a faith that will land you short of Heaven…Morality may keep you out of jail, but it takes the blood of Jesus Christ to keep you out of hell…If you do not find salvation in Christ, you will never find it elsewhere."
Charles Spurgeon

"If we are not changed by grace, we are not saved by grace."
A.W. Tozer

"The only people who want to change the Gospel are those who are unchanged by it."
Leonard Ravenhill

Bible Reading
1 Chronicles 1-2 | Philippians 1 | Psalm 145

Fragments.

John 6:11-13
"And Jesus took the loaves; and when he had given thanks, he distributed to the disciples, and the disciples to them that were set down; and likewise of the fishes as much as they would. When they were filled, he said unto his disciples, Gather up the fragments that remain, that nothing be lost."

Andrew had scoffed at the resources that were available.

John 6:9
"There is a lad here, which hath five barley loaves, and two small fishes: but what are they among so many? What are they among so many."

Oftentimes we look at what we have to offer the Lord, and our resources seem daunting in comparison to the need of the task at hand. Like Andrew, we tend to doubt the Lord's power and what is possible when all that we have is given to Him.

Just like the five barley loaves He broke apart, **God often breaks us so that we can be used of Him.** Christ gave the pieces of bread to the disciples so that they could then disperse them to the multitude. Once the people had their fill to eat, Christ commanded the disciples to gather up what was left. The disciples picked up every piece of bread that was leftover. Miraculously, there were twelve baskets full. One for each disciple. Each of them had in their hands a basket full of food that was in itself more than they started with. Not only did 5,000 men eat, and an undisclosed amount of women and children, but also the disciples had food for themselves and their families. **God had given them the fragments to serve as a reminder that with God nothing shall be impossible.** God always has a purpose for breaking us. He must break us in order to empty our vessels so that the Potter can begin to mold us into His image, and fill us with His Spirit.

What fragments do you have leftover? If you could gather them all up, they are sure to be even more than what you had when you gave the Lord the little you started with. Those fragments of your life now stand as a witness and reminder of God's power. We are nothing without Him, but when we surrender our lives to Him we are sure to find that He has done exceeding abundantly above all that we originally asked or thought.

Be thankful for your fragments.

Bible Reading
1 Chronicles 3-4 | Philippians 2 | Psalm 146

Two Offerings.

Genesis 4:1-5

"And Adam knew Eve his wife; and she conceived, and bare Cain, and said, I have gotten a man from the LORD. And she again bare his brother Abel. And Abel was a keeper of sheep, but Cain was a tiller of the ground. And in process of time it came to pass, that Cain brought of the fruit of the ground an offering unto the LORD. And Abel, he also brought of the firstlings of his flock and of the fat thereof. And the LORD had respect unto Abel and to his offering: But unto Cain and to his offering he had not respect. And Cain was very wroth, and his countenance fell."

Cain and Abel, the sons of Adam & Eve, were the first children to be born into this world. And as brothers often are, they were competitive with each other. Both wanted to bring from their work a sacrifice unto the Lord. Cain was a man who tilled and prepared the ground to bare crops, and was proud of his work. Abel worked in the fields keeping watch over his flock of sheep.

The Accepted Sacrifice

"And the LORD had respect unto Abel and to his offering:"
Abel's offering was different because his involved the shedding of blood. **It was the blood that was accepted.** For without the shedding of blood there is no remission. He not only chose to slay one of his flock, but it was a *"firstling"*. He had faith that the Lord would provide, and gave the Lord his best because He felt the Lord was worthy of nothing less. Abel was confident in the blood's atonement, which speaks of Christ's atoning blood for us.

The Rejected Sacrifice

"But unto Cain and to his offering he had not respect.
And Cain was very wroth, and his countenance fell."
Cain's sacrifice was from the work of his hands. He was dependent upon what good he had done and his own ability; therefore the Lord did not have respect for his offering. Cain was confident in himself and his works, which speaks of a works salvation. It is not by works of righteousness that we have done, but through the precious blood of Jesus Christ that we find salvation. **Because Cain's sacrifice did not include the blood, the Lord was not pleased.** He has no respect for any other means of salvation other than the blood of His Son.

What can wash away our sin? Nothing but the Blood of Jesus!
Bible Reading
1 Chronicles 5-6| Philippians 3 | Psalm 147 | 185

Considered.

Job 1:8
"And the Lord said unto Satan, Hast thou considered my servant Job, that there is none like him in the earth, a perfect and an upright man, one that feareth God, and escheweth evil?"

Job, the mature and upright man from the land of Uz, who feared God and departed from evil. He had a reputation with men as the greatest man in all of the east, but he also had a reputation with God. He was His servant. The Lord said there was none like him in all of the earth. Job had such a relationship with the Lord that he was chosen to be the example encased within the canon of Scripture of the permission from the Lord that Satan needs before he touches one of God's children.

Job 1:9-10
"Then Satan answered the Lord, and said, Doth Job fear God for nought? Hast not thou made an hedge about him, and about his house, and about all that he hath on ever side? thou hast blessed the work of his hands, and his substance is increased in the land."

Satan is aware of the hedge of protection the Lord has placed around His children. Be thankful for the hedge that surrounds you today. **If you are a child of God, nothing can happen to you unless God allows it.** When the Lord allows difficult circumstances to come into our lives, it is an opportunity for us to be an example to those around us, and shine our Light. Like Job, we can use the situation to turn our weeping into worship.

Job 1:20-21
"Then Job arose, and rent his mantle, and shaved his head, and fell down upon the ground, and worshipped…the Lord gave, and the Lord hath taken away; blessed be the name of the Lord. In all this Job sinned not, nor charged God foolishly."

Job could have easily quit. He could have gotten mad at God for all that he lost. Instead, Job chose to fall on his knees and worship his Lord. Examine your walk with the Lord today. Could you be considered upright and one that feareth God? **Rejoice when you are considered worthy to be a partaker of Christ's sufferings.**

1 Peter 4:13
"But rejoice, inasmuch as ye are partakers of Christ's sufferings; that, when his glory shall be revealed, ye may be glad also with exceeding joy."

Bible Reading

186 | 1 Chronicles 7-8 | Philippians 4 | Psalm 148

Integrity.

Job 2:3

"And the LORD said unto Satan, Hast thou considered my servant Job, that there is none like him in the earth, a perfect and an upright man, one that feareth God, and escheweth evil? and still he holdeth fast his integrity, although thou movedst me against him, to destroy him without cause."

Again. The first word of Chapter 2 of the Book of Job tells us the scene. Much like the first chapter, Satan comes to present himself to the Lord once again. While he is there, the Lord asks him, again, if he has considered His servant Job. **Times of testing and trial are never singular.** We see this in the Book of James as we read *"count it all joy when ye fall into divers temptations".* The text does not read temptation, but rather *"temptations".* It also does not say if ye fall, but rather *"when ye fall".* **Times of testing are inevitable.** The rain falls upon the just and the unjust.

Throughout all of his trials, Job held fast to his integrity despite what those around him had to say about his situation. Satan was given permission to destroy Job's children, servants, livestock, herdsmen, home and even his health. God allowed Satan to persecute Job, all the while knowing the bright future ahead. The Lord sees what we don't see. **Job only saw his current situation; yet he did not waver in his integrity.** He continued to trust God despite his circumstances. Even Job's wife thought he should give up because of the attacks.

Job 2:9

"Then said his wife unto him, Dost thou still retain thine integrity? curse God, and die."

How did Job respond? He rebuked her negativity. **Job understood that both blessings and trials come when we walk with the Lord.** Despite his wife's opinion and advice, Job stood strong and without sin during his trial. May we mirror his integrity when we endure trials. When we can't see anything but the storm, God holds us in the palm of His hand. He will never leave us nor forsake us; and because of that, we can have integrity.

Job 27:5-6

"God forbid that I should justify you: till I die I will not remove mine integrity from me. My righteousness I hold fast, and will not let it go: my heart shall not reproach me so long as I live."

Bible Reading
1 Chronicles 9-10 | Colossians 1 | Psalm 149

Wait & Seek.

Lamentations 3:24-25
"The Lord is my portion, saith my soul; therefore will I hope in him. The Lord is good unto them that wait for him, to the soul that seeketh him."

Remember playing hide & seek? Maybe you've had the chance to play it recently with a cute little kid who asked, and you couldn't say no. One person waits and counts to ten while the other player(s) go and hide. Then the counter has the task of seeking out where the others are hiding. God doesn't hide from us, but we can all learn from this game. **We must stop and wait while God is working in our lives, and begin to seek Him as we walk through this dark world, shining our Light as we go.** While we wait, we must seek God through prayer and reading His Word.

Why should we wait & seek God?
Because the Lord is Our Portion.
Psalm 73:26
"My flesh and my heart faileth: but God is the strength of my heart, and my portion for ever."

Because the Lord is Our Hope.
Psalm 31:24
"Be of good courage, and he shall strengthen your heart, all ye that hope in the Lord."

Wait.
Psalm 27:14
"Wait on the LORD: be of good courage, and he shall strengthen thine heart: wait, I say, on the LORD."

Seek.
1 Chronicles 16:11
"Seek the LORD and his strength, seek his face continually."

If we want to have strength in our walk, we must wait on the Lord; and while we wait, we must seek Him.

Decide today to quit running.
Stop, then begin to wait and seek the Lord.

Bible Reading
1 Chronicles 11-12 | Colossians 2 | Psalm 150

Hope & Quietly Wait.

Lamentations 3:26
"It is good that a man should both hope and quietly wait for the salvation of the LORD."

God wants us to have hope while we wait. **He desires us to have faith that He is working behind the scenes.** Hope develops Faith, and faith develops patience.

Romans 8:24-25
"For we are saved by hope: but hope that is seen is not hope: for what a man seeth, why doth he yet hope for? But if we hope for that we see not, then do we with patience wait for it."

Patience is not a fun quality to develop. We've all heard the saying, "Don't pray for patience." But we have not, because we ask not. Many times in the growing of our patience, we only hope for the waiting to be over. Instead, God wants us to quietly wait for Him. While we wait in silence, we can exercise our faith that He will come through. Hope is simply faith marked with a waiting period.

When the Lord makes us wait, He has a purpose.
He may delay something for His glory & our good.

Isaiah 30:18
"And therefore will the LORD wait, that he may be gracious unto you, and therefore will he be exalted, that he may have mercy upon you: for the LORD is a God of judgment: blessed are all they that wait for him."

Are you loudly waiting for the Lord?
Exercising only your jaws will not get you very far. God gave us two ears so that we could listen twice as much as we speak. We can't hear as well while we are talking. Let your words be few today.

Are you quietly waiting for the Lord?
Exercising your faith on your knees allows the Lord to lift you up in His timing. Humble yourself before Him today, and quietly wait with the faith that He does all things well.

Bible Reading
1 Chronicles 13-14 | Colossians 3 | Proverbs 1

Substance By Faith.

Hebrews 11:1
*"Now faith is the substance of things hoped for,
the evidence of things not seen."*

Substance here is defined as that which has foundation, is firm; the substantial quality or nature of a person or thing; the steadfastness of mind, courage, resolution; confidence and assurance. When cross-referencing the Greek word *hypostasis* used here, we find it used in the first chapter of Hebrews.

Hebrews 1:3
*"Who being the brightness of his glory,
and the express image of his person, and upholding all things
by the word of his power,
when he had by himself purged our sins, sat down
on the right hand of the Majesty on high;"*

That Person referenced here is none other than our Lord and Saviour Jesus Christ. The word *hypostasis* is also used in this verse for *"his person"*.

Without faith in Jesus Christ we have no substance.
We can have hope because of our faith in Him.

Through Him all the promises of God are made real to us,
for without Him we cannot experience any.

Ephesians 2:8
*"For by grace are ye saved through faith;
and that not of yourselves:
it is the gift of God:"*

It is because of that Gift of God we are saved,
through our faith in His finished work.

We can have substance today through faith in Him!

Bible Reading
1 Chronicles 15-16 | Colossians 4 | Proverbs 2

Called To Do Something.

Matthew 28:18-20
"And Jesus came and spake unto them, saying, All power is given unto me in heaven and in earth. Go ye therefore, and teach all nations, baptizing them in the name of the Father, and of the Son, and of the Holy Ghost: Teaching them to observe all things whatsoever I have commanded you: and, lo, I am with you alway, even unto the end of the world. Amen."

We find here three different parts to the Great Commission. **Each plays a vital role in the furtherance of the Gospel of Christ, and together they make up the team effort needed in order to fulfill Christ's direction for the church.** While most of the time these are lumped together as one task that everyone should fulfill, the reality is that not everyone can do all three. It takes teamwork.

Some are called to Go.
Your call to "Go" may not take you overseas to a different country and culture; or it may be across the street to your neighbor or the cashier at your local grocery store. This is one step that all of us are called to do.

Some are called to Teach.
Some are blessed with the task and ability to teach and train others in their walk with the Lord. Discipleship is crucial in the furtherance of the Gospel. If we do not teach others to reach others we have failed in the Great Commission.

Some are called to Baptize.
Some have answered the call to preach the Gospel and lead our churches as pastors. These men are specifically given the *"baptizing"* role of the Great Commission. In order for there to be people to baptize, others must be taught to reach people and obey the command to *"Go".*

All of us are called to do something. We may not be able to baptize or even teach others, but we can all go. Whether it is to another continent, another country, another state, another county, another town, another street, or simply another person. **Make an effort today to go & tell others.**

Matthew 28:18
"And Jesus came and spake unto them, saying, All power is given unto me in heaven and in earth."

Rest in that power today. Through this power you can go, teach and baptize. **Do your part to fulfill the Great Commission.**

Bible Reading
1 Chronicles 17-18 | 1 Thessalonians 1 | Proverbs 3 | 191

Pray For Your Country.

Romans 10:1
"Brethren, my heart's desire and prayer to God for Israel is, that they might be saved."

Paul had a burden for the people within his country. He didn't want them to just live a good life or serve others, he desired for them to be saved. He prayed that they would realize their need for a Saviour, then not only recognize it, but receive Him. In chapter 10 of Romans, we see that Paul addressed those that had religion, but not salvation. The people were *"going about to establish their own righteousness".* They relied on their good works and morality to be enough.

Paul went on to explain to them how simple salvation is, if only they would confess and believe. **He cared enough about their eternal state to express his concern and share the Truth of the Gospel with them.**

Romans 10:9-10,13
"That if thou shalt confess with thy mouth the Lord Jesus, and shalt believe in thine heart that God hath raised him from the dead, thou shalt be saved. For with the heart man believeth unto righteousness; and with the mouth confession is made unto salvation…For whosoever shall call upon the name of the Lord shall be saved."

Under the inspiration of the Holy Spirit, Paul pinned these verses that are typically used today when explaining the Gospel. The simplicity of the Truth of the Gospel is evident in them. The Gospel has not changed. The desire of the hearts of people has changed.

What is your desire for your country? Do you desire to see the people saved? If the answer is yes, then what are you doing about it?

People will not be saved unless they confess and believe, but how can they if they have not heard? Paul understood this, as he closed out the rest of the chapter. See verses 14-17.

We must do our part in order
for the Great Commission to be carried out.

Pray for your country today.
Pray for revival and a great awakening to the souls of men.

Bible Reading
1 Chronicles 19-20 | 1 Thessalonians 2 | Proverbs 4

If & Then.

2 Chronicles 7:14
"If my people, which are called by my name, shall humble themselves, and pray, and seek my face, and turn from their wicked ways; then will I hear from heaven, and will forgive their sin, and will heal their land."

"If..."
We can learn from the Lord instructions to Solomon. This verse reveals the steps we must take in order to see revival in our hearts and our country. There are conditions to God's blessing on our lives and our land.

We Must Humble Ourselves. James 4:6
"But he giveth more grace. Wherefore he saith, God resisteth the proud, but giveth grace unto the humble."

We Must Pray. James 5:16
"Confess your faults one to another, and pray one for another, that ye may be healed. The effectual fervent prayer of a righteous man availeth much."

We Must Seek His Face. 1 Chronicles 16:11
"Seek the LORD and his strength, seek his face continually."

We Must Turn From Our Wicked Ways. Acts 26:17-18
"Delivering thee from the people, and from the Gentiles, unto whom now I send thee, To open their eyes, and to turn them from darkness to light, and from the power of Satan unto God..."

"then..."
After He lays out the requirements for revival, the Lord shows what blessings we will receive through obeying His requests.

He Will Hear Us. Psalm 40:1
"I waited patiently for the LORD; and he inclined unto me, and heard my cry."

He Will Forgive Our Sin. 1 John 1:9
"If we confess our sins, he is faithful and just to forgive us our sins, and to cleanse us from all unrighteousness."

He Will Heal Our Land. Jeremiah 3:22
"Return, ye backsliding children, and I will heal your backslidings. Behold, we come unto thee; for thou art the LORD our God."

Bible Reading
1 Chronicles 21-22 | 1 Thessalonians 3 | Proverbs 5 | 193

Turn Away.

2 Timothy 3:5
"Having a form of godliness, but denying the power thereof: from such turn away."

We are living within the *"perilous times"* that the Bible has foretold of for thousands of years. Perilous here refers to times that are hard to bear. We watch as what was once thought right is now thought wrong, and what was wrong is not only tolerated but is now the norm. This passage is often referred to as speaking of the world in general during the last days. Paul is actually warning Timothy, his son in the faith, of what would within the churches during the last days. **Paul admonishes Timothy to continue in his faith despite the persecution he was sure to face.**

Today, amidst the turmoil of the world, some are seeking religion. Many churches are beginning to rise in attendance due to their inspirational words and lack of preaching against sin. There is both persecution from without, and corruption from within our churches. Jesus warned us of wolves in sheep's clothing, and Paul warns of those that have a form of godliness, yet deny the power in which they claim to have.

Many are called Christian in name, yet they only have religion, and no relationship. The word *"form"* speaks of a resemblance. These are those who look and act as if they are a Christian or a follower of Christ. They resemble what the world now considers a Christian, however to resemble something is not to possess it.

What does the Scripture say to do when we find people who only possess a form of godliness? Turn Away. **We are Biblically told to withdrawal ourselves and avoid them.**

Romans 16:17-18
"Now I beseech you, brethren, mark them which cause divisions and offences contrary to the doctrine which ye have learned; and avoid them. For they that are such serve not our Lord Jesus Christ, but their own belly; and by good works and fair speeches deceive the hearts of the simple."

This turning away does not mean we should not love them and share the Gospel with them. **We are simply not to fellowship with them.**

When you find a person or church with a form of godliness, but denying the power thereof...**turn away.**

Bible Reading
1 Chronicles 23-24 | 1 Thessalonians 4 | Proverbs 6

Continue.

2 Timothy 3:14
"But continue thou in the things which thou hast learned and hast been assured of, knowing of whom thou hast learned them;"

**In those times when we are required to turn away,
we must continue in what we know to be the Truth.**

Continue In Prayer.
Colossians 4:1-2
"Masters, give unto your servants that which is just and equal; knowing that ye also have a Master in heaven. Continue in prayer, and watch in the same with thanksgiving;"

Continue In The Word.
John 8:31-32
"Then said Jesus to those Jews which believed on him, If ye continue in my word, then are ye my disciples indeed; And ye shall know the truth, and the truth shall make you free."

Continue Abiding In His Love.
John 15:9-11
"As the Father hath loved me, so have I loved you: continue ye in my love. If ye keep my commandments, ye shall abide in my love; even as I have kept my Father's commandments, and abide in his love. These things have I spoken unto you, that my joy might remain in you, and that your joy might be full."

Continue In Him.
John 15:4-7
"Abide in me, and I in you. As the branch cannot bear fruit of itself, except it abide in the vine; no more can ye, except ye abide in me. I am the vine, ye are the branches: He that abideth in me, and I in him, the same bringeth forth much fruit: for without me ye can do nothing. If a man abide not in me, he is cast forth as a branch, and is withered; and men gather them, and cast them into the fire, and they are burned. If ye abide in me, and my words abide in you, ye shall ask what ye will, and it shall be done unto you."

**We can continue today through Him,
because we are nothing without Him.**

Bible Reading
1 Chronicles 25-26 | 1 Thessalonians 5 | Proverbs 7 | 195

The Bystander Effect.

Lamentations 1:12
"Is it nothing to you, all ye that pass by?"

When an accident or medical emergency happens, there are two types of witnesses, those that stop to help and those that stand back and watch. When individuals do not offer any means of help to a victim while other people are present, it is referred to as the Bystander Effect. This is a psychological phenomenon that is inversely related to the number of people present when it occurs. **The more people around, the less likely it is that someone will help.**

The person decides what they will do in one of three ways:
1. Direct Intervention - assisting themselves
2. Detour Intervention – calling on others to assist in the situation
3. Declined Intervention – passing by without offering any assistance

We see this effect within the Scripture through the story of the Good Samaritan in Luke 10. Jesus Christ tells this parable to an inquisitive lawyer admonishing him to help his neighbor. The priest saw the wounded man, and crossed the street to avoid him. The Levite came by and looked upon his wounds, then passed by as well, perhaps going to go get help. Then the Samaritan came to where he was and had compassion on him, bounding up his wounds and taking him to the inn to heal.

We are all bystanders most of the time. No, we may not witness an accident or medical emergency right before our eyes on a regular basis, but we see people all throughout the day that are lost and on their way to spend eternity in a place prepared for Satan himself, yet what do we tend to do? We pass by them. *"Is it nothing to you, all ye that pass by?"*

We neglect getting directly involved most of the time, and detour the responsibility to just those who are "called" to do the job…pastors and missionaries. We tell the "first responders", but then we sit back and watch from the sidelines. Detour intervention is not an excuse. **We are all called to proclaim the Truth of the Gospel.** Jesus commanded all of us to go & tell others. *"Go ye into all the world, and preach the gospel to every creature."*

If we are honest, we are all guilty of the Bystander Effect. When will we realize that we may be the only person who can reach a particular person with the Gospel? Are we going to pass them by? It is nothing to us? **Lord, help us to reach them before it is eternally too late.**

Bible Reading
1 Chronicles 27-29 | 2 Thessalonians 1 | Proverbs 8

Compassion In Action.

Luke 10:33-34
*"But a certain Samaritan, as he journeyed, came where he was:
and when he saw him, he had compassion on him,"*

Jesus used the Good Samaritan as an example to not only the lawyer in Luke 10, but for us today as we read through our Bibles. There is so much to be learned from this one man's display of compassion upon that stranger on the side of the road.

We must to go to them. *"...came where he was..."*
We must make an effort to reach out to others, and we cannot do that by sitting still. Jesus showed us this example by going to Samaria. He felt led to the very city that our Good Samaritan was from. **What might the Lord do if we would obey His leading to go to others?**

We must look at their need. *"...and when he saw him..."*
Our eyes will affect our heart if we are sincere. God will give us a desire to help those in need as an opportunity to share His love for them.

We must have compassion on them. *"...he had compassion on him."*
We find in Scripture that only some will have compassion, and those that do can make a difference. **When God gives us compassion, He gives us opportunity to reach people for His glory.**

Compassion is more than just an acknowledgement of a need; it compels us to do something. The Good Samaritan not only went to this man, but his compassion compelled him to bound up his wounds and take him to an inn to care for him. **Compassion in Action.**

The lost will not realize their need unless we show them through the love of Christ. The backslidden will not realize their condition unless we love them through their trouble. The hurting will not receive the help they need unless we bear their burdens through intercessory prayer for them. Speak the love of Christ by showing the love of Christ. **Compassion in Action.**

Do you know someone hurting today? Are you burdened for them? Show them you care. Do something to make a difference in their life today. An encouraging text or phone call, or a card in the mail. Just a simple gesture of love to remind them that you are praying for them can change their mindset. If you cannot think of someone or something to do, ask the Lord to place someone on your heart. Ask Him to show you what the person needs. **Put action behind your compassion today.**

Bible Reading
2 Chronicles 1-2 | 2 Thessalonians 2 | Proverbs 9 | 197

Pray For Your Pastor.

Romans 15:30
*"Now I beseech you, brethren, for the Lord Jesus Christ's sake,
and for the love of the Spirit, that ye strive together with me
in your prayers to God for me;"*

The Apostle Paul realized the demand the ministry requires, as well as the spiritual warfare and resistance that he faced on a daily basis would require people to stand in the gap and pray for him and the work. He begged for the prayers of the people. *"Now I beseech you, brethren…"* Does your pastor have to beg you to pray for him? **The Scripture tells us to pray for those that God has placed in authority.** It is our duty to lift up our pastor in prayer.

Pray that God will protect your pastor from the attacks of Satan.
2 Corinthians 2:11
*"Lest Satan should get an advantage of us:
for we are not ignorant of his devices,"*

Pray for your pastor that he will not grow weary in well doing.
Galatians 6:9
*"And let us not be weary in well doing: for in due season we shall reap,
if we faint not."*

Pray for your pastor that he will glean Truths from the Word of God.
Acts 6:4
*"But we will give ourselves continually to prayer,
and to the ministry of the word."*

Pray for your pastor because he prays for you.
Philippians 1:3-4
*"I thank my God upon every remembrance of you,
Always in every prayer of mine for you all making request with joy,"*

Spend some time today, and everyday, thanking the Lord for the man of God He has placed in your life.

The greatest gift you can give your pastor is to pray for him.

2 Corinthians 1:11
*"Ye also helping together by prayer for us, that for the gift
bestowed upon us by the means of many persons thanks
may be given by many on our behalf."*

Bible Reading
2 Chronicles 3-4 | 2 Thessalonians 3 | Proverbs 10

God Has More In Store.

1 Corinthians 2:9
*"But as it is written, Eye hath not seen, nor ear heard,
neither have entered into the heart of man, the things
which God hath prepared for them that love him."*

More beautiful than any sunset. More lovely than the purest melody.
Our hearts cannot comprehend all that God has planned for us.

This Truth brings comfort when we are amidst the battle or storm. Our affliction is but for a moment, because one day…God will reveal to us what He has been preparing.

He has more in store for us than we can see, hear, or even desire!

This world is not our home; we are just passing through on our way to our eternal dwelling place. While we walk along this life's journey, God is not only preparing our heavenly home, but He is working behind the scenes here as well. His plan is unfolding with each step of faith we take in His direction. Sometimes we veer off course when we make a decision outside of His guidance, but when we stop and ask for help, He begins to lead us once again to His purpose.

Take comfort today that God has your situation all under control.
He has a better plan that He is working out for your good, and His glory!

Psalm 31:19
*"Oh how great is thy goodness,
which thou hast laid up for them that fear thee; which thou hast wrought
for them that trust in thee before the sons of men!"*

Our eyes have never seen such goodness.
Our ears have never heard such goodness.
Our hearts cannot hold all the goodness that God is.

God is working things for our good, because He is Good!

Bible Reading
2 Chronicles 5-6 | 1 Timothy 1 | Proverbs 11 | 199

Revealed.

1 Corinthians 2:10
*"But God hath revealed them unto us by his Spirit:
for the Spirit searcheth all things, yea, the deep things of God."*

**As we walk along by faith,
God begins to reveal His plan for our lives.**

He does this through the Holy Spirit,
as we read His Word and ask for His direction.

We cannot receive God's direction if we are not seeking it by communicating with Him. Our walk with God is a two way street, just like our relationships with our friends and family members must be. We talk to God through prayer, and He speaks to us through the Scripture. If our Bible is always closed and sitting on the table, we are not hearing God's direction for our lives. If we do not come to God in prayer, our requests will not be heard.

When reading God's Word, we may read a verse that we have read several times before, yet we see something different within the Words. This is the Holy Spirit revealing the Truth to us. The Spirit searches our hearts and reveals the deep Truths of Scripture to us just when we need them.

**Ask the Lord to show you just what you need
within the pages of your Bible today.**

He is sure to reveal something that will help
you serve Him and shine the Light for His glory.

Bible Reading
2 Chronicles 7-8 | 1 Timothy 2 | Proverbs 12

Declare His Praise.

Isaiah 42:11-12
*"Let the wilderness and the cities thereof lift up their voice,
the villages that Kedar doth inhabit: let the inhabitants of the rock sing,
let them shout from the top of the mountains. Let them give glory unto the
LORD, and declare his praise in the islands."*

Whether we are in the middle of a wilderness, a big city, a village, or an island, we can give glory unto the Lord and declare His praise unto all those around us.

He is Worthy to be Praised.
2 Samuel 22:4
"I will call on the LORD, who is worthy to be praised..."

Praise Him for His Mercy.
2 Chronicles 20:21
"...Praise the LORD; for his mercy endureth for ever."

Praise Him for His Righteousness.
Psalm 7:17
*"I will praise the LORD according to his righteousness:
and will sing praise to the name of the LORD most high."*

Praise Him for His Word.
Psalm 56:10
"In God will I praise his word: in the LORD will I praise his word."

Praise His Name.
Psalm 148:13
*"Let them praise the name of the LORD: for his name alone is excellent;
his glory is above the earth and heaven."*

Praise Him All The Time!
Hebrews 13:15
*"By him therefore let us offer the sacrifice of praise to God continually,
that is, the fruit of our lips giving thanks to his name."*

Praise the Lord today for His mercy, His righteousness,
His Word, and above all, His Name!

Declare His praise to those around you today!

Bible Reading
2 Chronicles 9-10 | 1 Timothy 3 | Proverbs 13 | 201

Colossians 3:17
*"And whatsoever ye do in word or deed,
do all in the name of the Lord Jesus,
giving thanks to God and the Father by him."*

We externalize our feelings and actions in only two ways – by what we say, or what we do, in word or deed. Each time we express ourselves it is an opportunity to give thanks and glory to God. Paul admonishes the church of Colosse of this Truth.

When we are asked to do something, regardless of what it is, we have an opportunity to give thanks to the Lord! Whether it is to speak before a vast audience or pick up trash when no one is watching, we can glorify the One Who has given us the ability to do the task in the first place.

If we seek to do all things in the Name of the Lord Jesus Christ, we will become more aware of our reactions.

Philippians 2:14
"Do all things without murmurings and disputings:"

This is one of the most difficult verses in the Bible to apply to our lives, yet just as inspired as *"For God so loved the world"*. It is difficult to go an entire day, or maybe even an hour without going against this verse isn't it? We cannot *"do all in the name of the Lord Jesus"* if we are murmuring or disputing. Convicting thought.

It is possible to do all things without murmuring or disputing.

Philippians 4:13
"I can do all things through Christ which strengtheneth me."

1 Corinthians 10:31
*"Whether therefore ye eat, or drink, or whatsoever ye do,
do all to the glory of God."*

Seek to use every opportunity today.
Do all things in the Name of the Lord Jesus Christ.
The Name above all names!

Bible Reading
2 Chronicles 11-12 | 1 Timothy 4 | Proverbs 14

The Afflictions Of The Righteous.

Psalm 34:19
"Many are the afflictions of the righteous:
but the LORD delivereth him out of them all."

We are only righteous because of the righteousness of Jesus Christ has been imputed to us. His afflictions were many. He bore the weight of our sin, enduring the wrath of God for us. He was scourged and crucified; experiencing nearly every bodily wound suffered pain and agony beyond description. He was forsaken by God the Father because of our sin, yet despite all these afflictions…*"the LORD delivereth him out of them all."*

Christ rose from the grave victorious, defeating every affliction He had suffered. This is yet another example to us that God can deliver us from any affliction that we suffer. **We can cry to Him, and He will not only hear us, but He will deliver us!**

Psalm 34:17-22
"The righteous cry, and the LORD heareth, and delivereth them out of all their troubles. The LORD is nigh unto them that are of a broken heart; and saveth such as be of a contrite spirit. Many are the afflictions of the righteous: but the LORD delivereth him out of them all. He keepeth all his bones: not one of them is broken. Evil shall slay the wicked: and they that hate the righteous shall be desolate. The LORD redeemeth the soul of his servants: and none of them that trust in him shall be desolate."

When we trust in Christ's finished work on Calvary as payment for our sin, we have His righteousness imputed on us, or put to our account. Just as our sin was imputed onto Him when He took our punishment, we are imputed with His righteousness.

We are redeemed and delivered because of our trust in the Lord Jesus Christ! Our afflictions in this life may be many, but we can claim this promise: *"Many are the afflictions of the righteous: but the LORD delivereth him out of them all."*

Dwell in His presence today, and thank Him for imputing His righteousness upon you. **No matter what trouble you face today, you can have peace because He has promised to deliver you!**

Bible Reading
2 Chronicles 13-14 | 1 Timothy 5 | Proverbs 15

The Secret Place.

Psalm 91:1-2
"He that dwelleth in the secret place of the most High shall abide under the shadow of the Almighty. I will say of the LORD, He is my refuge and my fortress: my God; in him will I trust."

Do you ever wish you could just hide away for a little bit? Rowdy children, a stressful co-worker, or just from people in general can make us want to hide. Everyone needs a break every once and awhile. **There is a secret place that is always available and never too crowded under the shadow of the Almighty God.**

He is Our Shelter. Psalm 61:3
"For thou hast been a shelter for me, and a strong tower from the enemy."

Even in the good times where the sun is shining bright, shelter is needed. When the storms rush in and the winds are too hard to bear, we can seek shelter in Him.

He is Our Refuge. Psalm 46:1-2
"God is our refuge and strength, a very present help in trouble. Therefore we will not fear…"

We not only find shelter, but also strength in Him. Though trouble may abound, He is always there as a present help. There is such a comfort in knowing that He is a help right here and now. *"a very present help"*

He is Our Fortress. Psalm 71:3
"Be thou my strong habitation, whereunto I may continually resort: thou hast given commandment to save me; for thou art my rock and my fortress."

We are secure in Him! He will not only shelter us and give us strength, but He provides security like no other. When our enemies seem to prevail, He is our stronghold. We can come to Him continually for help. He desires for us to rest in Him. *"whereunto I may continually resort"*

The shelter, strength, and security that we find in Him bring us to the Truth of *"in him will I trust."*

Find that secret place today. Allow Him to be your hiding place.

Psalm 32:7
"Thou art my hiding place; thou shalt preserve me from trouble; thou shalt compass me about with songs of deliverance. Selah."

Bible Reading
2 Chronicles 15-16 | 1 Timothy 6 | Proverbs 16

Trust In His Wings.

Psalm 91:3-4
*"Surely he shall deliver thee from the snare of the fowler,
and from the noisome pestilence. He shall cover thee with his feathers,
and under his wings shalt thou trust:
his truth shall be thy shield and buckler."*

When we are caught off guard by the traps of our enemies, we can seek shelter under the wings of our Saviour. He will shield us from the wiles of the devil and the people who seek to do us harm. **We can trust that He will protect us.**

Psalm 57:1
*"Be merciful unto me, O God, be merciful unto me:
for my soul trusteth in thee: yea, in the shadow of thy wings
will I make my refuge, until these calamities be overpast."*

David speaks from experience. He knew what it was like to feel caught in the trap of his enemies' snare. He knew how it felt to be the prey that his enemy sought after, but he also knew what deliverance felt like. **He understood the shelter and comfort that is available under the Lord's wings.** He had the feathers of His wings intertwining around him to provide safety and security.

If we will ask the Lord to cover us with the feathers
of His mighty wings He will deliver us.

Trust in His wings today.

Psalm 61:4
*"I will abide in thy tabernacle for ever:
I will trust in the covert of thy wings. Selah."*

Bible Reading
2 Chronicles 17-18 | 2 Timothy 1 | Proverbs 17

Leaning To Confidence.

Micah 3:11
*"…yet will they lean upon the LORD, and say,
Is not the LORD among us? none evil can come upon us."*

When an injured or disabled person uses a cane or crutch to help them walk they must lean on the object for assistance and stability. They have confidence that the cane will bear their weight, and balance them, so that they can take the next step. The Lord should in no way be viewed as a cane or crutch, but there is a principle here that we can learn from and apply to our daily walk with Him. **We in our own ability can do nothing without Christ.** Have you ever had to be reminded that you are nothing without Him? When our pride gets in the way, He has a way of reminding us of this Truth while still supporting and guiding us at the same time as we lean on and acknowledge Him.

Proverbs 3:5-6
*"Trust in the LORD with all thine heart;
and lean not unto thine own understanding.
In all thy ways acknowledge him, and he shall direct thy paths."*

Thankfully, we can also be reminded by the confidence Paul had when he pinned, *"I can do all things through Christ which strengtheneth me."* **We are nothing without Christ, but through Him and His strength we can accomplish all things in His will.** We have the Lord on our side!

Psalm 118:6
"The LORD is on my side; I will not fear: what can man do unto me?"

Hebrews 13:6
"So that we may boldly say, The Lord is my helper, and I will not fear what man shall do unto me."

Seek Him for guidance and direction on how to address the situation you are facing. He will calm your fears.

Psalm 34:4
*"I sought the LORD, and he heard me,
and delivered me from all my fears."*

**When we lean on Him our fears will subside
and be replaced by confidence
that only comes from knowing He is on our side.**

Bible Reading
2 Chronicles 19-20 | 2 Timothy 2 | Proverbs 18

Have No Fear.

Psalm 46:2-3
*"Therefore will not we fear, though the earth be removed,
and though the mountains be carried into the midst of the sea;
Though the waters thereof roar and be troubled,
though the mountains shake with the swelling thereof. Selah."*

"...though the earth be removed..."
When the ground beneath your feet seems to have disappeared,
and you feel as if you are falling with no end in sight… **Have no fear.**

"...though the mountains be carried into the midst of the sea..."
When the protection around you seems to be destroyed, and you feel
vulnerable at where the next attack may come from… **Have no fear.**

"...Though the waters thereof roar and be troubled..."
When the storm raging around you makes your surroundings seems
disoriented, and you feel unsteady and off balance… **Have no fear.**

"...though the mountains shake with the swelling thereof."
When your plan is shattered, the details become dismantled,
and you are shaking in your core… **Have no fear.**

How can we have no fear?
Psalm 46:1
"God is our refuge and strength, a very present help in trouble."

**Make God your refuge and strength!
He is a very present help in time of trouble.**

Remember there is comfort in knowing
that He is there to help right here and now.
"...a very present help in trouble."

Have no fear today, Christian.

Bible Reading
2 Chronicles 21-22 | 2 Timothy 3 | Proverbs 19 | 207

Falling.

Psalm 37:24
*"Though he fall, he shall not be utterly cast down:
for the LORD upholdeth him with his hand."*

Some people are blessed with the gift of clumsiness where there are days when they can't seem to stay on their own two feet. Can you relate? When we trip and fall, we have a choice…to get up or to stay down.

Falling Is Inevitable.
"Though he fall…"
The Book of James not only warns us that it is not if but *"when"* we will be in a trial, but remember the wording of that verse…

James 1:2
"My brethren, count it all joy when ye fall into divers temptations;"

Falling is to be expected. We may fall because of a choice we made, or someone else's choice that affects us. When our faith is tried we have an opportunity to grow, but we must first return to our feet.

Falling Is Temporary.
Why are we not destroyed when we fall?
"for the Lord upholdeth him with his hand."

In the previous verse we are told that our steps are ordered by the Lord. **If He orders our steps, then our falls are appointments that He allows.** He uses our falls and disappointments to point us to Him, and while doing so we are supported by the very hand of God. There is no safer place to fall!

Psalm 34:19
*"Many are the afflictions of the righteous:
but the LORD delivereth him out of them all."*

Falling Is Not Failure.
Sometimes our falls seem like failures to us, but in God's eyes they are opportunities for His glory. When our flesh desires something contrary to what God has for us, we may get disappointed when we do not receive it… but it is for our good. He has something better in store! **We do not fail until we fail to get back up.**

Proverbs 24:16
"For a just man falleth seven times, and riseth up again…"

Bible Reading
2 Chronicles 23-24 | 2 Timothy 4 | Proverbs 20

Purpose In Patience.

James 1:4
*"But let patience have her perfect work,
that ye may be perfect and entire, wanting nothing."*

No one likes to be taught how to have patience. In today's modern society patience is lacking. We have coined the terms "rush hour" and "drive thru" because of our lack of wanting to wait. But when God makes us wait...He always has a reason that far exceeds our own plan at the time. We want the wait to be over, and get from point A to point B as soon as we possibly can. **Wonder what we miss sometimes because we refuse to wait?**

"But let patience..."
Allow patience to do the work God intended.

Waiting allows us to learn something.
Waiting allows us to do something else in the mean time.
Waiting allows us to avoid an otherwise catastrophe.
Waiting allows us to increase our dependence and trust in God.

There is purpose in patience.

When we rush our patience we limit the purpose God has us wait for in the first place, we miss the full effect of His plan. In order not to limit His plans, we must rejoice in our trials!

James 1:2
"My brethren, count it all joy when ye fall into divers temptations;"

Sometimes trials are what it takes to begin to see God's plan unfolding. We will not see His plan for our lives fully developed if we go ahead of His timing. Waiting allows God to work in ways that only He can, which always leads to results that can only bring the glory to Him. **It is worth the wait.**

Hebrews 10:35-36
"Cast not away therefore your confidence, which hath great recompence of reward. For ye have need of patience, that, after ye have done the will of God, ye might receive the promise."

Bible Reading
2 Chronicles 25-26 | Titus 1 | Proverbs 21 | 209

No Withholding.

James 1:5
*"If any of you lack wisdom, let him ask of God, that giveth
to all men liberally, and upbraideth not; and it shall be given him."*

King Solomon loved the Lord.
He was given the opportunity to ask the Lord for anything he wanted.

1 Kings 3:5
*"In Gibeon the LORD appeared to Solomon in a dream by night:
and God said, Ask what I shall give thee."*

Can you imagine? This was not some genie in a bottle that wanted to grant him three wishes. This was the very Creator of the Universe, the Almighty God. Would you have the mental capacity to make such a wise request as Solomon did? He had wisdom before he even asked for it.

1 Kings 3:9
*"Give therefore thy servant an understanding heart to judge thy people,
that I may discern between good and bad:
who is able to judge this thy so great a people?"*

The Lord was pleased with Solomon's request. He gave him the wisdom he asked for…and so much more. Just like Solomon, **God will give us wisdom if we only ask for it.** He will not withhold it, but will give it liberally not just to some, but to all who ask in faith.

Wisdom and discernment go hand in hand, and the two are severely lacking in our day. Why? Because we have not asked for them.

**Christian, you need wisdom in order to endure
and learn from the trial you are facing.**

Ask the Lord to give you an understanding heart through your trial.
**Ask Him to help you discern how to make the right decisions,
in accordance to His will for your life.**

Nothing Wavering.

James 1:6
*"But let him ask in faith, nothing wavering.
For he that wavereth is like a wave of the sea
driven with the wind and tossed."*

We see here that the only requirement in addition to asking for wisdom is that we *"ask in faith, nothing wavering."* **We can ask for wisdom, but if we do not believe that God will give us the understanding and discernment we seek, we are certain to not receive it.** To waver is to stagger between belief and unbelief, like a seesaw. We either believe God and His promises or we don't.

Abraham's Unwavering Faith.
Romans 4:20-21
*"He staggered not at the promise of God through unbelief;
but was strong in faith, giving glory to God; And being fully persuaded
that, what he had promised, he was able also to perform."*

God had promised that Abraham would be the father of many nations, and he believed that God would keep His promise despite his old age.

Abraham was not weak in his faith. He did not waver despite the circumstances. **He was strong in his faith, giving God the glory while he waited for the promise to be fulfilled.**

We must believe that God is not only able to give us wisdom, but also to make us wise because He promised He would do so, if only we would ask in faith.

Regardless of our current situation, we must believe God's promises that He has made unto us. **Seek to be an unwavering Christian.** Follow God's leading, and trust Him to carry out the plan that He has for your life.

Bible Reading
2 Chronicles 29-30 | Titus 3 | Proverbs 23 | 211

Turn Your Fear Into Faith.

Hebrews 13:6
*"So that we may boldly say, The Lord is my helper,
and I will not fear what man shall do unto me."*

Fearful times are an opportunity to realize our need to have faith that God can and will deliver us. Fear allows us to see our need to trust.

Psalm 56:3
"What time I am afraid, I will trust in thee."

David knew what it was like to be fearful, and for good reason. Countless times he was surrounded by his enemies that sought to take his life; yet, King David turned his fear into faith. If he found a way to exchange his fear for faith we can too.

Praise & Trust His Word.
Psalm 56:4
*"In God I will praise his word, in God have I put my trust;
I will not fear what flesh can do unto me."*

Pray & Press On In Faith.
Psalm 118:5-6
*"I called upon the LORD in distress: the LORD answered me,
and set me in a large place. The LORD is on my side;
I will not fear: what can man do unto me?"*

The Apostle Paul learned from David's experiences. He had read how David had turned his fear into faith, and we see all throughout the New Testament how Paul applied that wisdom to his own life & ministry.

Paul boldly proclaimed, *"The LORD is my helper, and I will not fear..."*, which allowed his faith to defeat his fleshly fear. **With the Lord on his side, he knew that no man could harm him unless God allowed it.**

These men have left us an example to apply to our own lives. When we remember the promise that He will never leave us nor forsake us, we too can boldly proclaim, *"The LORD is my helper..."*

Whatever you are fearful of today,
the Lord is able to help you overcome it.
Ask Him to help you turn your fear into faith.

Bible Reading
2 Chronicles 31-32 | Philemon | Proverbs 24

God Is The Strength Of My Heart.

Psalm 73:26
*"My flesh and my heart faileth:
but God is the strength of my heart, and my portion for ever."*

For those times when we feel like we just cannot go on.
When we just want to quit and never look back.
When the weight is too heavy to bear.
When it just does not seem worth it.
When our heart is just not in it.
When we just don't understand
how things will work out, or if they even will.
"...but God is the strength of my heart..."

The Lord helps us turn our fears into faith when we rely upon His strength.
Though our bodies are weak, we can be strong through His strength.
Though our hearts are hurting, we can be strong through His strength.

2 Samuel 22:33
"God is my strength and power: and he maketh my way perfect."

Psalm 62:7
*"In God is my salvation and my glory:
the rock of my strength, and my refuge, is in God."*

Isaiah 12:2
*"Behold, God is my salvation; I will trust, and not be afraid: for the LORD
JEHOVAH is my strength and my song; he also is become my salvation."*

Acknowledge your need for His strength today.
He will supply the grace to make it through.

2 Corinthians 12:9-10
*"And he said unto me, My grace is sufficient for thee: for my strength is
made perfect in weakness. Most gladly therefore will I rather glory in my
infirmities, that the power of Christ may rest upon me. Therefore I take
pleasure in infirmities, in reproaches, in necessities, in persecutions, in
distresses for Christ's sake: for when I am weak, then am I strong."*

We will never be strong in our faith unless we thank God for our trials,
and allow His grace to strengthen us.
Allow the Lord to be the Strength of your heart today.

Bible Reading
2 Chronicles 33-34 | Hebrews 1 | Proverbs 25 | 213

Stablished, Strengthened, Settled.

1 Peter 5:10
"But the God of all grace, who hath called us unto his eternal glory by Christ Jesus, after that ye have suffered a while, make you perfect, stablish, strengthen, settle you."

Notice the promise of what awaits us after we have suffered for a little while for our good and His glory.

Stablished In The Faith.
Colossians 2:7
"Rooted and built up in him, and stablished in the faith, as ye have been taught, abounding therein with thanksgiving."

Our faith can only be established when it is rooted in Jesus Christ, for it is His grace alone that brings salvation.

Strengthened With Might.
Ephesians 3:16
"That he would grant you, according to the riches of his glory, to be strengthened with might by his Spirit in the inner man;"

Our faith gives us boldness and access to Christ Jesus. We do not have to faint in our tribulations. We can bow on our knees, and ask God to give us the strength we need to press on.

Settled In Love.
Ephesians 3:17
"That Christ may dwell in your hearts by faith; that ye, being rooted and grounded in love,"

We can only live as stable Christians if we are grounded in the love that Christ has for us. God is Love, and because He dwells in our hearts by faith, we can be grounded in His love for us.

We can be encouraged today that our trials and tribulations are just for a moment. As a result of our suffering, we can be stablished, strengthened and settled in Jesus Christ.

Bible Reading
2 Chronicles 35-36 | Hebrews 2 | Proverbs 26

Refusing To Stand.

Jeremiah 6:16
"Thus saith the LORD, Stand ye in the ways, and see, and ask for the old paths, where is the good way, and walk therein, and ye shall find rest for your souls. But they said, We will not walk therein."

Repeatedly throughout the Word of God we see that God set out a path for His people, and inevitably someone veers off in a different direction or refuses to walk in the same way anymore. Each time this occurs the people involved that made a change, or refused to continue, reap the consequences.

Jeremiah 18:15-17
"Because my people hath forgotten me, they have burned incense to vanity, and they have caused them to stumble in their ways from the ancient paths, to walk in paths, in a way not cast up; To make their land desolate, and a perpetual hissing; every one that passeth thereby shall be astonished, and wag his head. I will scatter them as with an east wind before the enemy; I will shew them the back, and not the face, in the day of their calamity."

Does this not sound like modern day "Christianity"? **The contemporary religion of today is not without warning from the Scriptures.** Many of those that once served the Lord with gladness have since decided to turn to a "Christianity" filled with vanity and tolerance in an effort to draw more people.

"...they have caused them to stumble in their ways from the ancient paths..." **When one decides to compromise, a few others are likely to follow.** Often when changes start to be made, we fail to think of what repercussions could arise in the lives of others by our refusing to stand for the old paths.

What may seem like an innocent change can quickly escalate to tolerance. Worldly music and multiple translations of the Bible will only bring confusion.

Christians who have the Truth must stand for the Truth. If we refuse to take a stand and separate ourselves from the world, we will no longer be effective in shining the Light of Christ.

Instead of refusing to stand, we must refuse to compromise.

Bible Reading
Ezra 1-2 | Hebrews 3 | Proverbs 27

Be Willing.

Isaiah 6:8
*"Also I heard the voice of the Lord, saying,
Whom shall I send, and who will go for us?
Then said I, Here am I; send me."*

God desires for us to be willing to follow whatever He commands. He will not force us to believe in Him, trust in Him, or work for Him.

Willing to Serve.
Sometimes God calls us display His love by serving others.
Galatians 5:13
"For, brethren, ye have been called unto liberty; only use not liberty for an occasion to the flesh, but by love serve one another."

Willing to Stand.
Sometimes God calls us to take a stand against something that is wrong.
1 Corinthians 16:13
"Watch ye, stand fast in the faith, quit you like men, be strong."

Willing to Separate.
Sometimes God calls us to separate ourselves from others.
2 Corinthians 6:17
"Wherefore come out from among them, and be ye separate, saith the Lord, and touch not the unclean thing; and I will receive you,"

Willing to Suffer.
Sometimes God calls us to suffer for His sake.
1 Peter 4:16
"Yet if any man suffer as a Christian, let him not be ashamed; but let him glorify God on this behalf."

Willing to Sacrifice.
Sometimes God calls us to make a sacrifice for His glory.
Romans 12:1
"I beseech you therefore, brethren, by the mercies of God, that ye present your bodies a living sacrifice, holy, acceptable unto God, which is your reasonable service."

Unless we are willing to answer God's call, we will miss out on what could happen if we would only say to the Lord, *"Here am I; send me."*

Are you willing?

Bible Reading
Ezra 3-4 | Hebrews 4 | Proverbs 28

Vision Minded.

Proverbs 29:18
*"Where there is no vision, the people perish:
but he that keepeth the law, happy is he."*

Everything rises and falls on leadership.
A leader of any kind leads by one of two ways: by vision or by agenda.

Do you have a vision? Or do you have an agenda?
A vision leader has Spirit-led motives.
An agenda leader has self-serving motives.

To be vision minded is to be Spirit-led.
"Where there is no vision, the people perish..."

When an artist sets out to create a new painting, sculpture or graphic, they begin with the end in mind. They have a vision for how they desire their creative piece to turn out. Sometimes throughout the creative process, changes are made that will alter the finished product from what was originally intended; the creator allows those changes to be made for the good of the outcome of the project.

When we set out to accomplish something for the Lord, we must begin with the end in mind, checking our motives in the process. These characteristics show whether we have a Spirit-led vision or a self-serving agenda. Notice the difference.

Vision Minded
Desires God's glory & favor
Allows the Lord to lead in changes despite the plan
Acknowledges that God is in control
Often behind the scenes of the work

Agenda Minded
Desires attention & applause
Manipulates things to achieve their goal
Craves control of the situation
Often places themselves in the spotlight

Ask the Lord to give you a vision for your life and ministry. Follow Him when He guides you through the necessary changes in order for your vision to line up with His will. **Be vision minded.**

Bible Reading
Ezra 5-6 | Hebrews 5 | Proverbs 29 | 217

Where Is Your Reward?

Matthew 6:1-4

"Take heed that ye do not your alms before men, to be seen of them: otherwise ye have no reward of your Father which is in heaven. Therefore when thou doest thine alms, do not sound a trumpet before thee, as the hypocrites do in the synagogues and in the streets, that they may have glory of men. Verily I say unto you, They have their reward. But when thou doest alms, let not thy left hand know what thy right hand doeth: That thine alms may be in secret: and thy Father which seeth in secret himself shall reward thee openly."

Have you ever thought about where your reward is? **When we earn rewards, we receive them one of two places…here or there.**

When we do good things seeking the applause of those around us here on earth in order to be seen of them, we have our reward. When we do good things with only the motive of pleasing God, and we will receive eternal rewards as well as God's favor on our life.

What eternal rewards have been lost because we received our reward here? **When we seek to be seen or receive applause, we forfeit any eternal reward that could have been earned in order to cast back at the feet of Jesus.**

"…to be seen of them…"

These types of people are easy to spot. The ones who only pick up a broom or mop when someone is watching. The ones that only come to a service or event because the Pastor might notice them. The ones that give me-imonies instead of testimonies. **They have their reward.**

What do you desire more…the glory of men or the Glory of God?

If we desire to receive rewards from the Father, we must seek only to please Him and leave the rewarding up to Him. We can earn eternal rewards that we will be able to cast at His feet, and yet He still will reward us here by His infinite blessings and grace.

Where do you want to receive your reward? Here or there? **Make the choice today to forfeit earthly rewards for eternal gain.**

Bible Reading

Ezra 7-8 | Hebrews 6 | Proverbs 30

Faith Without Works.

James 2:14
"What doth it profit, my brethren, though a man say he hath faith, and have not works? can faith save him?"

We are saved by God's grace when we see ourselves as a sinner in need of a Saviour and place our faith in the finished work of Jesus Christ on the cross. Plus nothing minus nothing. The Scripture tells us in Titus 3:5, *"Not by works of righteousness which we have done, but according to his mercy he saved us."* We cannot earn our way to Heaven. There is not enough good works that we could do in order to get to Heaven. With these Truths in mind, our verse today may seem confusing when the context is not studied and applied. James 2:14-26 will gives us the context. If we see someone in need of clothing or food, and we have the means to help them yet choose not to, what do we earn? **Faith without works is dead.**

James 2:17-18
"Even so faith, if it hath not works, is dead, being alone. Yea, a man may say, Thou hast faith, and I have works: shew me thy faith without thy works, and I will shew thee my faith by my works."

Without works we cannot display our faith for others to see. **We have no evidence of our faith if we do not have works.**

Hebrews 11:1
"Now faith is the substance of things hoped for, the evidence of things not seen."

God sees our faith. But if faith is the evidence of things not seen, how can we show our faith to those around us if we do not have works? They cannot see our heart like God does. We must display our faith by the works we do for the cause of Christ and not for our own glory or else we will lose our eternal reward.

Display your faith today. Allow those around you to see your faith by the works you do in Christ's Name. He is worthy of our works, our love, and our lives…but it must start with faith in Him.

James 2:26
"For as the body without the spirit is dead, so faith without works is dead also."

Make your faith alive in the work that God has given you to do!

Bible Reading
Ezra 9-10 | Hebrews 7 | Proverbs 31 | 219

Share.

Matthew 10:27
*"What I tell you in darkness, that speak ye in light:
and what ye hear in the ear, that preach ye upon the housetops."*

**It is within the dark and stormy nights of our lives
that we learn to seek God in our time of need.**

Hebrews 4:16
*"Let us therefore come boldly unto the throne of grace,
that we may obtain mercy, and find grace to help in time of need."*

The Lord speaks peace to our hearts in the darkest times, and teaches us lessons that we would not have learned otherwise. God uses the darkness to point us to the Light. Sometimes, God sends a storm so that we will seek shelter in Him.

The word *"darkness"* here refers to in secret, private. When we seek what God has to say, He reveals His Truth to us in a way we have never experienced before. The sleeplessness that comes from instilling God's Word within our souls changes us to be more like Jesus Christ. The quiet nights when the Scripture speaks so loudly that we stand in awe of the Word of God strengthen our walk with Him.

In contrast, the word *"light"* in this verse refers to that which is exposed to the view of all, openly, publicly. What we learn and experience in the darkness is to be shared openly. **We are to freely share the Truths we learn during our alone time with the Lord.** When the Holy Spirit opens our hearts and eyes to a deeper Truth of God's Word it is sure to help us, but maybe that Truth is just what someone else needs in their situation. Often times God can use a caring friend who feels led to share with us a Truth that the Lord showed them to speak peace to our souls.

**Share with your friends, and encourage them to likewise share
with you what God is revealing to them through His Word.**
It will strengthen your friendship.

Bible Reading
Nehemiah 1-2 | Hebrews 8 | Psalm 1

He's Always There.

1 Chronicles 28:20
"And David said to Solomon his son, Be strong and of good courage, and do it: fear not, nor be dismayed: for the LORD God, even my God, will be with thee; he will not fail thee, nor forsake thee, until thou hast finished all the work for the service of the house of the LORD."

We see this same promise reiterated all throughout Scripture. **Our Lord will never fail us or forsake us.** He's always there!

Moses to Joshua
Deuteronomy 31:7-8
"And Moses called unto Joshua, and said unto him in the sight of all Israel, Be strong and of a good courage: for thou must go with this people unto the land which the LORD hath sworn unto their fathers to give them; and thou shalt cause them to inherit it. And the LORD, he it is that doth go before thee; he will be with thee, he will not fail thee, neither forsake thee: fear not, neither be dismayed."

David to Solomon
I Chronicles 28:20
"And David said to Solomon his son, Be strong and of good courage, and do it: fear not, nor be dismayed: for the LORD God, even my God, will be with thee; he will not fail thee, nor forsake thee, until thou hast finished all the work for the service of the house of the LORD."

To All Believers
Hebrews 13:5
"Let your conversation be without covetousness; and be content with such things as ye have: for he hath said, I will never leave thee, nor forsake thee."

This promise is true for all who trust in Christ as their Saviour. Once we receive Him, He promises to never leave us. **No matter how dark the journey may seem or how bleak the circumstances, He is always there.** He is as close as the mention of His Name…Jesus.

Regardless of what you are facing, cling to this promise today. He is there with you and for you. Read His Word, and meditate on the Truths and promises that He gives us all because He loves us. **He's always there!**

Bible Reading
Nehemiah 3-4 | Hebrews 9 | Psalm 2 | 221

Waiting Wisely.

Psalm 27:14
*"Wait on the LORD: be of good courage,
and he shall strengthen thine heart: wait, I say, on the LORD."*

When we do not have a clear yes or no in answer to something we have prayed and asked God for, we have two choices: proceed with caution, not knowing the Lord's will, or wait.

Our flesh wants action, but waiting involves being still without movement or proceeding ahead. **Waiting is hard, but beneficial because it allows us to rely on God.**

Psalm 46:10
*"Be still, and know that I am God:
I will be exalted among the heathen, I will be exalted in the earth."*

David knew firsthand what it was like to wait. He was chosen to be king of Israel, but had to wait many years before he ascended the throne. Think of what all transpired while David waited for his time to come. A selfish tyrant held the very title David knew would one day be his, and this same man sought David's life on more than one occasion. Saul's actions forced David to hide in caves fearing that his days were numbered; yet, he knew God had promised him that one day he would be king. His many days of waiting allowed his character to be shaped in such a way that he was later called *"a man after God's own heart".*

What character is the Lord shaping in you while you wait? David could have chosen to be angry and discouraged in his days of waiting; but instead, **he allowed God to use the waiting period to shape him into the man God wanted him to be.** While he waited, he was confident and expected the Lord to come through for him. He would not have been the same if it had not been for the trials and period of waiting that God chose to give him.

Waiting can produce a confident expectation that God will provide. Though we may get discouraged, we can use the waiting period to allow God to create within us a confidence that only comes from trusting Him.

While we wait, we can use our time wisely by spending it with our Saviour. Time spent with the Lord is never wasted. Ask Him to give you grace in your times of waiting. **Use your time of waiting wisely by spending it in His presence.**

Bible Reading
Nehemiah 5-6 | Hebrews 10 | Psalm 3

He Is Waiting.

Isaiah 30:18
"And therefore will the LORD wait, that he may be gracious unto you, and therefore will he be exalted, that he may have mercy upon you: for the LORD is a God of judgment: blessed are all they that wait for him."

Even when we have a specific timetable for our lives, the Lord wants us to wait on Him and His timing. We often get impatient, wondering why the Lord is making us wait, but have we ever considered if we are making the Lord wait? **He waits** for us to see our need of a Saviour and repent of our sin. **He waits** for us to serve Him. **He waits** for us to confess our sin and restore our fellowship with Him. **He waits** for us to forgive those who have wronged us. **He waits** for us to trust Him. **He waits** for us to take a step of faith. **He waits.**

Are you making the Lord wait?

The Lord told Jonah to go to Nineveh, but Jonah had other plans. God showed him mercy despite his disobedience, and waited for Jonah to go where He called him to go. In order to get Jonah's attention, God sent a storm. When the storm didn't get his attention, God had his shipmates throw him overboard. When that didn't work, God sent a great fish to swallow him up and give him time to realize what he needed to do. **What might God have to do in order to get your attention of what He wants you to do?**

The Lord is Longsuffering.
"And therefore will the LORD wait"
2 Peter 3:9
"The Lord is not slack concerning his promise, as some men count slackness; but is longsuffering to us-ward, not willing that any should perish, but that all should come to repentance."

The Lord is Merciful.
"that he may have mercy upon you"
Psalm 103:8
"The LORD is merciful and gracious, slow to anger, and plenteous in mercy."

He is waiting.
Decide today to do what He has laid on your heart.

Bible Reading
Nehemiah 7-8 | Hebrews 11 | Psalm 4

Absolutely Nothing.

John 15:4-5
*"Abide in me, and I in you. As the branch cannot bear fruit of itself,
except it abide in the vine; no more can ye, except ye abide in me. I am
the vine, ye are the branches: He that abideth in me, and I in him,
the same bringeth forth much fruit: for without me ye can do nothing."*

A branch is absolutely nothing in and of itself.
When it is broken off from the vine,
it loses its strength and ability to produce fruit.

To be fruitful Christians, we must abide in Christ.
We must depend upon Him and commune with Him.

The Vine never leaves the branches. If a branch becomes unfruitful, it is because it has broken away from the Vine, its Supplier and Sustainer. **It is absolutely necessary that the branch remain connected to the Vine**. A branch cannot produce any fruit or survive without the Vine.

2 Corinthians 3:5
*"Not that we are sufficient of ourselves to think any thing as of ourselves;
but our sufficiency is of God;"*

John 15:5
"...for without me ye can do nothing."

Philippians 4:13
"I can do all things through Christ which strengtheneth me."

Remind yourself today that as a branch,
you must stay connected to the True Vine, the Lord Jesus Christ.

**Take time today and every day to abide in Him,
for without Him we can do absolutely nothing.**

Bible Reading
Nehemiah 9-10 | Hebrews 12 | Psalm 5

He Chose Us.

John 15:16
"Ye have not chosen me, but I have chosen you, and ordained you, that ye should go and bring forth fruit, and that your fruit should remain: that whatsoever ye shall ask of the Father in my name, he may give it you."

He chose us.
Why? Because He loves us!

1 John 4:19
"We love him, because he first loved us."

He chose us before He even created us, and gives us the choice to accept Him or reject Him. He chose to give us freewill because He wants us to choose Him.

He had a purpose for us before the foundation of the world, and He still has that same purpose for us today. **He chose us, and has enabled us that we should go and bring forth fruit for His glory.** This is why it is so imperative that we as the branches stay connected to the Vine.

Our purpose is to spread the Gospel and bear fruit. Not a temporary fruit, but a fruit that will remain. This alludes to a true and genuine faith in the Gospel of Jesus Christ and His sacrifice that He paid on Calvary so that we could be His children.

If you feel fruitless today, it is not too late! There is still time to bear fruit for His glory. He tells us we just need to ask…*"that whatsoever ye shall ask of the Father in my name, he may give it you."*

He chose us, so that we could choose Him.

Bible Reading
Nehemiah 11-13 | Hebrews 13 | Psalm 6

A Clean Slate.

Psalm 51:10
"Create in me a clean heart, O God; and renew a right spirit within me."

Sometimes in order to get back on track toward the ending we hoped for, we have to go back to the beginning. A clean slate. A fresh start.

We all need to start over sometimes.
1 John 1:9
"If we confess our sins, he is faithful and just to forgive us our sins, and to cleanse us from all unrighteousness."

Our relationship does not change when we mess up. Once we are adopted into the family of God, He will always be our Father.

The setup of adoptions today in America is based upon this Biblical fact. A father and mother can rewrite their wills to legally exclude their own biological children if they choose to; however, when an adopted child is welcomed into the family, they can never be excluded. The adopted child has full rights to the Father's inheritance.

**When we have sin in our life we are still God's children,
but our fellowship with Him is broken.**
Psalm 66:18
"If I regard iniquity in my heart, the Lord will not hear me:"

David knew what it was like to be out of fellowship with the Lord. He wrote Psalm 51 after Nathan the prophet confronted him about his sins involving Bathsheba & Uriah. The Lord got ahold of David's heart and showed him his need for forgiveness. David wrote these verses asking for a clean heart and restored fellowship.

Psalm 51:10-12
*"Create in me a clean heart, O God; and renew a right spirit within me.
Cast me not away from thy presence; and take not thy holy spirit from me.
Restore unto me the joy of thy salvation;
and uphold me with thy free spirit."*

If you have broken your fellowship with the Lord, you can have it restored today. Read Psalm 51 as if it is your prayer to God, and you can be given a clean slate. **God is waiting with His faithful open arms of forgiveness, if we would only confess and ask.**

Bible Reading

Esther 1-2 | James 1 | Psalm 7

Precious Seed.

Psalm 126:5-6
"They that sow in tears shall reap in joy. He that goeth forth and weepeth, bearing precious seed, shall doubtless come again with rejoicing, bringing his sheaves with him."

A seed must be sown into the earth in order to produce fruit. **The *"precious seed"* that the sower bears here is none other than the Word of God.** We see this in Luke 8 as Jesus tells the parable of the sower.

If we are to sow effectively, there must be some tears. We must have a burden for the lost, but also we must also be a partaker of the sufferings of Christ to be more like Him.

Though it may be painful now, when we sow in spite of the tears, we will one day have our sadness turned to tears of joy. Reaping the benefit of suffering and of sowing in tears. *"They that sow in tears shall reap in joy."*

Our sorrows should not prevent us from sowing the Seed. For the Bible tells us that we will one day reap what we have sowed, and we will not be empty handed.

John 4:35-36
"Say not ye, There are yet four months, and then cometh harvest? behold, I say unto you, Lift up your eyes, and look on the fields; for they are white already to harvest. And he that reapeth receiveth wages, and gathereth fruit unto life eternal: that both he that soweth and he that reapeth may rejoice together."

When we sow a Seed we may not reap immediately, but we have done our part. Bear the *"precious seed"* of the Gospel, sow with tears knowing that God's Word will not return void, and **let God give the increase.**

1 Corinthians 3:6-8
"I have planted, Apollos watered; but God gave the increase. So then neither is he that planteth any thing, neither he that watereth; but God that giveth the increase. Now he that planteth and he that watereth are one: and every man shall receive his own reward according to his own labour."

What have you planted today?

Bible Reading
Esther 3-4 | James 2 | Psalm 8

Unashamed.

Romans 1:16
*"For I am not ashamed of the gospel of Christ:
for it is the power of God unto salvation to every one that believeth;
to the Jew first, and also to the Greek."*

We live in a day and hour where many want a form of godliness, but when tested their faith fades into the darkness. **Despite the persecutions and tribulations that the Apostle Paul faced, he remained unashamed of the Gospel of Jesus Christ.** If he could be unashamed, so can we.

Paul knew the difference that the Gospel had made in his life and wanted to share it with everyone he could. When we realize the difference that the Gospel has made in our lives, we will want to tell others.

We must proclaim the Gospel with boldness.
Ephesians 6:19-20
"And for me, that utterance may be given unto me, that I may open my mouth boldly, to make known the mystery of the gospel, For which I am an ambassador in bonds: that therein I may speak boldly, as I ought to speak."

Just as Paul felt as if he ought to speak boldly of the Gospel, so should we. Do we have a desire to proclaim the Gospel? The very eternities of those around us hang in the balance if we keep the Good News to ourselves.

We must be bold because the Gospel has life changing power.
"for it is the power of God unto salvation to every one that believeth"

Your life and eternity was changed when you believed the Gospel and put your faith in the finished work of Jesus Christ. **The power of the Gospel transformed your life.**

Are you willing to share that same life changing power with someone else? **Choose today to be unashamed.**

Bible Reading
Esther 5-6 | James 3 | Psalm 9

Faith To Faith.

Romans 1:17
*"For therein is the righteousness of God revealed from faith to faith:
as it is written, The just shall live by faith."*

From the moment we receive Christ as our Saviour, to the moment He calls us home to Heaven to spend eternity with Him, **our relationship with God is all about faith.** Our faith should grow as time passes, meaning the longer we are saved the more our faith should increase. There is none righteous outside of the Blood of Jesus Christ and the more we strengthen our relationship with Him, the more faith we will have in Him. We have no righteousness of ourselves; our righteousness is found in Him.

Philippians 3:9
*"And be found in him, not having mine own righteousness,
which is of the law, but that which is through the faith of Christ,
the righteousness which is of God by faith:"*

Jesus Christ is the Author and Finisher of our faith. **He gives us the faith to believe in His finished work on Calvary, and He gives us faith along our journey.**

Hebrews 12:2
"Looking unto Jesus the author and finisher of our faith; who for the joy that was set before him endured the cross, despising the shame, and is set down at the right hand of the throne of God."

We cannot please God without faith. **From start to finish, our lives must be filled with faith in Him.** As we seek Him, He will give us more faith to continue on our journey in accordance with His will.

Hebrews 11:6
*"But without faith it is impossible to please him:
for he that cometh to God must believe that he is,
and that he is a rewarder of them that diligently seek him."*

We only have one life to live for Him, and without faith in Him we will surely fail. Our time is running out. **Will we not choose to serve Him by faith?** He promises to reward us when we seek Him by faith.

Ask God to strengthen your faith today so that you can please Him. Seek to do His will. Search the Scriptures for the direction you need to follow Him. Choose to live a life of faith.

Bible Reading
Esther 7-8 | James 4 | Psalm 10 | 229

His Workmanship.

Ephesians 2:10
"For we are his workmanship, created in Christ Jesus unto good works, which God hath before ordained that we should walk in them."

We are new creatures in Christ Jesus.
Our faith in His substitutionary sacrifice has transformed us.

2 Corinthians 5:17
"Therefore if any man be in Christ, he is a new creature: old things are passed away; behold, all things are become new."

This new creation as *"his workmanship"* occurs as an internal transformation that happens gradually. We cannot contribute to this work on our own, for it is only God Himself Who must do the work by His grace.

We were dead in our sin, He quickened us together with Christ to make us alive unto His marvelous grace by His unfailing mercy and love. We are saved by His grace through our faith in His finished work on the Cross. **It is nothing we have done, but He is the Gift through which we obtain eternal life.**

If we could contribute or obtain this new life on our own, He knew we would boast about our achievements and successes. Instead, He freely gives us the choice to receive Him through faith or reject Him through unbelief.

We are not saved by works, but He desires us to work for Him so that others may see what a difference He has made in our life - a complete transformation. If our faith has no works associated with it, how will others see Christ in us? Because He has made us *"a new creature"*, we are able to perform good works for His glory. He desires for us to walk in these good works so that Christ Jesus will be glorified.

What are we doing for His glory today?

Bible Reading
Esther 9-10 | James 5 | Psalm 11

Strive Together.

Philippians 1:27
*"Only let your conversation be as it becometh the gospel of Christ:
that whether I come and see you, or else be absent, I may hear of your
affairs, that ye stand fast in one spirit, with one mind
striving together for the faith of the gospel;"*

The Lord sends people into our lives for a reason.
Sometimes for encouragement during a trial you are facing.
Sometimes for counsel to help you make the right decision.
Sometimes for strength to continue despite the enemy's attack.
And sometimes, because you need someone to strive together with for the sake of the Gospel of Jesus Christ. Someone you can earnestly contend for the faith along side. A friend in life. A friend in the ministry. **Every once in awhile God crosses your path with people that you can *"stand fast in one spirit, with one mind"* together.** Those kindred spirits with whom our hearts are knitted that can only come by the Lord's provision and grace.

Philippians 2:2
*"Fulfil ye my joy, that ye be likeminded, having the same love,
being of one accord, of one mind."*

Whether you have one or several, be thankful for those people in your life. They are invaluable to your life and to the ministry that God has called you to do for His glory. Sometimes they have been there for years before you realize how much they have invested in your life. Sometimes they come right when you are at the end of your rope and they willingly hold the rope of your life to allow you to climb back up. Sometimes they just show up beside you to encourage you to keep pressing on, and it seems as though they had been there your entire life.

They encourage you when your head hangs low.
They fill your life with fun and laughter.
They keep you accountable.
They make coffee taste sweeter.
They remind you of what is important.
They lead by example.

Whether you strive together hand-in-hand daily in ministry or miles or oceans separate you, God has placed these kindred spirits in your life to remind you how much **He loves you, and He knows exactly what you need.**

Bible Reading
Job 1-2 | 1 Peter 1 | Psalm 12 | 231

The Forbearance Of God.

Romans 3:25-26
"Whom God hath set forth to be a propitiation through faith in his blood, to declare his righteousness for the remission of sins that are past, through the forbearance of God; To declare, I say, at this time his righteousness: that he might be just, and the justifier of him which believeth in Jesus."

The Blood of Jesus Christ that He shed on the Cross of Calvary was for every single person that has ever been created. From Adam and Eve in the Garden to those walking on this earth today, and every person that will be born until Christ's Second Coming. **He died for us all that we might have faith in His shed blood and have a home for all eternity with God The Father in Heaven.**

Cain's sacrifice was insufficient to the more excellent sacrifice of Abel's because of the blood. Those who were before the Cross looked forward to His sacrifice just as we look back to that same Cross today for *"without shedding of blood is no remission"* of sin.

Jesus Christ was the Propitiation, the Atoning Sacrifice, for our sin.

1 John 2:2
"And he is the propitiation for our sins: and not for ours only, but also for the sins of the whole world."

1 John 4:10
"Herein is love, not that we loved God, but that he loved us, and sent his Son to be the propitiation for our sins."

Forbearance refers to the suffering of difficulties while continuing to love the person(s) in question. **God displayed His forbearing love for us by giving His Son's life on the Cross which took His life and gave us ours.** He patiently waited for the day we would see our need for a Saviour and place our faith in the finished work of Christ. He is also patiently waiting with longsuffering for those who still need to accept Him.

2 Peter 3:9
"The Lord is not slack concerning his promise, as some men count slackness; but is longsuffering to us-ward, not willing that any should perish, but that all should come to repentance."

Bible Reading
Job 3-4 | 1 Peter 2 | Psalm 13

Find, Save & Preserve.

Mark 8:35
"For whosoever will save his life shall lose it; but whosoever shall lose his life for my sake and the gospel's, the same shall save it."

**When we give our life to the Lord
and are willing to do whatever He pleases and purposes with us,
we shall find, save and preserve our life through Him.**

Matthew 16:25
*"For whosoever will save his life shall lose it:
and whosoever will lose his life for my sake shall **find** it."*

Luke 9:24
*"For whosoever will save his life shall lose it:
but whosoever will lose his life for my sake, the same shall **save** it."*

Luke 17:33
*"Whosoever shall seek to save his life shall lose it;
and whosoever shall lose his life shall **preserve** it."*

Isn't that just what Christ did in us?
He found us, when we could not find our way to Him.
He saved us, when we could not save ourselves.
He preserves us, because we could not keep our salvation on our own.

When we delight in Him,
He will change our fleshly aspirations
to the desires that fit His will for our lives.

If we want to find our purpose in life...
If we want to be saved from everlasting destruction...
If we want to be preserved from the turmoil of this life...
We must lose our lives to Him.

Give yourself to Him today.
He is waiting with open arms to receive you
and use you for His glory.

Exchange your desires for His.

Bible Reading
Job 5-6 | 1 Peter 3 | Psalm 14 | 233

Proverbs 11:24
*"There is that scattereth, and yet increaseth;
and there is that withholdeth more than is meet, but it tendeth to poverty."*

When we give our resources, time, or talent to be used by God, we are shining our Light for Him while also allowing Him to display His glory.

God has a way of multiplying our resources beyond our logic or comprehension. The Widow of Zarephath is a perfect example of this. She was down to the last meal for her and her son; yet, because she obeyed God's command to give, the barrel of meal and cruse of oil never wasted. She didn't understand how it happened; she just believed God had sustained her because of her obedience.

Luke 6:38
*"Give, and it shall be given unto you; good measure,
pressed down,and shaken together, and running over,
shall men give into your bosom. For with the same measure that ye mete withal it shall be measured to you again."*

On the flip side, when we withhold our resources and put them away "for safe keeping", we do more harm than good. **God will not multiply that which we have not given to Him.** We see this in the Parable of the Talents where the unprofitable servant *"digged in the earth, and hid his lord's money"* only later to have that talent taken from him and given to the one who had started with five, and wound up with not only ten, but eleven total. God multiplied what was given to Him, and decreased what was withheld.

Matthew 16:25
*"For whosoever will save his life shall lose it:
and whosoever will lose his life for my sake shall find it."*

Whatever you have,
no matter how much or how little,
give it away to the Lord.

You will not be disappointed or empty handed.

Bible Reading
Job 7-8 | 1 Peter 4 | Psalm 15

Go The Extra Mile.

Matthew 5:41-42
*"And whosoever shall compel thee to go a mile, go with him twain.
Give to him that asketh thee, and from him that would
borrow of thee turn not thou away."*

God wants us to go above and beyond what is expected of us.
If we are asked to go a mile, we should go the extra mile.

Be a Second Mile Christian.
"...compel thee to go a mile..."

Regardless of what is asked of us, when we feel compelled, we must not only participate, but do so willingly. **Submitting to the unreasonable demands of others allows us to display the love of Christ.** In this same passage Christ warns us of what is sure to happen when we live our lives by going the extra mile.

Matthew 5:44
*"But I say unto you, Love your enemies, bless them that curse you,
do good to them that hate you, and pray for them
which despitefully use you, and persecute you;"*

Christ knew exactly what it was like to have enemies. He knew what it was like to be cursed and hated. He prayed for those that despitefully used and persecuted Him. **When we live our lives in service to others, we will develop enemies.** We will be cursed at and hated, and we will definitely be despitefully used and persecuted – even by other Christians and those we consider our friends. However, we should never let that stop us from going the extra mile!

Matthew 5:46
*"For if ye love them which love you, what reward have ye?
do not even the publicans the same?"*

Going the extra mile is not always easy.
There will be attacks. There will be burdens.

Going the extra mile is always worth it.
There will be joy. There will be rewards.

**Those who go the extra mile for the Lord's glory
will never be disappointed.**

Bible Reading
Job 9-10 | 1 Peter 5 | Psalm 16 | 235

Most Unlikely.

1 Corinthians 1:26-27
"For ye see your calling, brethren, how that not many wise men after the flesh, not many mighty, not many noble, are called: But God hath chosen the foolish things of the world to confound the wise; and God hath chosen the weak things of the world to confound the things which are mighty;"

Have you ever noticed that God seems to call the "most unlikely" people to do His work? This is no accident, for there are no accidents or coincidences with God. **He chooses the most improbable people and situations to manifest His power, grace and love through**.

1 Corinthians 2:5
"That your faith should not stand in the wisdom of men, but in the power of God."

If He only used those who we in our human flesh deem worthy to be called we would put our faith in the ability of a person, instead of God's power to use them.

God gets the most glory when a situation seems most unlikely.
Luke 1:37
"For with God nothing shall be impossible."

Moses had a stammering tongue and considered himself to be a worthless speaker. God used him beyond Moses' ability and the opinions of others. He allowed Moses to lead the children of Israel through the wilderness and used him to display God's power in many miracles along the way. When they reached the Red Sea they had nowhere to turn. **That seemingly impossible moment allowed God to manifest His power in an incredible way that no one thought was possible at the time.**

You may feel like there is nothing you can offer the Lord in service to Him. That is how He wants us to feel, for it is then that He can work through us. He is not looking for the wisest person to do His work; He only wants the willing. Ask Him to use you in spite of you. **When we get ourselves out of the way, that is when He can use us for His glory.**

1 Corinthians 2:9
"But as it is written, Eye hath not seen, nor ear heard, neither have entered into the heart of man, the things which God hath prepared for them that love him."

Bible Reading
Job 11-12 | 2 Peter 1 | Psalm 17

What Shall We Drink?

Exodus 15:22-24

"So Moses brought Israel from the Red sea, and they went out into the wilderness of Shur; and they went three days in the wilderness, and found no water. And when they came to Marah, they could not drink of the waters of Marah, for they were bitter: therefore the name of it was called Marah. And the people murmured against Moses, saying, What shall we drink?"

Just after the children of Israel had experienced the Red Sea miracle, they journeyed three days through the wilderness of Shur where they were unable to find water. After days of traveling, they finally found water in Marah. The water must have looked so tasty and refreshing; yet, they when they drank of the waters they were bitter. The water's appeal was deceiving.

How often in our lives do we have a mountain top experience and pull back from the Water of the Word of God only to become thirsty again? **Sometimes we try to quench our thirst with something other than the Word only to be left disappointed.** The devil wants to deceive us into thinking something looks so appealing and refreshing, yet when we partake of it we end up with a bitter taste in our mouth.

After tasting the bitter waters, the flesh of the people showed as they murmured about their situation.

Just three days prior, these same people walked up to the Red Sea with nowhere to turn. God showed Moses just what to do, and after he obeyed the Lord's commands the unthinkable happened. What was once an uncrossable sea became standing walls of water with a dry path for them to walk across. **Did they forget the miracle they had seen just days before?** After hearing the people's complaints, Moses sought the Lord for help, and the Lord answered by showing him the solution to the situation.

Exodus 15:25

*"And he cried unto the LORD; **and the LORD shewed him a tree**, which when he had cast into the waters, the waters were made sweet…"*

May we follow Moses' example when we hear murmurings or if we ourselves begin to murmur. Ask the Lord for help in dealing with the situation. He will provide just as He provided for Moses and the children of Israel. **Choose to drink from the Water of the Word of Life today.**

Bible Reading
Job 13-14 | 2 Peter 2 | Psalm 18

A Tree Made The Difference.

Exodus 15:25-26
*"And he cried unto the LORD; and the LORD shewed him a tree,
which when he had cast into the waters, the waters were made sweet:
there he made for them a statute and an ordinance, and there he proved
them, And said, If thou wilt diligently hearken to the voice of the LORD
thy God, and wilt do that which is right in his sight, and wilt give ear to his
commandments, and keep all his statutes, I will put none of these diseases
upon thee, which I have brought upon the Egyptians:
for I am the LORD that healeth thee."*

Despite the complaints and murmuring of the people,
Moses pressed on and sought the Lord to provide for their need.

Exodus 15:25
"And he cried unto the LORD; and the LORD shewed him a tree…"

A tree made the difference.

After the water was turned sweet and was drinkable, Moses began to
preach to the people…He begged them to listen to the Lord.
*"and there he proved them, And said,
If thou wilt diligently hearken to the voice of the LORD thy God..."*

The Lord promised if they would do these things He would not bring any of
the diseases or plagues He put on the Egyptians on them.

He promised to heal them instead.

The Lord wants to heal us today as well. He is waiting for us to ask Him for
help and healing. Just like God used a tree to take the bitter water and
make it sweet, **God also used a Tree to make our salvation possible.**

1 Peter 2:24
*"Who his own self bare our sins in his own body on the tree,
that we, being dead to sins, should live unto righteousness:
by whose stripes ye were healed."*

Calvary hosted the Tree that held our Saviour in order for us to be healed
from our sin. The Source of our Restoration hung on the Tree that day with
all the sin of the world upon Him.

It was our Saviour upon the Tree that made the difference.

Bible Reading
Job 15-16 | 2 Peter 3 | Psalm 19

Lift Him Up.

John 12:32
"And I, if I be lifted up from the earth, will draw all men unto me."

Our life's purpose is to lift up the Name of Jesus!
Every church, every pastor, every Christian…our purpose is to lift Him up!

Jesus told Nicodemus why the Son of Man must be lifted up.
John 3:14-15
*"And as Moses lifted up the serpent in the wilderness,
even so must the Son of man be lifted up:
That whosoever believeth in him should not perish, but have eternal life."*

Jesus always exalted His Father.
John 8:28
*"Then said Jesus unto them, When ye have lifted up the Son of man, then
shall ye know that I am he, and that I do nothing of myself;
but as my Father hath taught me, I speak these things."*

The words *"I be lifted up"* not only refer to Christ being raised up on the Cross of Calvary, but they also show us that Jesus Christ is to be exalted and honored. May we follow Jesus' example and live our lives to exalt Him!

Exalt Him by worshipping at His feet.
Psalm 99:5
"Exalt ye the LORD our God, and worship at his footstool; for he is holy."

Exalt Him by praising His lovely name.
Isaiah 25:1
*"O LORD, thou art my God; I will exalt thee, I will praise thy name; for thou
hast done wonderful things; thy counsels of old are faithfulness and truth."*

We are to exalt Him so that others may see Him!
When we give Jesus Christ His proper place in our lives, we are shining His Light so that others may see. Why are we to shine our Light by exalting Him? So that He may draw sinners unto Himself.

Lift Him up today!

Bible Reading
Job 17-18 | 1 John 1 | Psalm 20 | 239

Search & Rescue.

Luke 19:10
"For the Son of man is come to seek and to save that which is lost."

In the Old Testament, the Lord revealed to the prophet Ezekiel the Truth of how the Lord Jesus would both search for and rescue His lost sheep.

Ezekiel 34:11-12
"For thus saith the Lord GOD; Behold, I, even I, will both search my sheep, and seek them out."

"...seek..." – **Jesus Searches For Us.**

He came to us when we were unable to come to Him. He searches for us when we think we cannot be found. When we have lost something, do we not search frantically until we find it? We must seek the lost diligently just like Jesus did. We must seek them with the purpose of winning their souls for Him.

Luke 15:4
"What man of you, having an hundred sheep, if he lose one of them, doth not leave the ninety and nine in the wilderness, and go after that which is lost, until he find it?"

"...save..." – **Jesus Rescues Us.**

As the Good Shepherd, He rescues the sheep that go astray. We are just like that lost sheep which left the fold that the Shepherd came and rescued as if we were His only child. He loves us that much.

Matthew 18:14
"Even so it is not the will of your Father which is in heaven, that one of these little ones should perish."

When we had no strength to come to Him, Jesus came and rescued us. As ungodly as we are, He gave His life so that we might have ours. Just as Jesus did, we should seek or search for the lost. We cannot save them, but we can perform a "Search & Rescue" and point them to the only One Who can be the Saviour they so desperately need.

Soulwinning is a spiritual discipline. It is something we inwardly choose to be obedient to, for the cause of Christ. Soulwinning is the greatest thing we can do in order to exhibit the image of Christ.

Proverbs 11:30
"The fruit of the righteous is a tree of life; and he that winneth souls is wise."

Bible Reading
Job 19-20 | 1 John 2 | Psalm 21

In The Middle Of It All.

John 20:19
*"Then the same day at evening, being the first day of the week,
when the doors were shut where the disciples were assembled
for fear of the Jews, came Jesus and stood in the midst,
and saith unto them, Peace be unto you."*

The doors were shut. They were closed in and assembled together. They were afraid. Yet, suddenly in the middle of it all…stood Jesus. He had been crucified and was now risen again, standing in the midst before them. He did not enter through a door. He is God and can do the impossible.

Have you ever been afraid of the circumstances around you, not knowing what to do next, when suddenly a peace fell upon your weary soul? In the midst of your trouble all the fear went away…because Jesus was in the midst.

There is Peace when Jesus is in the midst.
John 20:19
"…when the doors were shut where the disciples were assembled for fear of the Jews, came Jesus and stood in the midst, and saith unto them, Peace be unto you."
When we are fearful, He can speak peace if we will only stop and listen. What is He telling you today? Stand still and let Him lead you.

There is Payment when Jesus is in the midst.
John 19:18
"Where they crucified him, and two other with him, on either side one, and Jesus in the midst."
When we were in need of a Saviour, Jesus paid our debt so that we might be free and live with Him. We need to trust in His payment, while telling others about His payment.

There is Potential when Jesus is in the midst.
John 20:28
"And Thomas answered and said unto him, My Lord and my God."
When we are struggling with unbelief, our lack of faith can disappear when Jesus is in the midst. He can give us the faith to press on, to trust Him, and to believe that the impossible is possible with Him.

Whether you are in need of peace, of payment, or of potential today.
Invite Jesus in the middle of it all.

Bible Reading
Job 21-22 | 1 John 3 | Psalm 22 | 241

Answers To Prayer.

Psalm 143:1
*"Hear my prayer, O LORD, give ear to my supplications:
in thy faithfulness answer me, and in thy righteousness."*

Praise the Lord that we serve a God Who answers prayer! His ears are always open to our cry. He is never too busy to hear us, and He desires to hear from us often. When we pray…God always answers.

A Direct Answer.
It is encouraging to see our prayers answered just the way we asked. God allows our specific requests to encourage us to keep on asking. No detail is too small to pray about. No circumstance is too large that the Lord cannot deliver. Ask Him today for the small details and the big situations.

A Different Answer.
Sometimes the Lord answers in a totally different way than what we asked for or expected. He always has a greater plan. He may answer in an unexpected way that may have seemed impossible, for He is God. There is nothing too hard for Him. Allow God to use the different answers to your prayers to reveal His glory in your life.

A Denied Answer.
Though it may not be the answer we desire, He has still answered our prayer. When He says "No" it is always for our good, for He always know what is best. We must be satisfied and thankful even when your request is denied.

A Delayed Answer.
It may seem like He is four days late, but the Lord is always on time. Mary and Martha thought that all hope was lost when their brother died before Christ arrived in Bethany. Jesus was heartbroken at the loss of His friend, but He knew that it wasn't the end. Four days after he had died, Lazarus was raised from the dead. Sometimes the Lord allows time to pass and all hope to seem gone, just so that He can work a miracle in our lives. If your answer seems delayed, have no fear…He is always right on time.

God always answers, so why do we not always pray?

Let your requests be made known unto Him today.
He will always answer!

Bible Reading
Job 23-24 | 1 John 4 | Psalm 23

Strong. Courageous. Fearless.

Deuteronomy 31:6
*"Be strong and of a good courage, fear not, nor be afraid of them:
for the LORD thy God, he it is that doth go with thee;
he will not fail thee, nor forsake thee."*

Be Strong!
We can be strong when we admit our weakness, and allow it to be replaced by His strength. We must realize that we have no strength in or of ourselves. **Ask the Lord to strengthen your hands as you work for Him.**

Isaiah 35:3-4
*"Strengthen ye the weak hands, and confirm the feeble knees.
Say to them that are of a fearful heart, Be strong, fear not: behold, your God will come with vengeance, even God with a recompence;
he will come and save you.."*

Be Courageous!
When the Lord gives us a task we can courageously press on knowing that He will provide the ability and power needed to accomplish it. **God can give us a boldness to carry us through every day of our lives.**

Joshua 1:9
*"Have not I commanded thee? Be strong and of a good courage;
be not afraid, neither be thou dismayed:
for the LORD thy God is with thee whithersoever thou goest."*

Be Fearless!
Even when many enemies seem to be surrounding you, we must not be discouraged or intimidated. **We have no reason to fear, He is on our side!**

Isaiah 41:10
*"Fear thou not; for I am with thee: be not dismayed; for I am thy God:
I will strengthen thee; yea, I will help thee; yea, I will uphold thee with the right hand of my righteousness."*

We can be strong, courageous and fearless because He desires to fight our battles for us, if only we will let Him. When we fight our battles alone, we will surely lose. God wants us to stand still and allow Him to fight for us.

Exodus 14:14
"The Lord shall fight for you, and ye shall hold your peace."

Allow God to fight your battle.
Be strong, courageous, and fearless today.

Bible Reading
Job 25-26 | 1 John 5 | Psalm 24 | 243

Adversity.

Proverbs 24:10
"If thou faint in the day of adversity, thy strength is small."

Although we do not like to think about it, times of adversity are just as much appointed by God as times of prosperity. When it is our turn to partake in the sufferings of Christ, we must remind ourselves that trials and afflictions make us more like Him. It is comforting to know that our times of adversity are not described as years or even days, but rather a *"day"*. Though it may not seem like it at the time, while we are facing the challenge, in light of eternity it is sure to be only a day. **Our affliction is but for a moment!**

2 Corinthians 4:16-17
"For which cause we faint not; but though our outward man perish,
yet the inward man is renewed day by day.
For our light affliction, which is but for a moment,
worketh for us a far more exceeding and eternal weight of glory;"

For the Christian, suffering persecution is something we can count on. When we live our lives in service to God we are sure to suffer, just as Christ did when He walked on this earth. **It is not a matter of if, but rather when we shall face adversity.**

2 Timothy 3:12
"Yea, and all that will live godly in Christ Jesus shall suffer persecution."

Though we suffer, we can renew our strength by relying on the Lord to carry us through our troubles. When we yield our weakness to His strength we can run and walk boldly with Him. **We must face the adversity in our lives through His power and strength.**

Isaiah 40:29-31
"He giveth power to the faint; and to them that have no might he increaseth strength. Even the youths shall faint and be weary, and the young men shall utterly fall: But they that wait upon the LORD shall renew their strength; they shall mount up with wings as eagles; they shall run, and not be weary; and they shall walk, and not faint."

If we faint in our day of adversity it is because we are relying on our strength instead of His. Don't give in to the desire to faint or quit. Renew your strength today by waiting on the Lord to defeat the adversity you are facing.

Bible Reading
Job 27-28 | 2 John | Psalm 25

Comforting Promises.

Isaiah 43:1-2
"But now thus saith the LORD that created thee, O Jacob, and he that formed thee, O Israel, Fear not: for I have redeemed thee, I have called thee by thy name; thou art mine. When thou passest through the waters, I will be with thee; and through the rivers, they shall not overflow thee: when thou walkest through the fire, thou shalt not be burned; neither shall the flame kindle upon thee."

From the foundation of the world, God had a plan that included us. As He spoke the rivers and mountains into existence, we were on His mind. As He saw His Son walk to Calvary to give His life as a ransom for many, we were on His mind. Our verses today remind us of how much that the Lord has given, and the comforting promises that He will continually provide.

He Redeemed Us.
1 Peter 1:18-19
"Forasmuch as ye know that ye were not redeemed with corruptible things, as silver and gold, from your vain conversation received by tradition from your fathers; But with the precious blood of Christ, as of a lamb without blemish and without spot:"

He Called Us.
2 Timothy 1:9
"Who hath saved us, and called us with an holy calling, not according to our works, but according to his own purpose and grace, which was given us in Christ Jesus before the world began,"

We Are His!
2 Timothy 2:19
"Nevertheless the foundation of God standeth sure, having this seal, The Lord knoweth them that are his…"

He knows His children and regardless of our situation, He will never leave us. **When we face adversity, He promises that He will be with us.** Whether we face rain, rivers, or a raging fire, He is right there beside us each step of the way. We may get wet, but we will not drown. We may feel the heat of the flames, but we will not get burnt. When we trust in Him, our Saviour will rescue us no matter what circumstance we face. Trust Him to guide you each step of the way as you walk by faith.

Take time today to remember the Lord's comforting promises.

Bible Reading
Job 29-30 | 3 John | Psalm 26 | 245

Publish The Gospel.

Mark 13:10
"And the gospel must first be published among all nations."

As the disciples noticed the great buildings around the temple, Christ began to disclose what will happen during the end times. The descriptions Christ gives are very similar to those of today. *"wars and rumours of wars... nation shall rise against nation...earthquakes in divers places...famines and troubles".* However before the end can occur, Jesus Christ promises that *"the Gospel must first be published among all nations."*

The Great Commission is not limited to preachers and those in full-time Christian service. **Every Christian must *"Go ye into all the world, and preach the gospel".*** To preach is not just to get behind a pulpit during a service, but to proclaim the finished work of Jesus Christ so that all can be saved.

Live The Gospel.
The death, burial, and resurrection of Jesus Christ should be visible in our lives. We must die to ourselves. We must bury our own will in exchange for His. We must live again through Him by dying to ourselves, showing we are born again as a new creature.

1 Corinthians 9:14
"Even so hath the Lord ordained that they which preach the gospel should live of the gospel."

Give The Gospel.
Pray for opportunities to tell others of the Gospel of Christ. Be bold, and give the Gospel by telling others what Christ did for you.

Ephesians 6:19-20
"And for me, that utterance may be given unto me, that I may open my mouth boldly, to make known the mystery of the gospel, For which I am an ambassador in bonds: that therein I may speak boldly, as I ought to speak."

Leave The Gospel.
A Gospel tract can speak boldly to a person when a verbal conversation isn't possible. Tracts preach the Gospel after you leave. When the Word of God is printed and given, Seeds are sown. Only Heaven will reveal the fruit that has been yielded through the printed Word of the Gospel.

It is our responsibility to publish the Gospel among all nations.
Fulfill your purpose today,
and reach someone with the Gospel of Jesus Christ.

Bible Reading
Job 31-32 | Jude | Psalm 27

Whosoever.

Romans 10:13
"For whosoever shall call upon the name of the Lord shall be saved."

Whosoever: whatever person; anyone; no matter who.
Whosoever does not exclude anyone.
All are welcome. It's that simple.

The word *"whosoever"* appears in 163 verses in the Bible. Many of which describe anyone that is able or willing to do something.

Anyone Can Believe.
John 3:16
"For God so loved the world, that he gave his only begotten Son,
that whosoever believeth in him should not perish,
but have everlasting life."

Once you see yourself as a sinner, if you will simply *"call upon the name of the Lord"*, you can be saved from spending eternity in the Lake of Fire separated from God forever.

You may say…"It's not for me." or "I'll never be good enough."
But God said…Whosoever.

God is not willing that any should perish.
That includes you.

No call for salvation goes unheard.
When Peter was sinking in the water, the Lord heard him cry,
"Lord, save me", and rescued him.

When the Blind Man cried out,
"Jesus, thou Son of David, have mercy on me",
the Lord heard him and healed him.

If you will call upon His Name today He'll save you too.

This should also encourage us that anyone we share the Gospel with can be saved. It is our responsibility to share the Truth of the Gospel with those around us and allow God to work in their hearts for salvation.

Share the message with someone today.

Whosoever.

Bible Reading

The Least Of These.

Matthew 25:40
"And the King shall answer and say unto them, Verily I say unto you, Inasmuch as ye have done it unto one of the least of these my brethren, ye have done it unto me."

The Truth must be told to all those around us. When we comfort them by doing good works, even sharing a cup of water, we are showing the love of Christ. In this passage we find several examples of good works we can do unto others. Feed the hungry. Give a cup of water to the thirsty. Clothe the naked. Sit with the sick. Visit the prisons. **Christ said that when we do these things we have done them unto Him.**

Similar to our passage today, in Matthew 10, Jesus sent the disciples out to preach the Gospel. He told them to go even though their needs weren't met ahead of time. He wanted them to go by faith and without fear. He wanted His disciples to trust that God would supply their need through those around them.

We see missionaries leave their home for the place where they are called to spread the Gospel and reach *"the least of these"*. They answer the call that God has placed on their lives, and willingly go by faith that He will supply their needs. God often uses those around us to supply our needs! After the missionaries leave their home, the place where they were sent becomes home because they are where God would have them to be. Home is wherever God places us because He is there!

Where has God called you to reach *"the least of these"*?

It may be across the world on another continent or across the country in another state. It may be across town where you work, or within the walls of your own household. Wherever God has placed you, remember that even giving a cup of water can be done for Christ.

God can use you if only you will give your life to Him.

Matthew 10:39
"He that findeth his life shall lose it: and he that loseth his life for my sake shall find it."

Bible Reading
Job 35-36 | Revelation 2 | Psalm 29

Show His Strength.

Psalm 71:15-18
*"My mouth shall shew forth thy righteousness and thy salvation all the day;
for I know not the numbers thereof. I will go in the strength of the Lord
GOD: I will make mention of thy righteousness, even of thine only.
O God, thou hast taught me from my youth: and hitherto have I declared
thy wondrous works. Now also when I am old and greyheaded,
O God, forsake me not; until I have shewed thy strength
unto this generation, and thy power to every one that is to come."*

When we go forth to pursue the calling that God has placed on our lives, we do not have go alone or under our own ability. **We can confidently press on through His strength!**

Psalm 73:26
*"My flesh and my heart faileth:
but God is the strength of my heart, and my portion for ever."*

Our strength will fail us and cause us to doubt the decision we have made to follow Him. From the small details to the big events, if we go forth on our own power, we will be disappointed every time. It is in those times when we must stop and ask God for His help in all that we do.

Psalm 71:9
*"Cast me not off in the time of old age;
forsake me not when my strength faileth."*

We must remind ourselves how frail we are without the Lord. **We can only truly show His strength when we yield our own strength to His.** Do not allow your flesh to delay or prevent you from fulfilling the Lord's purpose for your life. If you submit your will to Him today, rest assured you will not be disappointed. Have you ever heard of someone who has ever fully given his or her life to be used by God and regretted it? Nope.

Let God use your life for His glory. **Wherever the Lord has placed you, strive to show His strength and power to everyone around you.** If you aren't exactly sure where God would have you to serve, do not fret.

Start where you are.

Bible Reading
Job 37-38 | Revelation 3 | Psalm 30 | 249

Praying With Purpose.

Colossians 1:9-12
*"For this cause we also, since the day we heard it,
do not cease to pray for you, and to desire that ye might be filled with
the knowledge of his will in all wisdom and spiritual understanding; That
ye might walk worthy of the Lord unto all pleasing, being fruitful in every
good work, and increasing in the knowledge of God; Strengthened with
all might, according to his glorious power, unto all patience and
longsuffering with joyfulness; Giving thanks unto the Father…"*

There is no doubt the Lord has blessed you with some special people in your life. Take a moment to reflect on those that have made a difference in your life. **The greatest thing you can do for someone you care about is to pray for them.** Intercessory prayer is vastly important. **If we desire others to pray for us, we must have a burden to pray for others.** What a privilege it is to go   before the throne of grace and bear the burdens of our loved ones. In the first chapter of Colossians we find a strategy for praying with purpose for the people God has given us.

Pray for them often. Colossians 1:3
*"We give thanks to God and the Father of our Lord Jesus Christ,
praying always for you,"*

Pray for them to obtain knowledge & wisdom. Colossians 1:9
*"For this cause we also, since the day we heard it, do not cease to pray for
you, and to desire that ye might be filled with the knowledge of his will in
all wisdom and spiritual understanding;"*

Pray for them to be fruitful. Colossians 1:10
*"That ye might walk worthy of the Lord unto all pleasing, being fruitful in
every good work, and increasing in the knowledge of God;"*

Pray for them to be strengthened. Colossians 1:11
*"Strengthened with all might, according to his glorious power, unto all
patience and longsuffering with joyfulness;"*

"We never know how God will answer our prayers, but we can expect that He will get us involved in His plan for the answer. If we are true intercessors, we must be ready to take part in God's work on behalf of the people for whom we pray." – Corrie ten Boom

Who are you praying with purpose for today?

Bible Reading
Job 39-40 | Revelation 4 | Psalm 31

Deuteronomy 27:10
"Thou shalt therefore obey the voice of the LORD thy God, and do his commandments and his statutes, which I command thee this day."

Sacrifice.
Exodus 5:17
*"But he said, Ye are idle, ye are idle: therefore ye say,
Let us go and do sacrifice to the LORD."*

We are not to be idle in our work or service for the Lord. When we remain idle we cannot yield fruit or give glory to God. We can sacrifice our time for Him. How long do we spend wasting time on other things when we could spend it at His feet?

Serve.
1 Kings 17:13
"And Elijah said unto her, Fear not; go and do as thou hast said: but make me thereof a little cake first, and bring it unto me, and after make for thee and for thy son."

Think of the blessing that the Widow of Zarephath would have missed if she had neglected to obey and serve Elijah. Not only would she have missed the miracle, she wouldn't have managed to survive. God not only sustained her and her son, but He allowed them to witness a miracle each day of their lives until the famine was over. What miracles have we missed in our lives because we neglected to serve and obey?

Show Mercy.
Luke 10:37
*"And he said, He that shewed mercy on him.
Then said Jesus unto him, Go, and do thou likewise."*

We want to be shown mercy when we have done wrong or disregarded something that was our responsibility; yet, when the tables are turned are we as willing to show mercy as we are to receive it? If we want to obtain mercy, we must show mercy to others. Forgive. Let go of the bitterness or anger. Have compassion.

May we go and do as He has said today.
Sacrifice. Serve. Show Mercy.

Bible Reading
Job 41-42 | Revelation 5 | Psalm 32 | 251

Be Of Good Cheer.

John 16:33
*"These things I have spoken unto you,
that in me ye might have peace. In the world ye shall have tribulation:
but be of good cheer; I have overcome the world."*

Even in the midst of our trials and tribulations, we can be of good cheer! Why? Jesus Christ has overcome the world! Through Him we can always be victorious no matter what our circumstances.

Be of Good Cheer...
Because our sins are forgiven!
Matthew 9:2
*"And, behold, they brought to him a man sick of the palsy, lying on a bed:
and Jesus seeing their faith said unto the sick of the palsy;
Son, be of good cheer; thy sins be forgiven thee."*

Because our Saviour is with us!
Matthew 14:26-27
*"And when the disciples saw him walking on the sea, they were troubled,
saying, It is a spirit; and they cried out for fear. But straightway
Jesus spake unto them, saying, Be of good cheer; it is I; be not afraid."*

Because we can believe what God has said!
Acts 27:25
*"Wherefore, sirs, be of good cheer: for I believe God,
that it shall be even as it was told me."*

**Regardless of your situation,
remember you can be of good cheer today!**

Bible Reading
Ecclesiastes 1-2 | Revelation 6 | Psalm 33

In Trouble.

Psalm 46:1
"God is our refuge and strength, a very present help in trouble."

God is Our Refuge.
Psalm 62:7-8
"In God is my salvation and my glory: the rock of my strength, and my refuge, is in God. Trust in him at all times; ye people, pour out your heart before him: God is a refuge for us. Selah."

God is Our Strength.
2 Corinthians 12:9-10
"And he said unto me, My grace is sufficient for thee: for my strength is made perfect in weakness. Most gladly therefore will I rather glory in my infirmities, that the power of Christ may rest upon me. Therefore I take pleasure in infirmities, in reproaches, in necessities, in persecutions, in distresses for Christ's sake: for when I am weak, then am I strong."

God is Our Present Help.
Hebrews 13:6
"So that we may boldly say, The Lord is my helper, and I will not fear what man shall do unto me."

If only when could remember these Truths when trouble comes. When a phone call, text, or meeting delivers unexpected news, where do we turn? Our first instinct is usually to panic or plea for help from a friend…but what if we paused and consulted the Friend Who is ready and able to help regardless of the circumstance?

He is our Refuge.
He is our Strength.
He is our Present Help.

If you are in trouble today, all you have to do is call upon Him!

Hebrews 4:16
"Let us therefore come boldly unto the throne of grace, that we may obtain mercy, and find grace to help in time of need."

Bible Reading
Ecclesiastes 3-4 | Revelation 7 | Psalm 34 | 253

In His Own Eyes.

Judges 17:6
*"In those days there was no king in Israel,
but every man did that which was right in his own eyes."*

Is this not much like the world we live in today? People seem to think they have all the answers as to what is right as long as it feels good at the time. We are constantly advised, "Follow your heart!" when trying to make a decision. But what does the Bible say about our heart?

Jeremiah 17:9
*"The heart is deceitful above all things,
and desperately wicked: who can know it?"*

We can clearly see that our hearts cannot be trusted. We are wicked on the inside, desperately wicked. Our flesh wants to please itself no matter the cost. This is why we have the inner struggle between our old nature and the new creature we have become through Christ. It is a daily battle that we all have to deal with, but thankfully we do not have to fight alone.

Proverbs 12:15
*"The way of a fool is right in his own eyes:
but he that hearkeneth unto counsel is wise."*

Ask the Lord to give you the counsel you need. **The Bible should be our first and final authority for all that we say or do.** Then, we are to seek Godly counsel from our trusted pastors and friends. We are wise when we have a multitude of counselors around us.

Proverbs 21:2
*"Every way of a man is right in his own eyes:
but the LORD pondereth the hearts."*

We look on the outward appearance of people and make our own opinion, but God looks upon our hearts. We are desperately wicked without Him. Instead of doing what we think is right, may we consult the Word of God in all that we do. Base your life choices upon the Bible and you can never go wrong. Trust in the Lord. Seek His will for your life, and allow Him to direct your path to what is right for you. **Rather than doing what seems right within our own eyes, may we seek to follow Him.**

Bible Reading
Ecclesiastes 5-6 | Revelation 8 | Psalm 35

Bear Their Burden.

Galatians 6:2
"Bear ye one another's burdens, and so fulfil the law of Christ."

It is a privilege to bear the burdens of others
and help with what they are going through.

Sometimes we can actively get involved.
Remember the friends who climbed up the side of the house and ripped off the roof in order to get their friend to Jesus? They were determined to get their friend the help he needed.

Mark 2:5
*"When Jesus saw their faith, he said unto the sick of the palsy,
Son, thy sins be forgiven thee."*

Our friend may not need us to rip the roof off a house for them, but how far are we willing to go in order to help those we care about?

Sometimes all we can do is pray for them and the situation.
Prayer is the greatest thing we can do for someone else. Intercessory prayer is probably one of the most neglected resources today. To intercede at the Throne of Grace on someone else's behalf is to follow Christ's example. Did He not pray for others? He not only prayed for His disciples, He even prayed for those that persecuted and crucified Him.

Job 42:10
*"And the LORD turned the captivity of Job,
when he prayed for his friends:
also the LORD gave Job twice as much as he had before."*

Even though his friends had wronged him, he prayed for them. When Job began to intercede for his friends, God turned the tide of Job's situation. He not only restored all that Job had lost, but He blessed Job with twice as much as he had before. **It is a blessing to pray for others!**

If a friend or family member is in need right now, make an effort to help them bear their burden. If the situation does not allow for you to actively be involved in the solution, take the time to persistently pray for them and their need. God is sure to intervene and as He provides the solution, you will be blessed at how the Lord has delivered.

Bible Reading
Ecclesiastes 7-8 | Revelation 9 | Psalm 36

Their Faith.

Mark 2:5
*"When Jesus saw their faith, he said unto the sick of the palsy,
Son, thy sins be forgiven thee."*

It wasn't the faith of the one who had the problem that was mentioned.
"When Jesus saw their faith..."

Jesus saw the faith of the others.
Those who got actively involved in helping their friend.

How much faith do you have that the Lord can meet someone else's need?
If it is possible to help someone, do you jump in and offer assistance or do you just sit back and watch them go through something? We have a choice to pass them by or be the Good Samaritan and get involved.

**What are you doing
to demonstrate your faith within someone else's life?**

Galatians 6:2
"Bear ye one another's burdens…"

When we take time to evaluate how much faith we display in the lives of those around us we may be disappointed. In today's society, we tend to get so caught up in our own problems and circumstances that we neglect to show our friends how much we care.

Would you be willing to climb up the side of someone's house and tear the roof off if that was required in order to get your friend help? Sounds drastic, doesn't it? It was for the friends that wanted to see their friend healed by Jesus. These friends put aside their own issues and focused on their hurting friend's need. Can we not do the same?

Do you have a friend who is ill? Visit or call them.
Do you have a friend who is discouraged? Send them a card or text.
Do you have a friend who is grieving? Make them smile or laugh.
Remind your friend you are praying for God to help them.
It's the little things that matter the most.

**Show your faith that God will provide whatever the need,
then watch and rejoice when the Lord shows up.**

Bible Reading
Ecclesiastes 9-10 | Revelation 10 | Psalm 37

Mixed With Faith.

Hebrews 4:2
*"For unto us was the gospel preached, as well as unto them:
but the word preached did not profit them,
not being mixed with faith in them that heard it."*

Many people, even in our churches today, know a great deal about Jesus Christ, yet they do not have a personal relationship with Him.

They know of Him, but they do not know Him.

To know Christ is to combine our knowledge of Him with faith in His finished work on Calvary. We must believe in Him, and put our faith into action as we read, hear and learn more about Him.

Romans 10:17
"So then faith cometh by hearing, and hearing by the word of God."

The Word of God must be preached to be heard, and once heard must be mixed with faith to be profitable. Those around us cannot express faith in Christ if we do not first proclaim the Gospel to them.

Isaiah 55:11
*"So shall my word be that goeth forth out of my mouth:
it shall not return unto me void, but it shall accomplish that which I please,
and it shall prosper in the thing whereto I sent it."*

The Lord has promised that when His Word is sent out, It shall prosper and accomplish what the He pleases. We can rest assured that when we proclaim the Gospel, God will bless our effort.

Bible Reading
Ecclesiastes 11-12 | Revelation 11 | Psalm 38 | 257

Be Wise.

Proverbs 11:30
*"The fruit of the righteous is a tree of life;
and he that winneth souls is wise."*

"It is the greatest pleasure of living to win souls to Christ."
D.L. Moody

Dwight Lyman Moody was saved on April 21, 1855, while working in a shoe store in Downtown Boston. His Sunday School teacher, Edward Kimball, visited him and explained to him the Gospel once more. **That Sunday School teacher did not know what fruit would come from his visit that day.** D.L. Moody would go on to reach countless souls for Christ and train his disciples to reach others.

Moody's Sunday School teacher was a soulwinner. He planted the Seed of the Gospel week by week, and ended up seeing the increase of his labour for Moody's soul that day he stopped in the shoe store. He led one of the greatest soulwinners to the Lord. Moody would go on to reach two continents with the Gospel, and win countless souls for the cause of Christ. **Think of the fruit his Sunday School teacher obtained because he used his time wisely that day in Boston.**

During Moody's ministry, a man named Wilber Chapman accepted Christ. Chapman later became an evangelist preaching meetings across the country. A professional baseball player named Billy Sunday attended one of Chapman's meetings, and realized his need for Christ that night. Sunday would later quit baseball and begin preaching evangelistic meetings.

Think of the thousands that came to know the Lord as a result of one Sunday School teacher's faithfulness to give the Gospel to his students. This story is just one example of how *"The fruit of the righteous is a tree of life; and he that winneth souls is wise."*

What will your tree of souls look like? How many generations of people will hear the Gospel because of your faithful planting of the Seeds of the Gospel?

**Be wise today.
Share the Gospel with someone.**

Bible Reading
Song of Solomon 1-2 | Revelation 12 | Psalm 39

Obey God.

Acts 5:28-29

"Saying, Did not we straitly command you that ye should not teach in this name? and, behold, ye have filled Jerusalem with your doctrine, and intend to bring this man's blood upon us. Then Peter and the other apostles answered and said, We ought to obey God rather than men."

In a day when our religious liberty is declining, we must take a stand for what is right! Religion is typically welcomed all around us, but not when it involves the Name of Jesus. The day has come, and will continue to occur, that we are rebuked for teaching in His Name.

There is just something about the Name of Jesus!

Any religion outside of Christianity is tolerated, and even some "forms" of Christianity as well...those that do not pray in the Name of Jesus Christ.

May we continue to *"Go, stand and speak"* just as the angel of the Lord told disciples when they were in prison. They obeyed, and so should we.

Though persecution from the government or our fellow citizens may come, we must remember, *"We ought to obey God rather than men."*

Regardless of what anyone else tells you, obey God.

**You may suffer persecution,
but you can never go wrong when you obey God!**
He will deliver you!

2 Timothy 3:11
*"...what persecutions I endured:
but out of them all the Lord delivered me."*

Bible Reading
Song of Solomon 3-4 | Revelation 13 | Psalm 40 | 259

We Have Not Arrived.

1 Corinthians 10:12
"Wherefore let him that thinketh he standeth take heed lest he fall."

When pride gets involved, we are in trouble. Just when we think we have arrived or are doing something right, God has a way or reminding us Who we must rely upon. Paul writes of the children of Israel and their falling in the wilderness as an example to us today.

1 Corinthians 10:11
"Now all these things happened unto them for ensamples: and they are written for our admonition, upon whom the ends of the world are come."

We are to read and learn from the result of their prideful spirit.

Proverbs 16:18
"Pride goeth before destruction, and an haughty spirit before a fall."

God hates pride.

Proverbs 8:13
"The fear of the LORD is to hate evil: pride, and arrogancy, and the evil way, and the froward mouth, do I hate."

Despite our fleshly desires to let pride creep into our lives, we must remember that God hates our pride. We must fear the Lord in all we do, and remind ourselves that we are not above the chastening hand of God.

Romans 11:20-21
"...Be not highminded, but fear: For if God spared not the natural branches, take heed lest he also spare not thee."

No one is exempt from falling. We all have a tendency to let pride creep in, but it is how we react to our pride that matters. We choose to whether to exalt or humble ourselves.

James 4:10
"Humble yourselves in the sight of the Lord, and he shall lift you up."

Anything we achieve is because of the Lord Jesus Christ working in us and through us. **We have not arrived, for we are nothing without Him.**

John 15:5
"...for without me ye can do nothing."

Bible Reading
Song of Solomon 5-6 | Revelation 14 | Psalm 41

Tomorrow.

Proverbs 27:1
*"Boast not thyself of to morrow;
for thou knowest not what a day may bring forth."*

We have no way of knowing what tomorrow holds.

On September 10th, 2001, thousands of Americans had no idea that their lives would end or be forever changed the next day when our country was attacked by terrorists.

You may receive a phone call today that will completely change your tomorrow, or you may not see it at all, for we are not promised tomorrow. As depressing as those realities are, we can take comfort in the fact that God inhabits eternity. He is already in our tomorrow.

God is already aware of what we will face tomorrow. He sees what we cannot see. We are to trust Him at all times, regardless of how bleak our surroundings may look to us. **We do not know what tomorrow holds, but we do know Who holds tomorrow.**

*I don't know about tomorrow
It may bring me poverty
But the One Who feeds the sparrow
Is the One Who stands by me
And the path that be my portion
May be through the flame or flood
But His presence goes before me
And I'm covered with His blood.
Many things about tomorrow
I don't seem to understand
But I know Who holds tomorrow
And I know Who holds my hand.*
Ira Stanphill

**He is already in our tomorrow,
while also right by our side today.**

Bible Reading
Song of Solomon 7-8 | Revelation 15 | Psalm 42

Psalm 55:1-5

*"Give ear to my prayer, O God; and hide not thyself from
my supplication. Attend unto me, and hear me: I mourn in my complaint,
and make a noise; Because of the voice of the enemy, because of the
oppression of the wicked: for they cast iniquity upon me, and in wrath they
hate me. My heart is sore pained within me: and the terrors of death are
fallen upon me. Fearfulness and trembling are come upon me,
and horror hath overwhelmed me."*

When the employees in the offices of the Twin Towers reported to work on the morning of September 11, 2001 they had no idea of the events that would unfold after 8:46am that fateful day. **They had woken up just like any other Tuesday.**

Once the hijacked planes turned around, the eternal fate of thousands of Americans was about to begin. The passengers aboard the four planes, the employees at the Pentagon, as well as the pedestrians and tourists beneath the Towers, never expected the day of terror they received. **Within seconds, their lives and the life of our nation were forever changed.**

Our hearts pained, and the terror of the unknown flooded our minds as we learned our country was under attack. Fearfulness. Trembling. Horror. As people rushed out the buildings, first responders rushed in trying to save as many as they could.

The days following unveiled a unity of our people, and a need for God that our country had not seen in many years or has since. Many saw their need for a Saviour because of their experiences on that dreadful day. **God can use any situation to point others to Him.**

The world around us today is full of fearfulness, trembling and horror. Many wake up daily with the fear of not knowing what will befall them before the sun goes down. **We do not know how a day may unfold, but we serve the One Who is in control of everything.**

We have the Solution to every problem, yet we often refuse to rush in like the first responders, amidst the terror around us and tell of the Good News of the Gospel of Jesus Christ. **May we use every opportunity to point someone to Jesus, our Ultimate First Responder.**

Bible Reading
Isaiah 1-2 | Revelation 16 | Psalm 43

Nearer.

James 4:8
"Draw nigh to God, and he will draw nigh to you. Cleanse your hands, ye sinners; and purify your hearts, ye double minded."

God not only wants us to draw nearer to him, He promises that if we do, He will draw nearer to us. If we take one step, He takes one too. He wants us to seek Him by faith, and He rewards us by revealing more of Himself to us.

In order to get closer to Him, we must rid ourselves of the sin in our lives. We must cleanse our hearts and our habits. It can be painful to change what you do or who you hang around, but it is necessary if we are sincere about getting closer to God.

Matthew 15:8-9
"This people draweth nigh unto me with their mouth, and honoureth me with their lips; but their heart is far from me. But in vain they do worship me, teaching for doctrines the commandments of men."

Many people say they want to get closer to God. Their lips say one thing, but their actions say another. God calls this double minded, and unstable.

Actions speak louder than words.
Hebrews 10:22
"Let us draw near with a true heart in full assurance of faith…"

Psalm 73:28
*"But it is good for me to draw near to God:
I have put my trust in the Lord GOD, that I may declare all thy works."*

The Psalmist realized that it was good for him to draw near to God. If it was good for him, it is surely good for us as well. **Let us put our trust in Him today as we make every effort to draw nearer to Him as we proclaim His Gospel.**

Remember His promise,
"Draw nigh to God, and he will draw nigh to you."

Draw nearer to Him today.

Bible Reading
Isaiah 3-4 | Revelation 17 | Psalm 44

Proverbs 3:5-6
"Trust in the LORD with all thine heart;
and lean not unto thine own understanding.
In all thy ways acknowledge him, and he shall direct thy paths."

Trust, n.
1. To have confidence in; reliance or resting of the mind on the integrity, justice, friendship or other principle of another person or thing.

We can have confidence in our Saviour! **In the big things and all the little details, we can trust Jesus for He knows what is best.** All throughout the Scripture we find reasons we can trust in Him. There are many examples from the lives of His children and promises that He will always be there for us.

Trust In Him When You Don't Understand.
Job 13:15
"Though he slay me, yet will I trust in him:
but I will maintain mine own ways before him."

Trust In Him When You Need Deliverance.
Psalm 37:40
"And the LORD shall help them, and deliver them: he shall deliver them from the wicked, and save them, because they trust in him."

Trust In Him When You're In Trouble.
Nahum 1:7
"The LORD is good, a strong hold in the day of trouble;
and he knoweth them that trust in him."

Trust In Him At All Times.
Psalm 62:8
"Trust in him at all times; ye people, pour out your heart before him:
God is a refuge for us. Selah."

Trust in Him with all your heart today. Do not depend on what you think you know. Acknowledge that He knows what is best for you and your situation. Allow Him to direct your paths in accordance with His will for your life. **Regardless of your situation, you can trust in Him.**

Bibles Reading
Isaiah 5-6 | Revelation 18 | Psalm 45

Looking Or Listening?

1 Kings 19:11-12

"And he said, Go forth, and stand upon the mount before the LORD. And, behold, the LORD passed by, and a great and strong wind rent the mountains, and brake in pieces the rocks before the LORD; but the LORD was not in the wind: and after the wind an earthquake; but the LORD was not in the earthquake: And after the earthquake a fire; but the LORD was not in the fire: and after the fire a still small voice."

Elijah looked at the wind, the earthquake, and even in the fire; yet, the Lord was not in any of them. It was not until Elijah listened to that *"still small voice"* that he heard the Lord. It was so powerful that he covered his face with his mantle and went out to stand at the opening of the cave. The Lord had gotten his attention, and was now about to speak to Elijah.

Instead of looking for signs around him, Elijah began to listen. Once he heard and acknowledged the *"still small voice"*, he was then able to hear what the Lord had for him.

Wonder what we miss in our daily lives as Christians because we are looking for God to give us signs and wonders of what He would have us to do, instead of allowing ourselves to be still and listen for His direction? We can trust in the Lord and allow Him to direct our paths, but in order to hear His direction, we must stop and acknowledge Him while patiently waiting for Him to direct our paths.

As Elijah stood with his mantle wrapped around his face at the opening of the cave, God asked him, *"What doest thou here, Elijah?"* It wasn't that God didn't know the answer, He simply wanted Elijah to answer honestly. He desires the same thing for us today.

Are we looking or listening for God's direction today?

Psalm 46:10

"Be still, and know that I am God..."

Bible Reading
Isaiah 7-8 | Revelation 19 | Psalm 46

Follow Him.

Matthew 4:19
"And he saith unto them, Follow me, and I will make you fishers of men."

Follow. The first command to the Disciples. The Lord Jesus did not tell the men to follow someone else, He told them to, ***"Follow me"***. The Creator of the very earth they walked upon told them to follow Him. Those that obeyed showed their faith in Jesus immediately. **They knew nothing about the Man, yet they were compelled to follow Him.** What great faith these men had, which must have been why Christ chose them.

He was not looking for the most talented or skilled, only the most willing. The same is true today. When the Holy Spirit tugged on our hearts through the power of His conviction, He told us to follow Him. Praise God for the faith He gave us to believe and put our trust in Jesus Christ alone for our salvation.

Some of the disciples were fishermen by trade, yet Jesus changed the type of fish they sought after. They may have still caught fish in the sea to sustain them, but after they followed Him they desired to fish for men.

The Lord also desires for us to be fishers of men. There is no greater joy than that of leading someone else to the Lord. If this is something you have not experienced yet, it is not too late. **God only desires you to be willing, and He will use you for His glory.** The greatest tool in winning souls for Christ is simply sharing with others what Jesus did for you. Tell someone the difference Christ has made in your life.

God only wants us to be willing to be used by Him.
May we give our lives for His glory, and submit our will to Him today.

Mark 8:34
"And when he had called the people unto him with his disciples also, he said unto them, Whosoever will come after me, let him deny himself, and take up his cross, and follow me."

Follow Him today.

Bible Reading
Isaiah 9-10 | Revelation 20 | Psalm 47

Last Place.

Matthew 20:16
*"So the last shall be first, and the first last:
for many be called, but few chosen."*

Have you ever known someone who always wants to be first in line? When dinner is called, they are the first to fill their plate. When they meet another car at the drive thru they wouldn't even dream of allowing them to go first for fear they might have to wait for their French fries. They won't hold the door for someone and allow them to get ahead of them in line at the Post Office. Faces may be flooding your mind, or maybe you even feel a little convicted.

Jesus used the Parable of the Labourers In The Vineyard for us to learn how to be a servant. Those that were hired in the eleventh hour were paid the same amount that those hired the third hour. The eleventh hour labourers were paid first. When the third hour labourers saw this, they assumed they would receive more money since they had worked all day. They were wrong, and they began to murmur among themselves against their employer. The ones that worked an hour received the same pay as those who had *"borne the burden and heat of the day".*

Our flesh wants to sympathize with those who had worked all day long and yet received the same pay as those who barely broke a sweat. Can we not relate with their hurt feelings? Sure, we all can; but we should not let that prevent us from serving. **Jesus was teaching His disciples, and us today, that we should have a heart to serve others.**

Jesus had a servant's heart. He is our Ultimate Example of a Servant. He even washed the feet of His disciples. **We have opportunities every day to show the love of Christ by serving others.** It is a Biblical principle to allow others to go before you. Do not allow your hurt feelings of the past to keep you from serving. Start today and when it comes to serving, strive for last place.

**God promises us in His Word
that He will bless those who put others first.**

Bible Reading
Isaiah 11-12 | Revelation 21 | Psalm 48 | 267

Commissioned.

Acts 13:2-3
"As they ministered to the Lord, and fasted, the Holy Ghost said, Separate me Barnabas and Saul for the work whereunto I have called them. And when they had fasted and prayed, and laid their hands on them, they sent them away."

Here we see two missionaries being commissioned by the church to go and serve. Paul and Barnabas traveled far and wide proclaiming the Gospel. God used their surrendered lives as the church sent them away to reach others. There are many other examples in the Bible of those who surrendered their lives for God's glory. Esther, Daniel, David, Paul, etc.

Be willing.
Isaiah 6:8
"Also I heard the voice of the Lord, saying, Whom shall I send, and who will go for us? Then said I, Here am I; send me."

Though you may not feel called to leave home to reach others, you can still be used if you are willing. Isaiah was willing to do whatever the Lord asked of him. Are you?

Have the right motive.
When Hudson Taylor was the Director of the China Inland Mission, he asked missionary candidates, "Why do you wish to go as a foreign missionary?"

He received several responses: "Because Christ commanded us." "Because millions are perishing without Christ." And many others. Hudson Taylor then responded, "All of these motives, however good, will fail you in times of testings, trials, tribulations, and possible death. There is but one motive that will sustain you in trial and testing: namely, the love of Christ."

The Love of Christ makes the missionary's duty a delight.
What is your motive for serving?

Matthew 28:18-20
"And Jesus came and spake unto them, saying, All power is given unto me in heaven and in earth. Go ye therefore, and teach all nations, baptizing them in the name of the Father, and of the Son, and of the Holy Ghost: Teaching them to observe all things whatsoever I have commanded you: and, lo, I am with you alway, even unto the end of the world. Amen."

Remember today that we have been commissioned!

Bible Reading
Isaiah 13-14 | Revelation 22 | Psalm 49

Walk Toward Them.

Colossians 4:5
"Walk in wisdom toward them that are without, redeeming the time."

A missionary is one who has surrendered their life to *"Walk in wisdom toward them that are without".* Their heart's desire is to go to those who do not know Christ that they to may have eternal life. They live many different lives; but regardless of their situation, they no doubt walk in their field praying that God would open a door of opportunity for them to share the Gospel and the love of Christ.

Colossians 4:2-4
"Continue in prayer, and watch in the same with thanksgiving; Withal praying also for us, that God would open unto us a door of utterance, to speak the mystery of Christ, for which I am also in bonds: That I may make it manifest, as I ought to speak."

They live in a variety of living conditions and locations. Some live in the middle of an urban city, some in the middle of a jungle or village. Some can be found in the middle of nowhere, and some in a rural neighborhood. Why? **Because everywhere you can possibly go on this earth, people need the Gospel.**

No "job description" is the same, and it likely changes from day to day. A day full of inviting may be followed by a day of Bible studies. One day they may travel to town to get supplies and visit their people, the next they may be digging holes on their property while also trying to file reports, and mail prayer letters to their supporters. Why such unpredictable schedules? **Because in order to be effective in the ministry, you must be flexible.**

If you thought a missionary's life only consisted of teaching and preaching, you probably haven't met very many missionaries. With every task that is needed, there is a common theme… **To show the love of Christ and what He did for them.**

The truth is, **we are all called to be missionaries.** We may not all be in what we refer to as "full time service", but we all have an opportunity to *"Walk in wisdom toward them that are without".* **There are people all around us who need the Gospel.**

People need the Lord!
Be a missionary today, and walk toward them!

Bible Reading
Isaiah 15-16 | Romans 1 | Psalm 50 | 269

It Is Not Your Battle.

2 Chronicles 20:15
"And he said, Hearken ye, all Judah, and ye inhabitants of Jerusalem, and thou king Jehoshaphat, Thus saith the LORD unto you, Be not afraid nor dismayed by reason of this great multitude; for the battle is not your's, but God's."

The crowd around us can sometimes deter us from our purpose or duty. When we feel as if there is a great company against us and we don't know what to do, we must turn our eyes upon Jesus!

When all of Judah stood before the LORD with anticipation of how He would help them, the Spirit of the LORD came upon Jahaziel in the midst of the congregation. The LORD used him to proclaim our verse today.

When you read the verse did a current battle you are facing come to mind? **Be encouraged that it is not your battle to fight!** We must stand still, lay down our arms, and allow God to fight the battle for us.

Exodus 14:14
"The LORD shall fight for you, and ye shall hold your peace."

We often want to do whatever we can to help get ourselves out of the situation we are in, and of course we want to win! If we fight on our own, we often do more harm than good; but when we stand still and surrender our will in the fight, we allow God to move as only He can.

Psalm 27:1
"The LORD is my light and my salvation; whom shall I fear? the LORD is the strength of my life; of whom shall I be afraid?"

We have the Almighty God on our side, whom shall we fear? We must turn our eyes upon the Lord Jesus and begin to stand still and wait.

As we allow Him to fight our battles for us, we are able to wait for Him to bring the victory.

The battle is never easy or enjoyable, but when the Lord is in control we will not only be victorious, we can shine His Light to others through our battle. This is when God receives the glory He so rightfully deserves.

Allow Him to shine!

Regardless of the opposition you face today, have no fear.
It is not your battle to fight!

Bible Reading
Isaiah 17-18 | Romans 2 | Psalm 51

Walking In The Midst Of The Fire.

Daniel 3:24-25
"Then Nebuchadnezzar the king was astonied, and rose up in haste, and spake, and said unto his counsellors, Did not we cast three men bound into the midst of the fire? They answered and said unto the king, True, O king. He answered and said, Lo, I see four men loose, walking in the midst of the fire, and they have no hurt; and the form of the fourth is like the Son of God."

A familiar story. King Nebuchadnezzar had made an image of gold, and gathered together all sorts of dignitaries for the dedication of it, then a command was given.

Daniel 3:5-6
"That at what time ye hear the sound of the cornet, flute, harp, sackbut, psaltery, dulcimer, and all kinds of musick, ye fall down and worship the golden image that Nebuchadnezzar the king hath set up: And whoso falleth not down and worshippeth shall the same hour be cast into the midst of a burning fiery furnace."

There were only three Hebrew boys, Shadrach, Meshach, and Abednego, who chose to stand when all the others were bowing. **They refused to compromise their belief in God despite the threat of the burning fiery furnace.** They were not afraid of the opposition, but rather had faith that their God would deliver them, or else they were willing to die for their faith.

Daniel 3:17-18
"If it be so, our God whom we serve is able to deliver us from the burning fiery furnace, and he will deliver us out of thine hand, O king. But if not, be it known unto thee, O king, that we will not serve thy gods, nor worship the golden image which thou hast set up."

They chose to take a stand, and the Lord went into the fire with them.

1 Peter 1:7
"That the trial of your faith, being much more precious than of gold that perisheth, though it be tried with fire, might be found unto praise and honour and glory at the appearing of Jesus Christ:"

Regardless of the opposition or peer pressure around you, choose to take a stand for what the Bible says is right. God is sure to bless your faith and deliver you from both the enemy and the fiery furnace. **You can walk in the midst of your fire today with the Lord by your side.**

Bible Reading
Isaiah 19-20 | Romans 3 | Psalm 52

Shaken.

Acts 4:31
"And when they had prayed, the place was shaken where they were assembled together; and they were all filled with the Holy Ghost, and they spake the word of God with boldness."

The place was shaken because they prayed in one accord.
Acts 4:24
"And when they heard that, they lifted up their voice to God with one accord, and said, Lord, thou art God, which hast made heaven, and earth, and the sea, and all that in them is:"

What if we prayed in one accord? We can only imagine what could happen! **We must pray in order to see the power of prayer.** God is ready and able to move in our churches and our lives if only we would ask.

When we pray…Our Churches Will Be Shaken.
"…where they were assembled…"
In order for our churches to be shaken, we must first assemble together. God desires for His people to assemble together. The Holy Ghost inspired the writer of Hebrews to call out *"as the manner of some is"*, those who even in that day where forsaking the assembling of the church. God knew this would be an ongoing issue among our churches.

Hebrews 10:25
"Not forsaking the assembling of ourselves together, as the manner of some is; but exhorting one another: and so much the more, as ye see the day approaching."

When we pray…Our Character Will Be Changed.
"…and they were all filled with the Holy Ghost…"
We wonder why we do not have the power of God, yet did even we ask for His help? If we do not pray, we will not be changed.

When we pray…Our Courage Will Be Spoken.
"…and they spake the word of God with boldness."
We cannot speak for God until we have spoken with God. If we want to be bold for Him, we must hear what He has to say within His Word, and ask Him for His help in every area of our lives.

Do you want your life to be shaken for God's glory?
Pray.

Bible Reading
Isaiah 21-22 | Romans 4 | Psalm 53

Unshakeable Faith.

Luke 6:47-49

*"Whosoever cometh to me, and heareth my sayings, and doeth them,
I will shew you to whom he is like: He is like a man which built an house,
and digged deep, and laid the foundation on a rock: and when the flood
arose, the stream beat vehemently upon that house, and could not shake
it: for it was founded upon a rock. But he that heareth, and doeth not, is
like a man that without a foundation built an house upon the earth; against
which the stream did beat vehemently, and immediately it fell;
and the ruin of that house was great."*

We must pray not only for our churches and our lives to be shaken by God's power, but also for our faith to be unshakeable.

Anyone can have unshakeable faith.

"Whosoever cometh to me, and heareth my sayings, and doeth them"

Anyone can have unshakeable faith, if it is founded upon The Rock.

"and could not shake it: for it was founded upon a rock."

That Rock is Jesus Christ. God's Son, and our Saviour. Jesus used this picture of a builder for us to envision the simplicity of this Truth. The man building the house dug deep until he found rock, and then he laid the foundation upon that rock. He later tells us what happens to the houses that are without a foundation and built upon the earth.

We must dig deep. This doesn't imply that it is difficult to find Christ has our Rock, but rather refers to finding out what the Bible says about Him.

We must lay the foundation. We must build upon our faith in Jesus by learning what the Scriptures say, and developing our beliefs based upon the Truth. Just as a foundation is crucial to the integrity of a structure, without Jesus Christ our faith has no foundation!

Anyone can have their faith shaken without a Foundation that is built upon Jesus Christ. There was another man who built his house upon the earth, and saw it fall when the vehement stream came, *"and immediately it fell; and the ruin of that house was great".* **Any faith that is built on something else other than Jesus Christ alone will fall.**

**We can stand upon the Rock of Ages,
because He never changes.**

Bible Reading
Isaiah 23-24 | Romans 5 | Psalm 54 | 273

The Harvest.

Jeremiah 8:20
"The harvest is past, the summer is ended, and we are not saved."

Perhaps the most terrifying verse in the entire Bible.

What if today was the last day we had to plant the Seeds of the Gospel and watch as the Lord of the Harvest brings the increase?

Our time is running out.

Who can we reach before it is too late?
It is our job to plant and water the Seeds, and leave the rest up to God.

1 Corinthians 3:6-7
*"I have planted, Apollos watered; but God gave the increase.
So then neither is he that planteth any thing, neither he that watereth;
but God that giveth the increase."*

That day is coming. The trumpet will sound and God will call His children to meet the Lord Jesus in the air. Those on earth who have rejected the Gospel will not have another chance to accept Christ as their Saviour.

Will your friend be saved? Will your coworker trust Christ before it is eternally too late? Will that family member you have prayed for as long as you can remember finally listen and accept the Truth of the Gospel in time?

It is up to us to share the Truth.
Are you a harvester of the Gospel?

Luke 10:2
"Therefore said he unto them, The harvest truly is great, but the labourers are few: pray ye therefore the Lord of the harvest, that he would send forth labourers into his harvest."

The harvest is waiting.
Will you labour to reach them with the Gospel today?

Bible Reading
Isaiah 25-26 | Romans 6 | Psalm 55

The Value Of One.

Luke 15:3-7
"And he spake this parable unto them, saying,
What man of you, having an hundred sheep, if he lose one of them, doth
not leave the ninety and nine in the wilderness, and go after that which is
lost, until he find it? And when he hath found it, he layeth it on his
shoulders, rejoicing. And when he cometh home, he calleth together his
friends and neighbours, saying unto them,
Rejoice with me; for I have found my sheep which was lost. I say unto you,
that likewise joy shall be in heaven over one sinner that repenteth, more
than over ninety and nine just persons, which need no repentance."

The picture of a Shepherd and His Sheep in reference to Jesus and His children is one of the most precious recorded in Scripture. What tender love and care the Good Shepherd has for His sheep!

A lost sheep is completely helpless on it's own, and needs a Saviour to save it and bring it back to the fold. When the sheep is found, the Shepherd lovingly picks it up, gently speaks Words of comfort, and carries it home on His shoulders.

Psalm 23:1,3
"The LORD is my shepherd…He restoreth my soul"

Matthew 18:11-14
"For the Son of man is come to save that which was lost. How think ye? if a man have an hundred sheep, and one of them be gone astray, doth he not leave the ninety and nine, and goeth into the mountains, and seeketh that which is gone astray? And if so be that he find it, verily I say unto you, he rejoiceth more of that sheep, than of the ninety and nine which went not astray. Even so it is not the will of your Father which is in heaven, that one of these little ones should perish."

Although the ninety and nine may be safe, the Shepherd goes after the one. Aren't you glad He came and found you when you were astray? He is not willing that any should perish. **Just imagine the rejoicing in Heaven when a sinner repents and trusts Christ to save them.** Jesus came to earth with one purpose, to reach the lost; there is nothing else gives Him more joy. **May we strive to bring more rejoicing in Heaven by being faithful to share the Gospel with the lost sheep all around us.**

Bible Reading
Isaiah 27-28 | Romans 7 | Psalm 56

Excuses.

Luke 14:16-18

*"Then said he unto him, A certain man made a great supper, and bade many: And sent his servant at supper time to say to them that were bidden, Come; for all things are now ready.
And they all with one consent began to make excuse…"*

The master had given the servant instructions to bid others to come to the supper that had been prepared. The servant obeyed, and went inviting others to come, but they all began to give their excuses why they could not. Sound familiar? We hear excuses from people from two different sides of the ministry. Those who are too busy to see their need for Jesus Christ, and those who too busy to serve Him.

Some use vacation or leisure as an excuse. Luke 14:18
"…The first said unto him, I have bought a piece of ground, and I must needs go and see it: I pray thee have me excused."

Some use possessions or material goods as an excuse. Luke 14:19
"And another said, I have bought five yoke of oxen, and I go to prove them: I pray thee have me excused."

Some use family as an excuse. Luke 14:20
"And another said, I have married a wife, and therefore I cannot come."

The people's excuses made the master angry, and gave the willing servant more work.
Luke 14:21
"So that servant came, and shewed his lord these things. Then the master of the house being angry said to his servant, Go out quickly into the streets and lanes of the city, and bring in hither the poor, and the maimed, and the halt, and the blind."

The willing servant brought the poor, the maimed, the halt, and the blind to the master's house, and yet there was room for more! **There is always room at the Master's house.** People will always make excuses for their sin and need for salvation, but we cannot let that stop us from inviting them to the Master.

On the flip side, when will we stop making excuses for putting off what we know the Lord would have us to do? **Those that have answered the call of salvation and placed their faith in Christ are also called to serve Him. Stop the excuses.** Find a place within your local church and be a willing servant.

Bible Reading
Isaiah 29-30 | Romans 8 | Psalm 57

The Work Of His Hand.

Isaiah 64:8
*"But now, O LORD, thou art our father; we are the clay,
and thou our potter; and we all are the work of thy hand."*

To most of us, a lump of clay is just a pile of dirt; but an artist sees the potential that lies within the clay even before it becomes the work of his hands. As clay within the Potter's hand, we are in the hand of the Lord.

He is the Potter. We are the clay.

Jeremiah 18:6
*"O house of Israel, cannot I do with you as this potter? saith the LORD.
Behold, as the clay is in the potter's hand, so are ye in mine hand,
O house of Israel."*

The Potter transforms and fashions the clay according to His will. Who are we to question what He is doing in our lives? Though we may not understand, He is working all things for our good and His glory.

Romans 9:20-23
*"Nay but, O man, who art thou that repliest against God?
Shall the thing formed say to him that formed it, Why hast thou made me
thus? Hath not the potter power over the clay, of the same lump to make
one vessel unto honour, and another unto dishonour?
What if God, willing to shew his wrath, and to make his power known,
endured with much longsuffering the vessels of wrath fitted to destruction:
And that he might make known the riches of his glory on the vessels of
mercy, which he had afore prepared unto glory,"*

When sin gets in our lives, we become marred and need to be reworked on the Potter's wheel before we become a vessel of dishonour. **The clay must submit to the will of the Potter in order to be used.** Shall we not submit to the Lord's will for our lives?

You may see yourself or your life as just a lump of clay, but the Lord sees your potential. Don't allow the devil to convince you otherwise.

Trust the hands of the Potter as He molds you into His image.

Bible Reading
Isaiah 31-32 | Romans 9 | Psalm 58 | 277

Grace & Mercy.

John 5:6-7

"When Jesus saw him lie, and knew that he had been now a long time in that case, he saith unto him, Wilt thou be made whole? The impotent man answered him, Sir, I have no man, when the water is troubled, to put me into the pool: but while I am coming, another steppeth down before me."

Sin can cripple and immobilize us in such a way that we are helpless on our own. This impotent man who had an infirmity for 38 years lay beside the Pool of Bethesda hoping someone would help him reach the water. This pool was beside the sheep market in Jerusalem and had five porches. It was well known for having a great multitude of people gathered upon the porches awaiting an angel that would come and trouble the water. It was a custom that the first person to step in after the troubling of the water *"was made whole of whatever disease he had".*

Because of his infirmity, this impotent man routinely missed the opportunity to be healed at the water. This was before Jesus went up to Jerusalem. Upon seeing him lying there, Jesus asked him a simple question, already knowing his answer.

"Wilt thou be made whole?"

The man must not have realized Who had asked him the question or His ability to heal him without even touching the water. **Jesus showed this man grace.**

"Sir, I have no man"

He made an excuse. Just as we tend to make excuses when Jesus asks us a question. He allowed him to give his reasoning, and then commanded him to do something. **Jesus showed this man mercy.** Instead of a excuse this time, the man simply obeyed and the results were life changing.

"Rise, take up thy bed, and walk."

Immediately, the infirmity left the impotent man, and he took up his bed, and walked just as Jesus had told him to do so.

The number of porches of the Pool of Bethesda was not a coincidence. There were five resting places for the people in need of the grace of God. The word Bethesda in the Hebrew tongue refers to a "house of mercy". The impotent man was shown mercy that day when Jesus visited him beside the pool. The Pool of Grace & The House of Mercy. **It is the grace and mercy of our Lord Jesus Christ which carries us through each day of our lives.**

Bible Reading

Isaiah 33-34 | Romans 10 | Psalm 59

What's In Your Hand?

Exodus 4:2
*"And the LORD said unto him, What is that in thine hand?
And he said, A rod."*

Moses refuted against God's directive and told Him that the people would not believe that the Lord had appeared unto him. This was just after Moses had asked God what the His Name was, and He answered.

Exodus 3:14
"And God said unto Moses, I AM THAT I AM: and he said, Thus shalt thou say unto the children of Israel, I AM hath sent me unto you."

Where was Moses' faith? He had his eyes on the people around him instead of on the Almighty God.

The Lord was patient with Moses. He did not cast him aside and find someone else to use. He knew how to speak to Moses for him to understand and obey. He simply asked Moses what he had in his hand, what he had available to use for God's glory.

"And he said, A rod."
God used that rod to instill a faith in Moses that God could use him regardless of his inabilities or insecurities.

The rod that became a serpent and caused Moses to fear was the same one that returned to be the rod when he conquered his fear and took the serpent by the tail as the Lord commanded. **God wanted to use what Moses had in his hand to show the people that God had met with Moses.**

Exodus 4:5
"That they may believe that the LORD God of their fathers, the God of Abraham, the God of Isaac, and the God of Jacob, hath appeared unto thee."

That same rod was used when God parted the Red Sea.
That same rod was used to smite the rock in Horeb.
But that same rod was also used in disobedience, and Moses suffered the consequence of not bringing the people into the Promised Land.

What's in your hand? God can use it for His glory.
Will you obey and watch God perform miracles for His glory, or will you choose to disobey? **God can use whatever is in your hand, if only you will allow Him to use it.**

Bible Reading
Isaiah 35-36 | Romans 11 | Psalm 60 | 279

Asked Of Us.

Deuteronomy 10:12-13
*"And now, Israel, what doth the LORD thy God require of thee,
but to fear the LORD thy God, to walk in all his ways, and to love him,
and to serve the LORD thy God with all thy heart and with all thy soul,
To keep the commandments of the LORD, and his statutes,
which I command thee this day for thy good?"*

To require something of someone is simply to ask them to do something. Parents ask their children to clean their rooms and respect their elders. Teachers ask their students to pay attention to the lesson and do their best on their assignments. **What has the Lord asked of us?** We find five simple instructions in our verses today that the Lord told Moses to speak unto the children of Israel that He also is asking of us.

Fear the Lord.
Proverbs 1:7
*"The fear of the LORD is the beginning of knowledge:
but fools despise wisdom and instruction."*

Walk in the Way of the Lord.
Micah 6:8
*"He hath shewed thee, O man, what is good;
and what doth the LORD require of thee, but to do justly,
and to love mercy, and to walk humbly with thy God?"*

Love the Lord.
Psalm 31:23
*"O love the LORD, all ye his saints: for the LORD preserveth the faithful,
and plentifully rewardeth the proud doer."*

Serve the Lord.
Psalm 100:2
"Serve the LORD with gladness: come before his presence with singing."

Obey the Word of the Lord.
Jeremiah 42:6
*"Whether it be good, or whether it be evil, we will obey the voice of the
LORD our God, to whom we send thee; that it may be well with us,
when we obey the voice of the LORD our God."*

**These five principles can vastly change our lives,
if we are willing to do what the Lord has asked of us.**
Bible Reading
Isaiah 37-38 | Romans 12 | Psalm 61

Choose.

Joshua 24:15
*"And if it seem evil unto you to serve the LORD,
choose you this day whom ye will serve;
whether the gods which your fathers served that were on the other side of
the flood, or the gods of the Amorites, in whose land ye dwell:
but as for me and my house, we will serve the LORD."*

Joshua took a stand that day with the children of Israel. He laid it out for them that they had to make a choice of Who they were going to serve, while boldly proclaiming that he and his family would serve the Lord God of Jehovah.

We must make a choice today.

If we choose not to serve the Lord, we choose to be against Him. There are no gray areas when it comes to serving Him. A professing Christian who does not separate themselves from the ways of the world is doing more harm than good to the Name of Christ.

Luke 11:23
*"He that is not with me is against me:
and he that gathereth not with me scattereth."*

James 4:4
"Ye adulterers and adulteresses, know ye not that the friendship of the world is enmity with God? whosoever therefore will be a friend of the world is the enemy of God."

We cannot claim to be a Christian, live like the world, and think we are making a difference. **Choose today to make the choice to serve Him with your whole heart.** It has been said before that no person who chooses to serve the Lord has ever regretted that decision, but there are many who chose not to serve and were full of regret.

What choice will you make today?

Bible Reading
Isaiah 39-40 | Romans 13 | Psalm 62 | 281

A Precious Reunion.

Psalm 116:15
"Precious in the sight of the LORD is the death of his saints."

Losing someone we love is never easy.

As difficult as it is for us to understand, when the Lord calls one of His saints home to be with Him in Heaven, it is a precious experience. Although we that remain feel the loss and pain of no longer seeing our loved one, we can take comfort in the Blessed Hope that we have through our Lord Jesus Christ.

When a saint crosses over to the other side, the burden of the flesh is removed, and joy that awaits them as they see our Saviour face to face. **To be absent from the body is to be present with the Lord.** Our loved ones are not suffering anymore because they trusted in what Jesus did on the Cross of Calvary to give them a home in Heaven.

Through our faith in Jesus' sacrifice, God has freed us from the sting of death; but not from death itself. **Thank God we have the victory through Christ Jesus our Lord!**

1 Corinthians 15:55-57
"O death, where is thy sting? O grave, where is thy victory? The sting of death is sin; and the strength of sin is the law. But thanks be to God, which giveth us the victory through our Lord Jesus Christ."

The pain we feel when we lose someone we love is unbearable in our own strength, but God gives us grace and strength to get through. **How reassuring it is that to know Christ is to never have to truly say goodbye!**

What a precious reunion day awaits us!
What a day that will be!

Bible Reading
Isaiah 41-42 | Romans 14 | Psalm 63

The Winning Side.

Psalm 98:1
*"O sing unto the LORD a new song; for he hath done marvellous things:
his right hand, and his holy arm, hath gotten him the victory."*

All throughout Scripture we find reference to the *"right hand"*, which often refers to the Lord Jesus Christ. Here we find another mention of *"his right hand, and his holy arm, hath gotten him the victory."* Jesus won the ultimate victory when, after giving His life on Calvary, He arose victoriously after three days in the tomb. **God always gets the victory!**

1 Chronicles 29:11
*"Thine, O LORD, is the greatness, and the power, and the glory,
and the victory, and the majesty: for all that is in the heaven
and in the earth is thine; thine is the kingdom, O LORD,
and thou art exalted as head above all."*

He is God. Any greatness, power, glory, or victory we have is because of Him! **When we exalt Him to His rightful place in our lives, we can be on the winning side!**

We find near the end of the Book of Revelation that after Satan is loosed for a little season, he will receive his ultimate fate and be cast into the place created just for him, the Lake of Fire, never to deceive men again. He knows that his time is short and he will never win in the end, so he has chosen to make havoc of the world we live in. The outlook may be bleak, but the uplook is bright!

**Do not fret or fear today,
but remind yourself that you are on the winning side!**

*He's the keeper of my soul since I gave Him full control,
And He placed me on the winning side.
Well, I am on the winning side, yes, I am on the winning side,
Out in sin no more will I abide;
I've enlisted in the fight for the cause of truth and right,
Praise the Lord, I'm on the winning side!*
Hale Reever

Bible Reading
Isaiah 43-44 | Romans 15 | Psalm 64

Mark 8:34
"And when he had called the people unto him with his disciples also, he said unto them, Whosoever will come after me, let him deny himself, and take up his cross, and follow me."

All throughout Scripture we see the word *"whosoever"*.
A simple way to define this is simply anyone.

"...Whosoever will come after me, let him deny himself, and take up his cross, and follow me."

Anyone can follow Christ. We must simply die to ourselves and exchange our own will for His. Today we will look at some Biblical Truths that we can learn from this one simple word. **Take the time to read through the verses that contain the word *"whosoever"*, and see the Truth that we can apply to our lives.**

Anyone can hurt you..Matthew 5:38-40
Anyone can be used by God....................................Matthew 16:25
Anyone can be humble...Matthew 18:4
Anyone can serve..Matthew 20:26-28
Anyone can be proud...Matthew 23:12
Anyone can follow Christ..Mark 8:34
Anyone can have faith in God.................................Mark 11:22-24
Anyone can believe in Jesus...................................John 3:15-16
Anyone can drink of His water.................................John 4:13-14
Anyone can see His light..John 12:46
Anyone can have their sins erased...........................Acts 10:43
Anyone can be judgmental......................................Romans 2:1
Anyone can be saved...Romans 10:13
Anyone can resist...Romans 13:1-2
Anyone can be guilty...James 2:10
Anyone can be distracted.......................................James 4:4
Anyone can sin..1 John 3:4-5
Anyone can have love..1 John 4:14-16
Anyone can go to hell..Revelation 20:15

Whosoever.

Bible Reading
Isaiah 45-46 | Romans 16 | Psalm 65

1 John 1:9
"If we confess our sins, he is faithful and just to forgive us our sins,
and to cleanse us from all unrighteousness."

Throughout the Scriptures we see conditional blessings, where **God promises to grant us something, if we will simply do what He says.** God wants to give us so many things, yet so often we miss out on His blessings because we are unwilling to obey His commands.

If we confess, He will forgive and cleanse us.

We want His forgiveness. We want Him to cleanse us from all unrighteousness; yet we often neglect to confess our sins. We desire to be cleaner, but are rarely willing to do what it takes to be clean. He is faithful to forgive and cleanse, if only we will confess. Are we as faithful to confess, as He is to forgive and cleanse us?

If we will humble ourselves and pray,
seek His face and turn from our wicked ways,
He will hear, forgive and heal us.

2 Chronicles 7:14
"If my people, which are called by my name, shall humble themselves,
and pray, and seek my face, and turn from their wicked ways; then will I
hear from heaven, and will forgive their sin, and will heal their land."

We want Him to hear us. We desire His forgiveness. We beg for His healing; yet we do not receive because we are not willing to humble ourselves - much less pray, seek and turn.

There are many more examples of conditional blessings in the Bible. **Seek to notice what blessings can be ours <u>if</u> we will simply obey God's direction.**

Bible Reading
Isaiah 47-48 | John 1 | Psalm 66

The Truth Hurts.

Galatians 4:16
"Am I therefore become your enemy, because I tell you the truth?"

Knocking on a door, smiling cordially and greeting the resident as they wonder why you are standing on their doorstep is the easy part. The conversation is usually friendly, until you tell them you are with so and so Baptist church and are out in the area inviting people to come to church. Suddenly, the look on the homeowner's face changes from friendly to annoyed. They nod and make an excuse as to why they haven't been to church in years, and they may or may not be surprised as you turn the conversation to ask them that all important question…"If you died today, are you 100% sure you'd go to Heaven?" The annoyed expression has turned again, but this time to intrusive and distant. **The Truth hurts.**

Jesus told Nicodemus the Truth
when he acknowledged that Jesus was come from God.
John 3:3
"Jesus answered and said unto him, Verily, verily, I say unto thee, Except a man be born again, he cannot see the kingdom of God."

Have you ever asked a friend, "hey, can we talk?" and you can tell they instantly get the feeling that something is wrong? The defensive maneuvers go up as they prepare for an assumed attack of some sort and a guilty look appears on their face. **The truth hurts.**

The Lord sent Nathan to rebuke David for his sin
with Bathsheba and Uriah.
2 Samuel 12:1,7
"And the Lord sent Nathan unto David… And Nathan said to David, Thou art the man…"

We do not like to be told that we are in the wrong. Our flesh oftentimes shoots the messenger so to speak…perhaps you know the feeling. To be treated like the enemy is never fun, but how else will they, or we, learn the truth? **Someone must tell them, and someone must tell us.**

Sometimes we are the ones that need told we are wrong.
The truth hurts sometimes, but the Truth is needful.

The Word of God is our Final Authority and the Source of Truth.
Allow the Scripture to bring out the Truth in your life today.

Bible Reading
Isaiah 49-50 | John 2 | Psalm 67

Deceived.

Galatians 6:7
*"Be not deceived; God is not mocked:
for whatsoever a man soweth, that shall he also reap."*

To be deceived, one must be misled to go astray and commit sin. Who is the one who deceives? Does God deceive us? The Lord? The Holy Spirit? Absolutely not. **Deception starts with the deceiver.** The devil uses people, possessions, and pride to deceive us. We must resist the deceiver and not be ignorant of his devices.

Deceived By Alcohol.
Proverbs 20:1
*"Wine is a mocker, strong drink is raging:
and whosoever is deceived thereby is not wise."*

Many focus on the first part of the verse and dwell on the Truth of it, while leaving out the latter part. We learn from this verse that wine and strong drink can deceive people. **In order to partake of wine or strong drink, you must be deceived.** A person who is deceived by the devil in partaking of wine or strong drink may have their reasons why they feel it is okay for a Christian to do so; however, the Bible tells us that they are not wise.

Deceived By Pride.
Galatians 6:3
*"For if a man think himself to be something,
when he is nothing, he deceiveth himself."*

To be deceived by someone or something else is one thing, but many times we forget how often we deceive ourselves. Pride is followed by shame and destruction. God hates pride, so shouldn't we?

The Fate of the Deceiver.
Revelation 20:10
"And the devil that deceived them was cast into the lake of fire and brimstone, where the beast and the false prophet are, and shall be tormented day and night for ever and ever."

It is encouraging to remember the fate that awaits the deceiver. After all is said and done, he will be cast into the lake of fire; yet it is sobering to think of how many will choose to reject Christ and spend eternity with the devil.

Resist the deceiver today.

Bible Reading
Isaiah 51-52 | John 3 | Psalm 68 | 287

Discouragement.

Deuteronomy 1:21
*"Behold, the LORD thy God hath set the land before thee:
go up and possess it, as the LORD God of thy fathers hath said unto thee;
fear not, neither be discouraged."*

Discouragement is a tool of the devil.

He discourages us in order to distract us from our God-given purpose. He desires to make us less effective in what God has called us to do for Him. The devil knows what discourages us, and he also knows how to use people to accomplish just that. **Resist him today, and drive the discouragement away.**

James 4:7
*"Submit yourselves therefore to God.
Resist the devil, and he will flee from you."*

We can be encouraged today because the Lord is with us
wherever we go, whatever we do, whomever we are with.

We have no reason to be discouraged or afraid with Him by our side!

Joshua 1:9
*"Have not I commanded thee? Be strong and of a good courage;
be not afraid, neither be thou dismayed:
for the LORD thy God is with thee whithersoever thou goest."*

Resist the discourager.
Be strong because the Lord is on your side!

Discouragement does not have to get you down today.

Bible Reading

Isaiah 53 | John 4 | Psalm 69

The Bright Side.

2 Corinthians 4:6-10
"For God, who commanded the light to shine out of darkness, hath shined in our hearts, to give the light of the knowledge of the glory of God in the face of Jesus Christ. But we have this treasure in earthen vessels, that the excellency of the power may be of God, and not of us. We are troubled on every side, yet not distressed; we are perplexed, but not in despair; Persecuted, but not forsaken; cast down, but not destroyed; Always bearing about in the body the dying of the Lord Jesus, that the life also of Jesus might be made manifest in our body."

"...the light of the knowledge of the glory of God..."
Find the bright side of your situation. There is a positive aspect to whatever you are going through today. It may not seem like it on the surface, but God has a reason for whatever your circumstance is today. A reason that is both for your good, and His glory.

"..this treasure in earthen vessels..."
We have the light of Christ in our hearts; a treasure that this world cannot compare. **No matter what you are up against today, you have an opportunity to let the light of Christ shine through you.** If you neglect to shine the light, you miss out on the blessings available to you despite the struggle you are facing.

Look on the bright side…
You may be troubled, perplexed, persecuted and cast down…
but you do not have to be distressed, in despair, forsaken, or destroyed.

Matthew 5:16
"Let your light so shine before men, that they may see your good works, and glorify your Father which is in heaven."

When we shine so that others can see God, He gets the glory.
Allow the bright side of to shine in your life today.

Bible Reading
Isaiah 54-55 | John 5 | Psalm 70 | 289

Through Faith

2 Timothy 3:15
"And that from a child thou hast known the holy scriptures, which are able to make thee wise unto salvation through faith which is in Christ Jesus."

It is through faith that we receive anything of eternal value.
It is through faith that we understand the Scriptures.
It is through faith that we believe in Him!

When we take the time to know the Scriptures, we receive wisdom. **We learn that through faith in Jesus Christ, we are given so many blessings that our minds cannot fully comprehend.**

Through faith, we have atonement for our sins because of His Blood.
Romans 3:24-25
"Being justified freely by his grace through the redemption that is in Christ Jesus: Whom God hath set forth to be a propitiation through faith in his blood, to declare his righteousness for the remission of sins that are past, through the forbearance of God;"

Through faith, we are saved by His grace.
Ephesians 2:8
"For by grace are ye saved through faith; and that not of yourselves: it is the gift of God:"

Through faith, we inherit God's promises.
Hebrews 6:11-12
"And we desire that every one of you do shew the same diligence to the full assurance of hope unto the end: That ye be not slothful, but followers of them who through faith and patience inherit the promises."

Through faith, we can see God do the impossible.
Hebrews 11:11
"Through faith also Sara herself received strength to conceive seed, and was delivered of a child when she was past age, because she judged him faithful who had promised."

We must believe to receive, and we can only believe through faith in God's ability to provide. **All things are possible, if only we would place our faith in Him!**

Matthew 19:26
"...but with God all things are possible."

Bible Reading
Isaiah 56-57 | John 6 | Psalm 71

Purpose & Prayer.

Daniel 1:8

"But Daniel purposed in his heart that he would not defile himself with the portion of the king's meat, nor with the wine which he drank: therefore he requested of the prince of the eunuchs that he might not defile himself."

Daniel was a man of Purpose. Regardless of the consequences, he refused to compromise what the Lord had told him to do. May we be as willing to obey the Lord's commands in spite of pressure of the world around us to go against them. Perhaps the Lord has been working in your heart about something He has in mind for you to do. **What will you purpose in your heart to do for the Lord?**

Daniel pointed people to God, for he knew that only He could help them. Many people today point to themselves instead of the God in Whom they say they serve. In Matthew 6, we read that they have their reward only here on earth, but those who do not seek to glory in themselves have a reward in Heaven. **Where will you choose to receive your reward?**

Daniel 9:17-19

"Now therefore, O our God, hear the prayer of thy servant, and his supplications, and cause thy face to shine upon thy sanctuary that is desolate, for the Lord's sake. O my God, incline thine ear, and hear; open thine eyes, and behold our desolations, and the city which is called by thy name: for we do not present our supplications before thee for our righteousnesses, but for thy great mercies. O Lord, hear; O Lord, forgive; O Lord, hearken and do; defer not, for thine own sake, O my God: for thy city and thy people are called by thy name."

Daniel was a man of Prayer. He faithfully prayed unto the Lord, his God. He confessed. He exalted the Name of the Lord. He was persistent in his prayers, and the Lord blessed him for his efforts. He prayed because he knew he had a purpose to fulfill...to glorify and honor the Lord.

We cannot fulfill our purpose for the Lord without prayerfully seeking Him.

What are you purposefully praying about today?

Bible Reading
Isaiah 58-59 | John 7 | Psalm 72

Person To Person.

Acts 20:20-21
*"And how I kept back nothing that was profitable unto you,
but have shewed you, and have taught you publickly, and from house to
house, Testifying both to the Jews, and also to the Greeks, repentance
toward God, and faith toward our Lord Jesus Christ."*

The Apostle Paul preached not only publicly to the multitudes, but also from person to person. He traveled from house to house with a soul winning partner. The Scriptures teach us that Jesus sent the disciples out in pairs to reach the people, person to person.

Mark 6:7
*"And he called unto him the twelve,
and began to send them forth by two and two…"*

Paul followed the example set by his Saviour. Most of those who were saved under the ministry of Jesus Christ, as recorded in the Gospels, were won person to person.

Nicodemus – John 3:1-21
Philip – John 1:43
Bartimaeus – Mark 10:46-52
Zacchaeus – Luke 19:1-10
The Thief on the Cross – Luke 23:39-43

Soul winning must be a personal effort.
We must go forth with urgency to reach them, person to person. We must be persistent in our effort to win the lost. Revisiting those we have talked to before must not be neglected in our outreach.

Acts 5:42
*"And daily in the temple, and in every house,
they ceased not to teach and preach Jesus Christ."*

**The Gospel must be preached in our churches,
but it must also be proclaimed personally to those around us.**

Bible Reading
Isaiah 60-61 | John 8 | Psalm 73

Such As I Have.

Acts 3:6
"Then Peter said, Silver and gold have I none; but such as I have give I thee: In the name of Jesus Christ of Nazareth rise up and walk."

Peter did not have silver or gold, but he knew the One that had power to heal the lame man. His healing must have meant so much more to him than silver or gold. There was no power in Peter to heal the man, but he spoke in the power of the Name of Jesus Christ.

We may not have much money or material goods, but *"such as I have"*. Like Peter, we have no power within ourselves to heal or save anyone…but we know the One Who can. We too can speak the Name of Jesus Christ and tell of what He did for us.

If you have Jesus, you can give Jesus.
When we give Jesus, we do not lose anything, but we give everything.

If we had the cure for cancer, we would surely give it to those in need. If we had the ability to defeat terrorism, we would step up and fight. If we had the solution to for our friend's problem, we would not wait to solve it.

Every cure, ability, or solution that someone is seeking can be found by placing faith in Jesus Christ.

He is the Answer, yet we tend to hide our faith in Him.

"…such as I have give I thee…"
Who have you told about Jesus today?

Bible Reading
Isaiah 62-63 | John 9 | Psalm 74

Desired Criticism.

Luke 15:1-2
*"Then drew near unto him all the publicans and sinners for to hear him.
And the Pharisees and scribes murmured, saying,
This man receiveth sinners, and eateth with them."*

It was nothing new to have the Pharisees and scribes murmuring. **The more people that drew near to Jesus, the more the onlookers complained.** Jesus was used to it, and perhaps so are you. When we seek to do something for the Lord, regardless of how or what we do, there will be people who complain and murmur. Sometimes because they are jealous, sometimes because they are content right where they are, and sometimes just because its their nature.

Jesus did not let their criticism stop Him, and neither should we.

This time, the cause of the complaints was due to the type of people that Jesus was reaching…publicans and sinners. What the Pharisees and scribes failed to remember was that these were the people He came to save.

Luke 5:31-32
*"And Jesus answering said unto them, They that are whole
need not a physician; but they that are sick.
I came not to call the righteous, but sinners to repentance."*

Could it be said of us that we receive sinners? Oh, may we be found guilty! This is the type of criticism we should desire to receive. **To be criticized the same way our Saviour was is nothing but a compliment.**

Luke 5:30
*"But their scribes and Pharisees murmured against his disciples, saying,
Why do ye eat and drink with publicans and sinners?"*

Jesus sat down with them to show His love for them, so that they might see their need for Him. May we remember the example that our Saviour set for us. We can love the sinner while still being separated from their sin.

Have you been criticized for showing people their need for Jesus?

Bible Reading
Isaiah 64-66 | John 10 | Psalm 75

Direction & Correction.

Jeremiah 10:23-24
"O LORD, I know that the way of man is not in himself: it is not in man that walketh to direct his steps. O LORD, correct me, but with judgment; not in thine anger, lest thou bring me to nothing. "

Jeremiah, the weeping prophet, knew that there was nothing in him that could direct his steps down the right path.

He wept for God's direction.
"O LORD, I know that the way of man is not in himself..."

He wept for God's correction.
"O LORD, correct me..."

We cannot know which way to take through our own wisdom.
When did we last weep for God's direction and correction?

Proverbs 16:1-2
"The preparations of the heart in man, and the answer of the tongue, is from the LORD. All the ways of a man are clean in his own eyes; but the LORD weigheth the spirits."

Proverbs 16:9
"A man's heart deviseth his way: but the LORD directeth his steps."

Proverbs 21:2
"Every way of a man is right in his own eyes: but the LORD pondereth the hearts."

We may appear to be on the right path through our own eyes, but the Lord knows our heart. Jeremiah confessed, *"The heart is deceitful above all things, and desperately wicked".* Should we rely on our heart and our own wisdom to direct our steps?

Sometimes we need God's correction before we receive His direction.
Determine today to seek the Lord for both His direction & correction.

Bible Reading

Happiness.

Proverbs 16:20
*"He that handleth a matter wisely shall find good:
and whoso trusteth in the LORD, happy is he."*

True happiness is only found by trusting in the LORD.

Psalm 2:12
*"Kiss the Son, lest he be angry, and ye perish from the way, when his wrath
is kindled but a little. Blessed are all they that put their trust in him."*

Psalm 34:8
*"O taste and see that the LORD is good:
blessed is the man that trusteth in him."*

To trust in the Lord is to wait on Him.
There is grace and mercy in waiting and trusting.

Isaiah 30:18
*"And therefore will the LORD wait, that he may be gracious unto you, and
therefore will he be exalted, that he may have mercy upon you: for the
LORD is a God of judgment: blessed are all they that wait for him."*

To trust in the Lord is to hope in Him.

Jeremiah 17:7
*"Blessed is the man that trusteth in the LORD,
and whose hope the LORD is."*

Psalm 146:5
*"Happy is he that hath the God of Jacob for his help,
whose hope is in the LORD his God:"*

**May we seek today to wait and hope in the Lord
and trust that He does all things well,
for then we will find true happiness.**

Bible Reading
Jeremiah 3-4 | John 12 | Psalm 77

Humility.

James 4:10
"Humble yourselves in the sight of the Lord, and he shall lift you up."

Humility is not thinking less of ourselves, but rather thinking of ourselves less. We often get this backward. When we intentionally think less of ourselves to call ourselves humble, we are sadly mistaken. To call ourselves humble is very prideful indeed.

James 4:6
"But he giveth more grace. Wherefore he saith, God resisteth the proud, but giveth grace unto the humble."

1 Peter 5:5-7
"Likewise, ye younger, submit yourselves unto the elder. Yea, all of you be subject one to another, and be clothed with humility: for God resisteth the proud, and giveth grace to the humble. Humble yourselves therefore under the mighty hand of God, that he may exalt you in due time: Casting all your care upon him; for he careth for you."

The first mention of the word *"humble"* is found in Exodus. Just as God had given these words for Moses and Aaron to speak unto Pharoah that day, He also gave them to Moses to pen down for us today.

Exodus 10:3
*"And Moses and Aaron came in unto Pharaoh, and said unto him, Thus saith the LORD God of the Hebrews, **How long wilt thou refuse to humble thyself before me?** let my people go, that they may serve me."*

**How long will we refuse to humble ourselves
before a thrice-holy God?**

If we want God to dwell with us, **we must humble ourselves.**
Isaiah 57:15
If we want to be exalted, **we must humble ourselves.**
Matthew 23:12
If we want to receive more grace, **we must humble ourselves.**
James 4:6
If we want to be more like Jesus, **we must humble ourselves.**
Philippians 2:8

Bible Reading
Jeremiah 5-6 | John 13 | Psalm 78 | 297

Noticeable.

Acts 4:13
"Now when they saw the boldness of Peter and John, and perceived that they were unlearned and ignorant men, they marvelled; and they took knowledge of them, that they had been with Jesus."

They were thought to be unlearned and ignorant men,
but that is exactly the kind of people that God specializes in using.

1 Corinthians 1:26-29
"For ye see your calling, brethren, how that not many wise men after the flesh, not many mighty, not many noble, are called: But God hath chosen the foolish things of the world to confound the wise; and God hath chosen the weak things of the world to confound the things which are mighty; And base things of the world, and things which are despised, hath God chosen, yea, and things which are not, to bring to nought things that are: That no flesh should glory in his presence."

It was noticeable to the people that Peter and John had been with Jesus. Their boldness allowed others to see Jesus in them. Can the same thing be said of us? Can people tell that we have spent time in His presence?

It's a humbling thought, if we are truthful. Do we live our lives in such a way that those around us cannot refute what Christ has done in us?

May we be noticeable Christians making Him known!

Acts 4:10
"Be it known unto you all, and to all the people of Israel, that by the name of Jesus Christ of Nazareth, whom ye crucified, whom God raised from the dead, even by him doth this man stand here before you whole."

They could not deny that a noticeable miracle had taken place!

If we are saved by the Blood of Jesus Christ, a miracle has also taken place in our lives, just as it did in the life of the healed man that day. **God desires to make us noticeable Christians so that others will see His Light shine through us!**

Bible Reading
Jeremiah 7-8 | John 14 | Psalm 79

In Secret.

Matthew 6:6
"But thou, when thou prayest, enter into thy closet, and when thou hast shut thy door, pray to thy Father which is in secret; and thy Father which seeth in secret shall reward thee openly."

We can only be noticeable Christians if we spend time with our Saviour in secret. Getting alone with God is not limited to a specific place or time. Our closet can be anywhere and anytime we set aside to come before Him. **In His presence we must humble ourselves before Him** and examine our hearts of any sin in our lives. Then, we can commune with Him. To pray in secret, we must take the time to set ourselves apart. He meets with us where two or three are gathered, but oh the sweetness of a one-on-one meeting with the Father. **Our time with Him is to be in secret.** When we pray so that others may hear us, we have received our reward by their consideration. To boast of the time spent or matter discussed is allowing pride to steal our reward.

The best answers to prayer are those that no one but Him knew you asked. He cares for the little minute details of our lives just as much as the big monumental moments.

We are left with many examples of those that prayed in secret and God's blessings upon their life because of their devotion to Him.
Jacob prayed in secret. Genesis 32:24-29
Elisha prayed in secret. 2 Kings 4:33
Peter prayed in secret. Acts 10:9
Jesus prayed in secret. Matthew 14:23; 26:36-39

George Müller is known for his prayer life. He built many orphanages with little to no resources. He acknowledged that it was not his power that built them, but that of the Almighty God in which he served. Müller never let the needs of his ministry known to anyone except God in prayer. In his journals, he recorded over fifty thousand specific answers to prayer throughout the years of his ministry. This man was full of faith and devout in his time of prayer. If God can openly reward Müller's faith that was prayed in secret, He can do the same for us! We serve the same God that he did, and He never changes. **What God did for George Müller, He wants to do for us, if only we will have the faith to ask Him in secret.** Shut the door to your surroundings today, and enter into His presence. What He sees in secret, He promises to reward us openly.

Bible Reading
Jeremiah 9-10 | John 15 | Psalm 80

Come To Jesus.

John 7:37
*"In the last day, that great day of the feast, Jesus stood and cried,
saying, If any man thirst, let him come unto me, and drink."*

Come to Jesus For Salvation
The water that our body needs will not quench our thirst forever. Just as Jesus explained to the woman at the well that day, He is the Living Water.

John 4:14
"But whosoever drinketh of the water that I shall give him shall never thirst; but the water that I shall give him shall be in him a well of water springing up into everlasting life."

Come to Jesus For Courage
When Peter asked the Lord *"bid me come unto thee"* he did not ask to walk on the water; he simply asked to come to Him. Once Christ told him to come, he had the courage to step out of the boat.

Matthew 14:29
"And he said, Come. And when Peter was come down out of the ship, he walked on the water, to go to Jesus."

Come to Jesus for Rest
Even in serving the Lord, we must take the time to rest. Whether we are physically, emotionally, or even spiritually tired…Jesus can give us rest if we will simply come to Him.

Matthew 11:28-29
"Come unto me, all ye that labour and are heavy laden, and I will give you rest. Take my yoke upon you, and learn of me; for I am meek and lowly in heart: and ye shall find rest unto your souls."

What do you need to come to Jesus for today?
Whatever your need, He is the Answer.

Bible Reading
Jeremiah 11-12 | John 16 | Psalm 81

He Thinks About You.

Psalm 40:17
*"But I am poor and needy; yet the Lord thinketh upon me:
thou art my help and my deliverer; make no tarrying, O my God."*

David acknowledged that he was in need of the Lord's help. He did not think much of himself, but God doesn't look on the outward appearance, He looks on the heart. He even called David *"a man after his own heart".*

Regardless of the situation or state you are currently in, the Lord thinks about you! He wants to help and deliver us, if only we will come to Him. **He not only thinks about you, the Bible says that many are His thoughts about us!**

Psalm 40:5
"Many, O LORD my God, are thy wonderful works which thou hast done, and thy thoughts which are to us-ward: they cannot be reckoned up in order unto thee: if I would declare and speak of them, they are more than can be numbered."

How did David know that *"the Lord thinketh upon me"*? God had provided for David time and time again. **Take the time today to reflect on all the different ways that the Lord has provided for you.** Physical, emotional, financial, spiritual needs…every time one of your needs are met, the Lord has thought about you.

Psalm 139:17
"How precious also are thy thoughts unto me, O God! how great is the sum of them!"

You may feel unimportant, but **He thinks about you.**
You may think that no one cares, but **He cares for you.**

Jeremiah 29:11
"For I know the thoughts that I think toward you, saith the LORD, thoughts of peace, and not of evil, to give you an expected end."

Bible Reading
Jeremiah 13-14 | John 17 | Psalm 82 | 301

Perfect Peace.

Isaiah 26:3
"Thou wilt keep him in perfect peace,
whose mind is stayed on thee:
because he trusteth in thee."

No matter how the storm rages around you or how the struggle seems to weigh you down, you can have peace today by focusing your mind on the Lord. Not just any peace, perfect peace. Peace that this world cannot give.

His perfect peace surrounds us like a garrison around a city.
He wants to protect us from anything that would do us harm.

"Those that trust in God must have their minds stayed upon him, must trust him at all times, under all events, must firmly and faithfully adhere to Him, with an entire satisfaction in Him; and such as do so, God will keep in perpetual peace, and that peace shall keep them."
Matthew Henry

How do we obtain this perfect peace?
Only by fixing our heart and mind upon Him
can we have perfect peace.

To have our minds stayed on Him refers to leaning on Him, resting in Him, refreshing and sustaining ourselves in Him.
Lean on His everlasting arms.
Rest in His sufficient grace.
Find refreshing through Him as the Fountain of living water.
Find sustenance through Him as the Bread of Life.

Philippians 4:7
"And the peace of God, which passeth all understanding,
shall keep your hearts and minds through Christ Jesus."

No peace can be found outside of Jesus.

Bible Reading
Jeremiah 15-16 | John 18 | Psalm 83

Everlasting Strength.

Isaiah 26:4
*"Trust ye in the LORD for ever:
for in the LORD JEHOVAH is everlasting strength:"*

We can trust in the Lord to supply that perfect peace when we fix our hearts and minds upon Him. **If we trust in Him, we shall not only find that peace but we shall also receive strength, everlasting strength.**

Because of the flesh, our strength runs out quickly. His strength comes from the Rock of Ages, which Jesus said He would build His church upon and the gates of hell shall not prevail against it. He is the LORD JEHOVAH, which was, which is, and which is to come. He never changes, and His strength never runs out.

We find everlasting strength when we trust in Him.

Psalm 18:2
*"The LORD is my rock, and my fortress, and my deliverer;
my God, my strength, in whom I will trust; my buckler,
and the horn of my salvation, and my high tower."*

We must exchange our strength for His everlasting strength.

2 Corinthians 12:9-10
"And he said unto me, My grace is sufficient for thee: for my strength is made perfect in weakness. Most gladly therefore will I rather glory in my infirmities, that the power of Christ may rest upon me. Therefore I take pleasure in infirmities, in reproaches, in necessities, in persecutions, in distresses for Christ's sake: for when I am weak, then am I strong."

Choose today to trust Him.
Choose today to find everlasting strength in Him.

Bible Reading
Jeremiah 17-18 | John 19 | Psalm 84

Acts 4:10
"Be it known unto you all, and to all the people of Israel, that by the name of Jesus Christ of Nazareth, whom ye crucified, whom God raised from the dead, even by him doth this man stand here before you whole."

When asked how all these things were taking place, Peter proclaimed that it was only by the Name of Jesus Christ. **He took none of the credit.** He did not want the glory or honor, for he knew that it did not belong to him.

Acts 4:7
"...By what power, or by what name, have ye done this?"
Peter preached to the people when he was called upon. He was ready to give an answer. He was not only ready, he was full of the Holy Ghost and allowed Him to speak through him.

He made it known it was by the Saviour. *"by the name of Jesus Christ"*
He made it known it His strength. *"by him doth this man stand here"*
He made it known that his stature was restored. *"before you whole"*

Before this questioning and proclaiming happened, Peter and John were cast into a holding place. They were in prison. It was not comfortable. It was inconvenient, but God had placed them there. **They suffered persecution, but there was a purpose for it.**

Acts 4:4
"Howbeit many of them which heard the word believed; and the number of the men was about five thousand."

Many not only heard the Word, but they believed the Word. They could have quit because of the opposition, but those five thousand would not have heard or believed. **God used their sufferings for His glory and the furtherance of the Gospel.** After the persecution, they were questioned. Peter rose to his feet, and made it known that all the glory belonged to Jesus Christ. Whether it was many or any that heard the Word and believed, it was worth the maltreatment.

When we suffer for Christ's sake there is a purpose for it. It is worth our discomfort and inconvenience if many or any are reached with the Gospel.

Let us make it known to those around us that it is all because of Him!

Bible Reading
Jeremiah 19-20 | John 20 | Psalm 85

Backward.

Jeremiah 7:23-24
*"But this thing commanded I them, saying, Obey my voice,
and I will be your God, and ye shall be my people: and walk ye in all the
ways that I have commanded you, that it may be well unto you. But they
hearkened not, nor inclined their ear, but walked in the counsels and in the
imagination of their evil heart, and went backward, and not forward."*

They were warned.
Jeremiah 7:3
*"Thus saith the LORD of hosts, the God of Israel, Amend your ways and
your doings, and I will cause you to dwell in this place."*

They were told to obey & walk in His ways.
"Obey my voice"
"walk ye in all the ways that I have commanded you"

They went backward because they did not listen and disobeyed.
*"But they harkened not, nor inclined their ear,
but walked in the counsels and in the imagination of their evil heart,
and went backward, and not forward."*

**We have been warned of how we must turn from our sinful ways
by repenting and believing on Jesus by faith.**
Mark 1:15
*"And saying, The time is fulfilled, and the kingdom of God is at hand:
repent ye, and believe the gospel."*

We have also been commanded to obey and walk in the way of the Lord.
Deuteronomy 13:4
*"Ye shall walk after the LORD your God, and fear him,
and keep his commandments, and obey his voice,
and ye shall serve him, and cleave unto him."*

If we do not listen to God by reading His Word or ask Him to help us, we will also go backward. On our own, we will always go in the opposite direction from where He would have us to be. **Neglecting prayer and Bible study will cause us to go backward.** If we are not striving to daily spend time with the Lord, we are not walking forward, we are not even standing still…we are walking backwards. Progress and growth cannot happen if we are not walking with Him. **Which way are you walking today?**

Bible Reading
Jeremiah 21-22 | John 21 | Psalm 86 | 305

A God Given Task.

Nehemiah 2:12
"And I arose in the night, I and some few men with me; neither told I any man what my God had put in my heart to do at Jerusalem: neither was there any beast with me, save the beast that I rode upon."

The wall of Jerusalem was broken down. When Nehemiah received the news, he was broken as he *"sat down and wept and mourned"*. His burden drove him to fast and pray to the God of Heaven. **Nehemiah put action to his burden.** He set out to do something about it, yet he told no other man. He brought his burden to the Lord as asked for His help. **God gave him to desire to do something.** A God-given task.

Mark 9:29
"And he said unto them, This kind can come forth by nothing, but by prayer and fasting."

What has God put on your heart for you to do for Him? Maybe you do not have something specific right now, but you desire to serve…ask the Lord to direct your heart towards what He would have you to do.

Ask the Lord to lead you.
Psalm 40:1-2
"I waited patiently for the LORD; and he inclined unto me, and heard my cry. He brought me up also out of an horrible pit, out of the miry clay, and set my feet upon a rock, and established my goings."

Allow Him to guide you.
Psalm 32:8
"I will instruct thee and teach thee in the way which thou shalt go: I will guide thee with mine eye."

After the command is clear…trust Him.
Psalm 37:5
"Commit thy way unto the LORD; trust also in him; and he shall bring it to pass."

Seek counsel from both the Word of God and the people of God.
Proverbs 11:14
"Where no counsel is, the people fall: but in the multitude of counsellors there is safety."

Bible Reading
Jeremiah 23-24 | Philippians 1 | Psalm 87

Opposition.

Nehemiah 2:19
"But when Sanballat the Horonite, and Tobiah the servant, the Ammonite, and Geshem the Arabian, heard it, they laughed us to scorn, and despised us, and said, What is this thing that ye do? will ye rebel against the king?"

The Plea - Nehemiah 2:17
As Nehemiah shared his burden with the people, he pleaded with them to help rebuild the wall. When we share our God given vision, He will send people to help us accomplish it.

The Preparation - Nehemiah 2:18
There were people who wanted to help with the purpose of the task. They did not go into it unprepared; they strengthened their hands for the work ahead. We must strengthen our hands and our hearts for the work God has given us to do.

The Pessimists - Nehemiah 2:19
Nehemiah ran into opposition as word began to spread about their God given task. Sanballat and his friends laughed at and despised the workers. They even asked a sarcastic question that was filled with scorn and disdain.

When we set out to do something for the Lord, there will be opposition. Nehemiah and his crew did not let it stop them, and neither should we. Oftentimes, the opposition comes from those we least expect. The devil knows that the people we are closest to have the most influence over us, and if he can get them to question our God-given task, he most certainly will.

The Response - Nehemiah 2:20
"Then answered I them, and said unto them, The God of heaven, he will prosper us; therefore we his servants will arise and build: but ye have no portion, nor right, nor memorial, in Jerusalem."
The first four words of Nehemiah's answer are exactly how we should respond to our opposition…*"The God of heaven"*. He did not respond with "I" or "we", because he knew that the task was not about them…it was all about Him. **If God gives us a task to complete for Him, we must not let anything stop us.**

Acts 5:39
"But if it be of God, ye cannot overthrow it; lest haply ye be found even to fight against God."

Bible Reading
Jeremiah 25-26 | Philippians 2 | Psalm 88 | 307

Distractions.

James 4:7
*"Submit yourselves therefore to God.
Resist the devil, and he will flee from you."*

We can only be effective in our service to the Lord, and ministering to others if our attention is on the right things. So often we waste our time on things that do not have any eternal value. When this happens we have allowed the devil to distract us from what God would have us to do.

1 Peter 5:8-9
*"Be sober, be vigilant; because your adversary the devil, as a roaring lion, walketh about, seeking whom he may devour:
Whom resist stedfast in the faith, knowing that the same afflictions are accomplished in your brethren that are in the world."*

Our adversary has a plan, and in order to defeat him we must also have a plan. We must develop a strategy against distractions, so that we use wisely the time God has given us.

Resist the devil.
When we resist him, he will go elsewhere. What is the best way to resist him? *"Submit yourselves therefore to God."*

Be aware of his devices.
He will use people, places and things to distract us. He will even use our thoughts against us, if we let him. Do not allow him to get the victory! **Be strong in the Lord and fight of his distractions by keeping your heart and mind fixed on Jesus.**

2 Corinthians 2:11
*"Lest Satan should get an advantage of us:
for we are not ignorant of his devices."*

Just focus on the important things.
**Do not allow the devil to distract you
from your God given purpose.**

Bible Reading
Jeremiah 27-28 | Philippians 3 | Psalm 89

Exchange.

Matthew 26:41-42
*"Watch and pray, that ye enter not into temptation:
the spirit indeed is willing, but the flesh is weak. He went away again the
second time, and prayed, saying, O my Father, if this cup may not pass
away from me, except I drink it, thy will be done."*

The moment that Jesus had come to earth for was approaching. His spirit
was willing to endure the horrific scourging and crucifixion that was about
to take place. He knew that He was the only One Who could pay the debt
for the sins of the world. **His spirit was willing, but His flesh was weak.** He
was God in the flesh, which meant He dealt with pain and exhaustion, just
as we do. The strength of His flesh was tiring, it wanted to give up and give
in. **Instead, Jesus Christ showed us the importance of exchanging our will
for the will of His Father.**

When we exchange our will for His, we receive strength.
Luke 22:41-43
*"And he was withdrawn from them about a stone's cast, and kneeled down,
and prayed, Saying, Father, if thou be willing, remove this cup from me:
nevertheless not my will, but thine, be done. And there appeared an angel
unto him from heaven, strengthening him."*

When we exchange our will for His, we can reach souls for Him.
Luke 5:4-6
*"Now when he had left speaking, he said unto Simon, Launch out into the
deep, and let down your nets for a draught. And Simon answering said
unto him, Master, we have toiled all the night, and have taken nothing:
nevertheless at thy word I will let down the net. And when they had this
done, they inclosed a great multitude of fishes: and their net brake."*

**We may not understand why things are happening the way they are,
because His thoughts are not our thoughts.**
Isaiah 55:8-9
*"For my thoughts are not your thoughts, neither are your ways my ways,
saith the LORD. For as the heavens are higher than the earth, so are my
ways higher than your ways, and my thoughts than your thoughts."*

We can trust Him today as exchange our will for His.

Bible Reading
Jeremiah 29-30 | Philippians 4 | Psalm 90 | 309

The Guardian.

Psalm 91:9-11
"Because thou hast made the LORD, which is my refuge, even the most High, thy habitation; There shall no evil befall thee, neither shall any plague come nigh thy dwelling. For he shall give his angels charge over thee, to keep thee in all thy ways."

With Christ as our Guardian, we have a refuge like no other. We must take the time to dwell in His presence; for it is there that we find safety, shelter, and salvation.

We can find safety in the shadow of His Wings.
Psalm 91:1-2
"He that dwelleth in the secret place of the most High shall abide under the shadow of the Almighty. I will say of the LORD, He is my refuge and my fortress: my God; in him will I trust."

We can seek shelter under His Wings.
Psalm 91:4
"He shall cover thee with his feathers, and under his wings shalt thou trust: his truth shall be thy shield and buckler."

We can obtain salvation under His wings.
Psalm 91:14-16
"Because he hath set his love upon me, therefore will I deliver him: I will set him on high, because he hath known my name. He shall call upon me, and I will answer him: I will be with him in trouble; I will deliver him, and honour him. With long life will I satisfy him, and shew him my salvation."

The Lord will sustain us, provide for us, protect us, and deliver us, for He is our Guardian.

"He that by faith chooses God for his Guardian
shall find in Him all that which he needs or can desire."
Matthew Henry

Choose to make the Lord your Guardian today.

Bible Reading
Jeremiah 31-32 | Colossians 1 | Psalm 91

He Knows Your Name.

Isaiah 45:3-4
*"And I will give thee the treasures of darkness,
and hidden riches of secret places, that thou mayest know that I, the LORD,
which call thee by thy name, am the God of Israel. For Jacob my servant's
sake, and Israel mine elect, I have even called thee by thy name:
I have surnamed thee, though thou hast not known me."*

As God called Cyrus by name, He did so for the Jews to know that He called their earthly redeemer by name. Cyrus would lead them out of captivity as their redeemer, as a type of Jesus as our Redeemer.

Throughout the Scriptures, we see the words that Jesus Christ spoke pinned in red. He rarely called people by their name; however, when He did there is something personal we can learn from each of them He did call by name.

Simon Peter – Matthew 16:17-18
He can use anyone to further the Gospel.

Martha - Luke 10:41
He sees our service to Him.

Mary – Luke 10:42
He wants us to choose to sit at His feet.

Zacchaeus - Luke 19:5
He sees anyone willing to come to Him.

Lazarus - John 11:43
He can work a miracle in anyone's life.

Thomas - John 20:29
He cares for those that have doubt.

Saul/Paul - Acts 9
He can change anyone.

Could you imagine Jesus Christ, God in the flesh, speaking your name? Although your name may not be pinned within the pages of Scripture, He knows your name just as well as those He uttered. You are included in Scripture as that *"whosoever"* that He spoke of so often.

Take comfort today that He knows your name.

Bible Reading
Jeremiah 33-34 | Colossians 2 | Psalm 92 | 311

What The Lord Hates.

Proverbs 6:16-19
"These six things doth the LORD hate: yea, seven are an abomination unto him: A proud look, a lying tongue, and hands that shed innocent blood, An heart that deviseth wicked imaginations, feet that be swift in running to mischief, A false witness that speaketh lies, and he that soweth discord among brethren."

It is no coincidence that all these things that the Lord hates revolve around our flesh, senses, and desires. These are what the devil seeks to control about us. He seeks to destroy our testimony in any way he can, and at every opportunity.

"A proud look"
Oh, be careful little eyes what you see!
Do we look prideful to others?

"a lying tongue"
Oh, be careful little mouth what you say!
Are we truthful? Can we be trusted to keep our mouth shut?

"and hands that shed innocent blood"
Oh, be careful little hands what you do!
Do we slay someone who is not guilty?

"An heart that deviseth wicked imaginations"
Oh, be careful little heart what you feel!
Does our heart try to convince us of something other than the truth?

"feet that be swift in running to mischief"
Oh, be careful little feet where you go!
What/Who is directing our steps? Where are we running to?

"A false witness that speaketh lies"
Oh, be careful little mouth what you say!
Do we speak that which is not truthful?

"and he that soweth discord among brethren."
God more than hate this, it is an abomination unto Him. We reap what we sow. Churches and Christians have been destroyed because of the discord sown by others. May we build up those around us, instead of tearing them down.

Remember today those things which the Lord hates, and avoid them. God will bless our efforts when we do not allow ourselves to be controlled by our flesh and our pride.

Bible Reading
Jeremiah 35-36 | Colossians 3 | Psalm 93

The Work Of Our Hands.

Acts 7:41
"And they made a calf in those days, and offered sacrifice unto the idol, and rejoiced in the works of their own hands."

They Made. They Offered. They Rejoiced.
While doing so, they had turned their backs on the God of Heaven that had brought them out of bondage, across the Red Sea on dry land, and provided for them in the wilderness. They deceived Aaron, and demanded that he make them gods to go before them while Moses was on Mount Sinai communing with the Lord.

Isaiah 2:8
"Their land also is full of idols; they worship the work of their own hands, that which their own fingers have made:"

How often do we rejoice in the works of our own hands?
This can be described in one word…Pride.

While the preacher is getting his message from God what idol are we worshipping? Our career, our children, our ambition, our character, our ministry, our own wisdom? We make idols out of the things that we want to take credit for, when it was the Lord Who gave them to us in the first place. What would we have if He had not given it?

John 3:16
"For God so loved the world, that he gave his only begotten Son, that whosoever believeth in him should not perish, but have everlasting life."
He gave us everything, including His Son. The works of our hands are merely blessings from Him; yet we often worship the things that we believe we have created or built ourselves. **We steal His glory in worshipping ourselves and our pride.** Without Him, we have nothing. We glory in ourselves, while neglecting to praise Him for His goodness and His blessings in our lives. Shame on us. **We must remember that there are consequences when we allow ourselves to glory in the work of our hands.**

Exodus 32:7 *"have corrupted themselves"*
Exodus 32:8 *"They have turned aside quickly out of the way"*
Exodus 32:9 *"a stiffnecked people"*

Any work of our hands is because He allowed it, and gave us the ability to accomplish it.

The work of our hands is not ours.

Bible Reading
Jeremiah 37-38 | Colossians 4 | Psalm 94

Step Out In Faith.

Matthew 14:28-29
"And Peter answered him and said, Lord, if it be thou, bid me come unto thee on the water. And he said, Come. And when Peter was come down out of the ship, he walked on the water, to go to Jesus."

It takes faith to go to the other side. He sent them away, seemingly alone. **God will sometimes set us apart to allow us to learn to depend on Him.**
Matthew 14:22
"And straightway Jesus constrained his disciples to get into a ship, and to go before him unto the other side, while he sent the multitudes away."

Sometimes God sends us a storm in order for us to step out in faith, but He never sends us into the storm alone. He is always there with us in the middle of the storm, even when we do not see Him.
Matthew 14:24-26
"But the ship was now in the midst of the sea, tossed with waves: for the wind was contrary. And in the fourth watch of the night Jesus went unto them, walking on the sea. And when the disciples saw him walking on the sea, they were troubled, saying, It is a spirit; and they cried out for fear."

Even in the middle of our storm, God will speak to us. **When we follow the Lord's command to step out of our comfort zone, He will allow us to walk on water.** Only when we get our eyes off of Him will we begin to sink, but He is always there waiting for us to call on Him for help.
Matthew 14:28-30
"And Peter answered him and said, Lord, if it be thou, bid me come unto thee on the water. And he said, Come. And when Peter was come down out of the ship, he walked on the water, to go to Jesus. But when he saw the wind boisterous, he was afraid; and beginning to sink, he cried, saying, Lord, save me."

We can learn from Peter's courage to step out in faith. He was the only one that had the faith to even ask to step out of the boat. Only a courageous disciple who trusted that the Master knew what was best for him would ask such a question. It took a lot of faith to even ask for permission. We all know what would have happened if Peter had not asked, and just took it upon himself to jump out of the boat. Jesus could have denied Peter's request, but He had a lesson both for him and us today to learn.

Miracles can happen if we have the courage to step out in faith.

Bible Reading
Jeremiah 39-40 | Galatians 1 | Psalm 95

Great Is His Faithfulness.

Lamentations 3:22-23
*"It is of the LORD's mercies that we are not consumed,
because his compassions fail not. They are new every morning:
great is thy faithfulness."*

What a comfort it is to know that God is Faithful!

We do not need to be consumed by the circumstances that surround us,
because of the Lord's mercies toward us.

**May we remember when we open our eyes to each new day
that God is Faithful.**

1 Corinthians 1:9
*"God is faithful, by whom ye were called unto the fellowship
of his Son Jesus Christ our Lord."*

1 Corinthians 10:13
*"There hath no temptation taken you but such as is common to man:
but God is faithful, who will not suffer you to be tempted above that ye are
able; but will with the temptation also make a way to escape,
that ye may be able to bear it."*

1 Thessalonians 5:24
"Faithful is he that calleth you, who also will do it."

We, like Jeremiah, can say to the Lord *"great is thy faithfulness"*, but can the
Lord say that of us? Does the Lord consider us faithful?

May we strive to be faithful to God because He is Faithful!

Bible Reading
Jeremiah 41-42 | Galatians 2 | Psalm 96 | 315

Great Is His Mercy.

2 Samuel 24:14
*"And David said unto Gad, I am in a great strait:
let us fall now into the hand of the LORD; for his mercies are great:
and let me not fall into the hand of man."*

David had acknowledged his sin, and God allowed David to choose his punishment. He gave him three choices.

2 Samuel 24:12-13
"Go and say unto David, Thus saith the LORD, I offer thee three things; choose thee one of them, that I may do it unto thee. So Gad came to David, and told him, and said unto him, Shall seven years of famine come unto thee in thy land? or wilt thou flee three months before thine enemies, while they pursue thee? or that there be three days' pestilence in thy land? now advise, and see what answer I shall return to him that sent me."

He could have chosen whichever punishment he felt was the easiest for him. **But David, a man after God's own heart, chose to let God choose.** Do we submit ourselves to the Lord in such a way? David allowed even his punishment to be chosen by God.

7 years. 3 months. 3 days. God chose the shortest amount of time showing His great mercy upon David. **His mercy endureth forever!**

Just as God bestowed His great mercy upon David, that same mercy is given to us today. **Through His great mercy we have also been given the choice to choose the punishment for our sin.** We can pay the penalty ourselves in the lake of fire, or choose Jesus and His payment for our sins upon the Cross of Calvary. **The choice is ours:** Heaven or Hell, life or death.

God is not willing that any should perish, but that all should come to repentance. If we choose Him and His will, we will receive eternal life in Heaven with Him. But if we reject Him and His will, we choose Hell as our eternal home.

Great is His mercy!

Bible Reading
Jeremiah 43-44 | Galatians 3 | Psalm 97

Full Of Faith.

Acts 6:8
*"And Stephen, full of faith and power, did great wonders
and miracles among the people."*

Don't keep your faith to yourself. We must take our faith among the people and allow God to do the work in their hearts.

Read through Acts 6 & 7 with this thought in mind – Stephen was a man full of faith. **We need more people that are full of faith, and not afraid to stand up for what they believe in – The Name of Jesus!**

Acts 6:9-10
"Then there arose certain of the synagogue, which is called the synagogue of the Libertines, and Cyrenians, and Alexandrians, and of them of Cilicia and of Asia, disputing with Stephen. And they were not able to resist the wisdom and the spirit by which he spake."

Even when people dispute us as we try to serve, we must keep our eyes on Jesus. The people disputed, stirred, and accused Stephen as they brought him before the council, but he remained silent. It was only when the high priest asked, *"Are these things so?"* that he began to speak.

In comparing Acts 7 with the Hall of Faith in Hebrews 11, we see the order of Stephen's message to the people matches what is pinned in the Chapter of Faith. **Stephen followed the example of faith that had been left by those before him, and now we have Stephen also as an example for us to follow.**

The Lord Jesus stood at the throne, because of Stephen was full of faith.

**Do we have enough faith that Jesus
would feel the need to stand at His throne?**

What a humbling thought.

Bible Reading
Jeremiah 45-46 | Galatians 4 | Psalm 98 | 317

Needful.

Luke 10:38-42

"Now it came to pass, as they went, that he entered into a certain village: and a certain woman named Martha received him into her house. And she had a sister called Mary, which also sat at Jesus' feet, and heard his word. But Martha was cumbered about much serving, and came to him, and said, Lord, dost thou not care that my sister hath left me to serve alone? bid her therefore that she help me. And Jesus answered and said unto her, Martha, Martha, thou art careful and troubled about many things: But one thing is needful: and Mary hath chosen that good part, which shall not be taken away from her."

Jesus Christ loved these two sisters, and their brother Lazarus. He had a special relationship with them. Both women give us a different picture of a type of relationship we can have with Jesus. These sisters were very different, but they had one thing in common, they both loved Jesus and wanted to serve Him.

Martha was a busy woman, *"cumbered about much serving"*. She asked Jesus questions demanding answers, and even gave orders to her Friend, *"bid her therefore that she help me".*

Mary was quiet and patient. Many times in Scripture we find her sitting at Jesus' feet. She anointed His feet with ointment and wiped them with her hair. **Every time she sat near Him, she listened to hear His Word instead of questioning Him.** Both of the sisters came to Him, but with different attitudes and demeanors.

Notice Jesus' response about each of them:
"Martha, Martha, thou are careful and troubled about many things: But one thing is needful: and Mary hath chosen that good part, which shall not be taken away from her."

One thing was needful for both these sisters and for us today. Only one of them chose the needful thing of sitting at Jesus' feet and hearing His Word.

We can only hear Jesus speak when we sit at His feet.

Bible Reading
Jeremiah 47-48 | Galatians 5 | Psalm 99

At His Feet.

John 12:3
*"Then took Mary a pound of ointment of spikenard, very costly,
and anointed the feet of Jesus, and wiped his feet with her hair:
and the house was filled with the odour of the ointment."*

Several times throughout the Scripture we find people at the feet of Jesus Christ. Some in desperation, some in reverence and some in worship, but each knew their need of Him. We can learn from each of these that bowed at His feet. Whether your need is to be healed, provided for, or just for fellowship with Him, **there is a place for you at the feet of Jesus!**

A Place of Healing – The Multitudes – Matthew 15:30
*"And great multitudes came unto him, having with them those that were
lame, blind, dumb, maimed, and many others,
and cast them down at Jesus' feet; and he healed them:"*
**What healing have we or others missed out on
because we neglected to sit at His feet?**

A Place of Honoring & Seeking – Jarius – Luke 8:41
*"And, behold, there came a man named Jairus,
and he was a ruler of the synagogue: and he fell down at Jesus' feet,
and besought him that he would come into his house:"*
**What opportunities to honor and seek Jesus have we missed
because we neglected to sit at His feet?**

A Place of Hearing – Mary & Martha – Luke 10:38-39
*"Now it came to pass, as they went, that he entered into a certain village:
and a certain woman named Martha received him into her house. And she
had a sister called Mary, which also sat at Jesus' feet, and heard his word."*
**What have we not heard from His Word
because we neglected to sit at His feet?**

A Place of Holding & Worship – Mary Magdalene & Mary – Matthew 28:9
*"And as they went to tell his disciples, behold, Jesus met them, saying,
All hail. And they came and held him by the feet, and worshipped him."*
**What worship have we missed out on
because we neglected to sit at His feet?**

We miss out on many things when we neglect to take the time
to sit at the feet of Jesus and spend time in His presence.
Spend time at His feet today.

Bible Reading
Jeremiah 49-50 | Galatians 6 | Psalm 100 | 319

The Lord Is.

Psalm 27:1
*"The LORD is my light and my salvation; whom shall I fear?
the LORD is the strength of my life; of whom shall I be afraid?"*

As we notice these three characteristics of the Lord, we must realize how much we need His light, His salvation and His strength in our lives.
The first mention of *"The Lord is"* is found in Genesis 28:16:
*"And Jacob awaked out of his sleep, and he said,
Surely the LORD is in this place; and I knew it not."*

This reminds us that He will never leave us nor forsake us, regardless if we are aware of His presence or not. Take time today to study these Truths of God's Word of what the Lord is to us.

The Lord is Righteous..Exodus 9:27 & Psalm 145:17
The Lord is my Strength and Song....................Exodus 15:2 & Psalm 118:14
The Lord is Longsuffering.................................Numbers 14:18 & 2 Peter 3:9
The Lord is God..Joshua 22:34
The Lord is Able..2 Chronicles 25:9
The Lord is my Shepherd...Psalm 23:1
The Lord is my Strength and my Shield...............................Psalm 28:7
The Lord is Good..Psalm 34:8 & Nahum 1:7
The Lord is our Defence...Psalm 89:18 & Psalm 94:22
The Lord is Merciful and Gracious.......................................Psalm 103:8
The Lord is Gracious and full of Compassion.......Psalm 111:4 & Psalm 145:8
The Lord is on my side...Psalm 118:6
The Lord is far from the wicked...Proverbs 15:29
The Lord is a God of Judgment...Isaiah 30:18
The Lord is Exalted..Isaiah 33:5
The Lord is our Judge, Lawgiver and King....................................Isaiah 33:22
The Lord is the True God..Jeremiah 10:10
The Lord is my Portion...Lamentations 3:24
The Lord is Risen...Luke 24:34
The Lord is at hand...Philippians 4:5
The Lord is Faithful...2 Thessalonians 3:3
The Lord is My Helper..Hebrews 13:6

Whatever your situation is today...the Lord is exactly what you need.

Bible Reading
Jeremiah 51-52 | Ephesians 1 | Psalm 101

All Things Are Possible.

Matthew 19:26
*"But Jesus beheld them, and said unto them,
With men this is impossible; but with God all things are possible."*

We serve the God Who can do the impossible. When all hope seems lost, we can still have victory with God on our side. **We serve the God Who can accomplish what we cannot even think of as a solution.**

Throughout Scripture we see miracle after miracle that came to pass by the hand of God. **These miracles were pinned so that we may have faith that the same God Who performed them could do the same for us.**

A family preserved by an ark.
A barren woman conceives.
A parting of the sea.
A giant that is defeated.
A peace to the storm.
A fire that does not burnout.
A den of lions that do not bite.
A barrel that does not waste.
A blind man sees.
A lame man walks.
A deaf man hears.
A dumb man speaks.
A dead man lives.
A multitude is fed.
A Saviour rises again.

How much more evidence do we need in order to believe that God can perform a miracle in our life? We need to believe that anything is possible with Him. Sometimes, He chooses to perform the impossible so that we can have the courage to ask and believe again. When God accomplishes the impossible within our lives, we must thank Him for what He has done, and give Him the honor that He alone deserves.

Luke 1:37
"For with God nothing shall be impossible."
There is nothing that God cannot do.

Bible Reading
Lamentations 1-3 | Ephesians 2 | Psalm 102

This Mind.

Philippians 2:5
"Let this mind be in you, which was also in Christ Jesus:"

This is none other than the mind of our Lord and Saviour, Jesus Christ. Paul desired for the Church at Philippi to allow their minds to be like Christ, and so should we. **We are to let the mind of Christ be in us.** Our mindset should seek to be like His. Our thoughts should strive to be like His. How can we seek to have the mind of Christ? By following His example.

Seek no status...*"But made himself of no reputation..."* In a world where status appears to be everything, we should seek no status outside of being found in Christ. He was God in the flesh, yet He sat among the sinners. He was royalty, yet He chose to be born in a manger. There is no respecter of persons with God because Jesus was no respecter of persons.

Seek to be a servant...*"and took upon him the form of a servant"* Those who refuse to serve others have little understanding about Jesus Christ and His purpose. He gave us the Ultimate Example of a Servant by giving His life as a ransom for our sin debt. He took our place so that we might go free and choose to serve those around us.

Seek to be humble...*"And being found in fashion as a man, he humbled himself,"* Christ did not think less of Himself, for He knew He was the Son of God; but He thought about Himself less than anyone ever has. He is our Supreme Example of Humility. He never promoted Himself, but pointed people to God the Father.

Seek to die daily...*"and became obedient unto death, even the death of the cross."* Even Christ had to make Himself willing. *"nevertheless not my will, but thine, be done."* We must die to ourselves, and exchange our will for His.

Hebrews 12:2
"Looking unto Jesus the author and finisher of our faith; who for the joy that was set before him endured the cross, despising the shame, and is set down at the right hand of the throne of God."

Although we will not obtain the mind of Christ until we receive our glorified bodies, we can still seek to be like Him each day of our lives until He calls us home.
"Let this mind be in you..."

Bible Reading
Lamentations 4-5 | Ephesians 3 | Psalm 103

Let Down Your Nets.

Luke 5:4
*"Now when he had left speaking, he said unto Simon,
Launch out into the deep, and let down your nets for a draught."*

Once we have the courage to launch out, the work has only begun. We cannot step out in faith and expect God to just hand us blessings and supply our needs. **We must labour for Him!**

Christ told Simon Peter to *"let down your nets for a draught."* **The nets were not serving their purpose if they stayed in the boat.** In the next verse, we see Peter's partial obedience…*"nevertheless at thy word I will let down the net."* Not only did he complain, he failed to follow Christ's directions. Christ said *"let down your **nets**"*, Peter responded, *"I will let down the **net**."* Peter chose to obey, but not completely. Instead of letting down multiple nets, he chose to only let down one. The result of Peter's partial obedience is a lesson we should all take to heart. **Partial obedience is disobedience.**

They were rewarded for their obedience by receiving a great multitude of fishes; yet because they only partially obeyed their instructions, they had an immediate problem on their hands. Both ships began to sink because they had caught so many fish with only one net. If Peter had followed Christ's specific command, the nets may not have broken, or they might not have lost some of the fish. After seeing what happened by not completely obeying the Lord, Peter saw himself differently.

Luke 5:8
*"When Simon Peter saw it, he fell down at Jesus' knees, saying,
Depart from me; for I am a sinful man, O Lord."*

The lives of Peter, James and John were never the same after they witnessed the event. They were astonished, and became fishers of men.

Luke 5:11
*"And when they had brought their ships to land,
they forsook all, and followed him."*

What would happen if we let down the nets of our lives?
We would be astonished at what Christ would allow us to see. We sing the lyrics to "I Surrender All", but do we really mean them in our hearts?

Let down your nets today, and follow Him.

Bible Reading
Ezekiel 1-2 | Ephesians 4 | Psalm 104

Who Will Go?

1 Samuel 26:6
"Then answered David and said to Ahimelech the Hittite, and to Abishai the son of Zeruiah, brother to Joab, saying, Who will go down with me to Saul to the camp? And Abishai said, I will go down with thee."

These six words describe the attitude that every Christian should have in regards to the Will of God and the Great Commission.

"Who will go...?"
"I will go."

Are we willing to utter those words?
With them comes both great responsibility and great rewards.

Mark 16:15
"And he said unto them, Go ye into all the world, and preach the gospel to every creature."

So few answer the call, yet God has not stopped calling. Many have stopped listening. **In order to hear God's call, we must first stop and listen.**

Isaiah 6:8
"Also I heard the voice of the Lord, saying, Whom shall I send, and who will go for us? Then said I, Here am I; send me."

Your call may not be into what we often refer to as "full time ministry", but God is calling. Your call may be to the place you work in, the school you attend, or the home you raise your children. **We are all called to serve Him full time.** Regardless of where, God is still calling. Have you answered Him?

Luke 5:4
"Now when he had left speaking, he said unto Simon, Launch out into the deep, and let down your nets for a draught."

Once we have answered the call to what God has for us, we must launch out. **We cannot accomplish the work of God by standing still.** When we launch out by faith, we may find ourselves in deep water, but we must let down our nets.

God is Faithful to protect us and provide for us as we follow His direction.
We must only be willing to answer, *"I will go".*

Bible Reading
Ezekiel 3-4 | Ephesians 5 | Psalm 105

A Willing Heart

Exodus 35:5
"Take ye from among you an offering unto the LORD:
whosoever is of a willing heart, let him bring it, an offering of the LORD;
gold, and silver, and brass,"

Anyone can have a willing heart; but in order for us to be willing, we must first have a giving heart. So often when we hear the word *"offering"* we think of ushers passing a plate throughout the congregation so that the church can pay the bills, the pastor, or help a ministry or missionary.

An *"offering"* is so much more than giving money for a cause.

Exodus 25:1-2
"And the LORD spake unto Moses, saying, Speak unto the children of Israel, that they bring me an offering: of every man that giveth it willingly with his heart ye shall take my offering."

When we give, we also receive. We can give our time, service, prayers, support, praise, worship, and so much more to our Lord. **Every time we give of ourselves willingly, He blesses us and rewards us.**

2 Corinthians 9:7
"Every man according as he purposeth in his heart, so let him give; not grudgingly, or of necessity: for God loveth a cheerful giver."

God desires us to give our hearts cheerfully and willingly.

Giving must come from the heart.
A giving heart gives us a willing heart.

Willing to serve.
Willing to give.
Willing to sacrifice.
Willing to suffer.
Willing to stand.
Willing to be still.
Willing to wait.

Are you willing today?

Bible Reading
Ezekiel 5-6 | Ephesians 6 | Psalm 106

Wrestling.

Genesis 32:24
"And Jacob was left alone;
and there wrestled a man with him until the breaking of the day."

Jacob was left alone. When we are left alone, it is easy to wrestle with our own thoughts and worries, or even burdens of others. We can even begin to wrestle with God when we do not understand why things happen the way they do. Sometimes we can wrestle all evening long, which leads to faithless and sleepless nights.

Genesis 32:25
"And when he saw that he prevailed not against him,
he touched the hollow of his thigh; and the hollow of Jacob's thigh
was out of joint, as he wrestled with him."

Wrestling brings discomfort.
Jacob's thigh was out of joint because of his match with the Man.

Genesis 32:26
"And he said, Let me go, for the day breaketh.
And he said, I will not let thee go, except thou bless me."

Jacob wrestled with Him all night long. Jacob was persistent; he refused to let go until he received something from the Lord. **Giving up is easy, but persistence in our prayer lives pays off.**

Genesis 32:27-28
"And he said unto him, What is thy name? And he said, Jacob. And he said,
Thy name shall be called no more Jacob, but Israel: for as a prince hast
thou power with God and with men, and hast prevailed."

Wrestling will change us. Jacob had his name changed to Israel, the home of God's chosen people. He named the place Peniel, *"or I have seen God face to face, and my life is preserved."*

God may not choose to change our name, but when we wrestle with Him and allow Him to change us, our lives will never be the same. We may get injured along the way, but God makes no mistakes. The pain is for our good and His glory.

Whatever you are wrestling with, give it to the Lord
and allow Him to change the situation as He changes you.

Bibl Reading
Ezekiel 7-8 | Mark 1 | Psalm 107

One Thing.

Psalm 27:4
"One thing have I desired of the LORD, that will I seek after;
that I may dwell in the house of the LORD all the days of my life,
to behold the beauty of the LORD, and to enquire in his temple."

David saw His beauty in the temple.
He understood that delighting in the Lord is the most important thing. He desired to see the beauty of the Lord, and be in His presence in the temple.

Mary chose to sit at His feet.
Luke 10:41-42
"And Jesus answered and said unto her, Martha, Martha, thou art careful
and troubled about many things: But one thing is needful: and Mary hath
chosen that good part, which shall not be taken away from her."

Mary had chosen to sit at the Lord's feet which only made her want to see and hear more. She even washed His feet with her hair to show her servitude to Him.

Paul pressed on.
Philippians 3:13-14
"Brethren, I count not myself to have apprehended:
but this one thing I do, forgetting those things which are behind,
and reaching forth unto those things which are before, I press toward the
mark for the prize of the high calling of God in Christ Jesus."

Paul did not dwell in the past. He wanted to fulfill God's purpose for his life, so he pressed on toward what God had for him.

Make today about one thing.

Bible Reading
Ezekiel 9-10 | Mark 2 | Psalm 108

Look.

Psalm 119:18
"Open thou mine eyes, that I may behold wondrous things out of thy law."

This should be our prayer before we ever read a Word of the Bible. Open your eyes. Help is available to you, if only you are looking in the right direction. There are many places we can look for help.

We can look at ourselves.
Romans 7:18
"For I know that in me (that is, in my flesh,) dwelleth no good thing: for to will is present with me; but how to perform that which is good I find not."

Paul acknowledged that there was nothing about him that was good. Romans also tells us that *"there is none that doeth good, no not one."*

We can look at our surroundings.
Matthew 14:29-30
"And he said, Come. And when Peter was come down out of the ship, he walked on the water, to go to Jesus. But when he saw the wind boisterous, he was afraid; and beginning to sink, he cried, saying, Lord, save me."

God wants to work miracles in our lives. He desires for us to walk upon the waters of the storm around us with our eyes focused on Him. If we allow the wind to get our attention, then like Peter, we will begin to sink.

We can look at our Saviour.
Hebrews 12:2
"Looking unto Jesus the author and finisher of our faith; who for the joy that was set before him endured the cross, despising the shame, and is set down at the right hand of the throne of God."

What better place to look but to the Saviour?
We cannot look on Him physically, so where should we look to see Him?

John 1:1,14
"In the beginning was the Word, and the Word was with God, and the Word was God...And the Word was made flesh, and dwelt among us, (and we beheld his glory, the glory as of the only begotten of the Father,) full of grace and truth."

Jesus Christ is the Word. We can hold the very Word of God in our hands, if only we will take the time to look and read. **When you want to look at Jesus, look at the Word.**

Bible Reading
Ezekiel 11-12 | Mark 3 | Psalm 109

Obtain.

1 Corinthians 9:24
*"Know ye not that they which run in a race run all,
but one receiveth the prize? So run, that ye may obtain."*

Those that run in the Olympics all have the same desire…Gold. They all want to win. There are many runners, but there can only be one winner. We as Christians are to *"run with patience the race that is set before us, Looking unto Jesus…"*

Paul referenced those who competed in athletic events. He also desired to win a prize, but this prize is not limited to only one winner.

We can all seek to obtain.

Philippians 3:14
*"I press toward the mark for the prize
of the high calling of God in Christ Jesus."*

What can we obtain when we come to Jesus?

Hebrews 4:16
"Let us therefore come boldly unto the throne of grace…"

We obtain mercy.
"…that we may obtain mercy…"
Mercy is not getting what we deserve, which is nothing short of everlasting punishment in hell. But God in His mercy and grace made a Way for us to come to Him through His Son, Jesus Christ.

We obtain grace.
"…and find grace…"
Grace is getting something that we do not deserve. Everything that is given to us is by the grace of God. We do not deserve anything outside of paying for our sin debt ourselves.

We obtain help.
"…to help in time of need."
When we come boldly to the throne of grace, we not only find God's mercy and grace, but we also find that the Lord is our Helper. We need not fear what anyone may do to us with the Lord on our side.

Today, run so that you may obtain.

Bible Reading
Ezekiel 13-14 | Mark 4 | Psalm 110

He Knows The Feeling.

Hebrews 4:14-15
*"Seeing then that we have a great high priest,
that is passed into the heavens, Jesus the Son of God,
let us hold fast our profession. For we have not an high priest
which cannot be touched with the feeling of our infirmities;
but was in all points tempted like as we are, yet without sin."*

He knows how we feel, because He experienced our pain. He was touched with the feeling of our infirmities. Every feeling that we feel, Jesus felt. **Those times when we feel like we are alone and no one understands the feeling of what we are going through...we can rest assured that Jesus does.**

Isaiah 53:4-5
*"Surely he hath borne our griefs, and carried our sorrows:
yet we did esteem him stricken, smitten of God, and afflicted.
But he was wounded for our transgressions, he was bruised for
our iniquities: the chastisement of our peace was upon him;
and with his stripes we are healed."*

In the dark of night the devil can begin to convince us that no one has ever dealt with the same set as circumstances, and that no one even cares what we are going through. He is the father of all lies for a reason; there is no truth in him. **Resist the devil as he tells you no one understands...because Jesus does.**

We can not only take comfort in the fact that Jesus knows the feeling of each and every thing that we face now, but also everything we will face in the future. He *"was In all points tempted like as we arc, yct without sin."*

Whatever you feel today...Jesus knows the feeling.

He felt it, but He remained the sinless Lamb of God.
May we strive to be like Him more with each passing day.

Bible Reading
Ezekiel 15-16 | Mark 5 | Psalm 111

The Less Spoken Of.

2 Kings 2:8
*"And Elijah took his mantle, and wrapped it together,
and smote the waters, and they were divided hither and thither,
so that they two went over on dry ground."*

Have you ever thought about the less spoken of miracles throughout the Scripture? Those that are just as miraculous as the well-known miracles, yet rarely referenced. The feeding of the…most would finish that phrase with 5,000 because it is the one to which we most often refer. The parting of the…most would say Red Sea. **The less spoken of miracles offer just as much truth and encouragement as those we hear about regularly.** They lie within the pages of Scripture waiting for us to notice.

The Feeding of the 4,000 - Matthew 15:32-38
There were seven loaves and a few little fishes, yet Christ fed 4,000 and the disciples collected seven baskets after all had eaten. Yes, it was less people with more supplies, but it was still a miracle performed by the hands of Jesus Christ.

The Parting of the Jordan - 2 Kings 2:8-14
It wasn't Moses at the Red Sea, but Elijah and Elisha at the Jordan. Different people and a different river, but a similar miracle. When they had nowhere else to go, they walked across on dry ground. The difference in this passage is that God parted the waters of the same river twice. Elisha asked for a double portion, and God proved His blessing on Elisha's life and ministry by performing the miracle all over again through him.

Do we get so complacent that we forget, or perhaps don't even realize, that each and every miracle is a miracle, and every blessing a blessing? May we avoid missing out on the blessing of the things that God does for us each and every single day.

Big or small, minor or major, every blessing is the same in God's eyes.

The less spoken of miracles can be spoken of more often,
if only we would take the time to realize what God has done for us.

Bible Reading
Ezekiel 17-18 | Mark 6 | Psalm 112

Run To The Rock.

Psalm 61:1-4
*"Hear my cry, O God; attend unto my prayer.
From the end of the earth will I cry unto thee,
when my heart is overwhelmed:
lead me to the rock that is higher than I.
For thou hast been a shelter for me,
and a strong tower from the enemy.
I will abide in thy tabernacle for ever:
I will trust in the covert of thy wings. Selah."*

What should we do when we feel overwhelmed?
Run to the Rock.
"...lead me to the rock that is higher than I..."

Psalm 18:2
*"The LORD is my rock, and my fortress, and my deliverer;
my God, my strength, in whom I will trust; my buckler,
and the horn of my salvation, and my high tower."*

When we are overwhelmed, we tend to forget even the simplest truths.
Our safety, strength, and salvation all comes from the Lord, our Rock.

Psalm 40:1-2
*"I waited patiently for the LORD; and he inclined unto me,
and heard my cry. He brought me up also out of an horrible pit,
out of the miry clay, and set my feet upon a rock,
and established my goings."*

This is not just any other rock or boulder, but the Rock of Ages. **Within this Rock is everlasting strength, and we can trust that He will be there whenever we cry unto Him.**
Isaiah 26:4
*"Trust ye in the LORD for ever:
for in the LORD JEHOVAH is everlasting strength:"*

Run to the Rock today.
When you don't know where to turn, He's there.

Bible Reading
Ezekiel 19-20 | Mark 7 | Psalm 113

Magnify Him.

Psalm 34:3
"O magnify the LORD with me, and let us exalt his name together."

Using a magnifying glass does not change the size of the object that is being viewed; it changes our perception. **As followers of Christ, we must be the magnifying glass through which the world sees our Lord.** We are to lift Him up, so that He can been seen more clearly.

We can magnify Him with rejoicing and love.
Psalm 40:16
"Let all those that seek thee rejoice and be glad in thee:
let such as love thy salvation say continually,
The LORD be magnified."

We can magnify Him with praise and thanksgiving.
Psalm 69:30
"I will praise the name of God with a song,
and will magnify him with thanksgiving."

We can magnify Him with our life and purpose.
Philippians 1:20
"According to my earnest expectation and my hope,
that in nothing I shall be ashamed, but that with all boldness,
as always, so now also Christ shall be magnified in my body,
whether it be by life, or by death."

Magnify Him so that others may see Him.
Let us exalt His Name together today.

Bible Reading
Ezekiel 21-22 | Mark 8 | Psalm 114

Deliverance.

Psalm 34:4
*"I sought the LORD, and he heard me,
and delivered me from all my fears."*

When David prayed, his fears were silenced. Just like him, we can exchange our fears for peace. **When we need delivered from our fears, we must realize there is a process to our deliverance.** We seek him. He hears us, and then He delivers us in His timing.

We cannot be delivered from our fears without Him first hearing our cry; and He cannot hear our plea, if we do not first seek Him for help. It all starts with seeking Him. **There is no deliverance, if we do not do our part of seeking Him.**

There are several examples in this chapter alone that can encourage us to seek the Lord's deliverance from the circumstances and troubles of our lives.

Psalm 34:6
*"This poor man cried, and the LORD heard him,
and saved him out of all his troubles."*

Psalm 34:17
*"The righteous cry, and the LORD heareth,
and delivereth them out of all their troubles."*

His ears are always open to our cries for help. There is no busy signal or need to stand in line and wait. **He is always there.**

Job tells us that our days will be full of trouble as we live for the Lord. We will suffer persecution; but **we can be thankful that though our afflictions are many, the Lord is there to deliver us from every one.**

Psalm 34:19
*"Many are the afflictions of the righteous:
but the LORD delivereth him out of them all."*

Bible Reading
Ezekiel 23-24 | Mark 9 | Psalm 115

Give Him Thanks.

Psalm 107:1
"O give thanks unto the LORD, for he is good:
for his mercy endureth for ever."

This exact verse is pinned five times throughout the Scriptures.
By His grace, we can give Him thanks.

Not just a day of thanks, not just a week of thanks, not just a month of thanks, or even a year…but **a life of thanks is what the Lord desires.**

Hebrews 13:15
"By him therefore let us offer the sacrifice of praise to God continually,
that is, the fruit of our lips giving thanks to his name."

Psalm 34:1
"I will bless the LORD at all times:
his praise shall continually be in my mouth."

Thank Him for what He has done in the past.
Thank Him for what He is doing in the present.
Thank Him for what He is going to do in the future.
Thank Him.

Psalm 92:1
"It is a good thing to give thanks unto the LORD,
and to sing praises unto thy name, O Most High:"

No matter what you face today, give Him thanks.

Bible Reading
Ezekiel 25-26 | Mark 10 | Psalm 116

A Thankful Heart.

Psalm 100
"Make a joyful noise unto the LORD, all ye lands.
Serve the LORD with gladness: come before his presence with singing.
Know ye that the LORD he is God: it is he that hath made us, and not we
ourselves; we are his people, and the sheep of his pasture. Enter into his
gates with thanksgiving, and into his courts with praise: be thankful unto
him, and bless his name. For the LORD is good; his mercy is everlasting;
and his truth endureth to all generations."

In this well-known Psalm we find the recipe for a thankful heart:

"Serve the LORD with gladness..."
There is serving the Lord, and then there is serving Him with gladness. We should be full of joy, not because of who we are, but Who we serve.

"Know ye that the LORD he is God..."
We forget sometimes that we serve the Lord, the Almighty God, the Creator of the universe. In all the chaos of life, we can tend to focus on the things and people around us instead of the One Who created us all.

"Enter into his gates with thanksgiving, and into his courts with praise..."
Thankgiving and praise go hand in hand. One cannot be truly felt without the other. When we thank Him, we praise Him. When we praise Him, we thank Him. Having our hands full of thankgiving and praise is a great way to approach His throne of grace.

"...be thankful unto him, and bless his name."
We can bless the Lord by coming to Him with a thankful heart.

Instead of focusing on being thankful during the Thanksgiving season, make an effort to carry a thankful heart into each day. Why? *"For the LORD is good; his mercy is everlasting; and his truth endureth to all generations."*

A thankful heart rests in the fact that the Lord is Good,
His mercy is everlasting,
and His truth endureth to all generations.

Bible Reading
Ezekiel 27-28 | Mark 11 | Psalm 117

Thankful In Every Thing.

1 Thessalonians 5:18
"In every thing give thanks:
for this is the will of God in Christ Jesus concerning you."

Here we find one of the places throughout Scripture where the will of God for our lives is plainly written and given to us. It is the will of God that we are thankful in every situation. **We may not be thankful for the circumstances, but we can be thankful while we are in them.** While that may seem confusing, it is actually quite simple. When we, or a loved one, receive a diagnosis for an incurable disease, we are not thankful for the situation, but we can be thankful while we are going through it.

God is still in control, and He is working things for our good and His glory. We may go through the fire, but we can come forth as gold. The trial of our faith can be found unto His praise, honor, and glory if only we remain thankful during it.

Job showed us how we can be thankful despite things not going how we had planned, or how we would prefer. Job lost all that he had, yet he remained thankful and God blessed him for it.

Job 1:21-22
"And said, Naked came I out of my mother's womb,
and naked shall I return thither: the LORD gave,
and the LORD hath taken away; blessed be the name of the LORD.
In all this Job sinned not, nor charged God foolishly."

He found himself in trial after trial, yet he never lost his thankful heart. He remained thankful and trusting the One he knew was working things for his good.

Job 13:15
"Though he slay me, yet will I trust in him:
but I will maintain mine own ways before him."

How can we remain thankful in every thing?
Pray about every thing.

Philippians 4:6
"Be careful for nothing; but in every thing by prayer and supplication
with thanksgiving let your requests be made known unto God."

Evaluate your thankfulness today.
Are you thankful in every thing?
Bible Reading
Ezekiel 29-30 | Mark 12 | Psalm 118 | 337

Contentment.

Philippians 4:11-12
*"Not that I speak in respect of want: for I have learned,
in whatsoever state I am, therewith to be content.
I know both how to be abased, and I know how to abound:
every where and in all things I am instructed both to be full
and to be hungry, both to abound and to suffer need."*

**Contentment involves being satisfied with what we have,
while trusting the Lord to provide for our needs each day.**

Paul had learned what it meant to be content. Where did he learn this? The Lord in which he rejoiced, requested all things, and respected. He learned while at His feet, and also while he graciously served and suffered for Him.

Philippians 4:13
"I can do all things through Christ which strengtheneth me."

He was bold and content, because he depended on Jesus Christ's strength and not his own. We can get through the good times, and the bad, by His strength. Whether we prosper or suffer, it is by His strength that we can flourish and endure.

1 Timothy 6:6
"But godliness with contentment is great gain."

Hebrews 13:5-6
*"Let your conversation be without covetousness; and be content with such things as ye have: for he hath said, I will never leave thee, nor forsake thee.
So that we may boldly say, The Lord is my helper,
and I will not fear what man shall do unto me."*

**We can find contentment
when we fill our lives with the Word of God.**

Bible Reading
Psalm 119

A Lowly Mind.

Philippians 2:3-4
"Let nothing be done through strife or vainglory; but in lowliness of mind let each esteem other better than themselves. Look not every man on his own things, but every man also on the things of others."

Ever know someone who not only has to be the center of attention, but must also be commended for nearly everything they do? Sometimes they seem to beg, whine, or even demand for pity or praise. According to Scripture this is far from how God would have us to portray ourselves.

A lowly mind goes right along with contentment and humility. **Nothing we do should intentionally promote us, nor should we have a false perception of ourselves.**

"Look not every man on his own things, but every man also on the things of others."

This does not refer to us comparing ourselves with those around us, but instead we should be concerned with the needs of others above our own: that is true humility.

Sometimes we get so blinded by what is going on in our own life that we neglect to see what others are going through. When we have a pity party about how something affects us, we are distracted from being a blessing to someone else.

Philippians 2:5
"Let this mind be in you, which was also in Christ Jesus:"

In Philippians 2, we read of Christ's example to us in His humility and lowliness of mind in how He looked upon our need instead of His own. It is through His sacrificial death for us that we can truly live.

Galatians 5:24-26
"And they that are Christ's have crucified the flesh with the affections and lusts. If we live in the Spirit, let us also walk in the Spirit. Let us not be desirous of vain glory, provoking one another, envying one another."

We must strive to have a lowly mind like Jesus.

Bible Reading
Ezekiel 31-32 | Mark 13 | Psalm 120

The Fruit Of The Spirit.

Galatians 5:22-25
"But the fruit of the Spirit is love, joy, peace, longsuffering, gentleness, goodness, faith, Meekness, temperance: against such there is no law. And they that are Christ's have crucified the flesh with the affections and lusts. If we live in the Spirit, let us also walk in the Spirit."

As we yield to the Holy Spirit, our lives will be filled with His fruit. **If we bear fruit, it is nothing that we have done; but the Spirit that lives within us.**

Notice that the Scripture says *"**fruit** of the Spirit"* and not fruits. Paul describes a nine-fold fruit which attributes are found in someone who truly walks in the Spirit. Think of an orange with nine pieces inside. In order to have the entire fruit, all nine pieces must be displayed.

As we become a new creature in Christ and begin to grow in Him, our life transforms into His image as we bear the fruit of the Spirit. **We either have the Fruit of the Spirit of we do not.** We cannot pick and choose. If we leave out even one of the qualities, we do not have the Fruit of the Spirit.

If we do not have love, we have no fruit.
If we do not have joy, we have no fruit.
If we do not have peace, we have no fruit.
If we do not have longsuffering, we have no fruit.
If we do not have gentleness, we have no fruit.
If we do not have goodness, we have no fruit.
If we do not have faith, we have no fruit.
If we do not have meekness, we have no fruit.
If we do not have temperance, we have no fruit.

**In order to have the Fruit of the Spirit,
we must be connected to the right Source.**

John 15:4-5
"Abide in me, and I in you. As the branch cannot bear fruit of itself, except it abide in the vine; no more can ye, except ye abide in me. I am the vine, ye are the branches: He that abideth in me, and I in him, the same bringeth forth much fruit: for without me ye can do nothing."

We cannot bear fruit on our own; for it is not our fruit in the first place, it belongs to Him. In order to bear fruit, we must abide in Him.

Abide in Him today, and be filled with the Fruit of the Spirit.

Bible Reading
Ezekiel 33-34 | Mark 14 | Psalm 121

The Fear Of Sinking.

Matthew 14:30
"But when he saw the wind boisterous, he was afraid; and beginning to sink, he cried, saying, Lord, save me."

Sometimes we allow the storm around us to shift our focus from where it should be. We learn this lesson from Peter as he stepped out of the boat and walked on the water toward Jesus. But why did he begin to sink? It was when *"he saw the wind"* that his courage disappeared only to be replaced by fear. But how do you see wind? You don't see it - you either feel it or only see the effects of the wind. **Sometimes we can't see the storm around us, we only feel it or see the effects of it.**

"...he was afraid..."
But what was he afraid of? The cause of his fear was *"he saw the wind boisterous"*. The effect of which was him *"beginning to sink"*. **When his faith decreased, he began to sink.** He was fearful; he didn't sink, but he was sinking. There is a difference between sinking and being sunk. **Sinking is reversible.** The Lord allowed Peter to begin to sink, so that he could see he needed a Saviour. Whatever your fear is today, it can be replaced with faith. Sinking can be reversed through faith in the Lord's ability to deliver us.

We must call for help before we sink.
The solution to fear is in crying for help - *"he cried, saying, Lord, save me."* Peter had faith that the Lord could save him. What a picture of salvation. He knew he couldn't save himself; but yet he had faith in the One that could reach down His hand to where Peter was. He simply called upon the Name of the Lord in faith, and he was saved. The Lord did not delay His deliverance.

Matthew 14:31
"And immediately Jesus stretched forth his hand, and caught him, and said unto him, O thou of little faith, wherefore didst thou doubt?"

If you feel as if you are sinking today, there is no need to doubt.
The Saviour is just a call away. Whatever your need, He's the answer.

Call upon Him today with faith
that He is able to deliver you from sinking.

Bible Reading
Ezekiel 35-36 | Mark 15 | Psalm 122

Rest In Him.

Psalm 37:7
"Rest in the LORD, and wait patiently for him:
fret not thyself because of him who prospereth in his way,
because of the man who bringeth wicked devices to pass."

When tiredness gets the best of us, we need to rest. Before we grow weary or begin to faint, we must rest in the Lord. **To truly rest in Him is to be silent or still before Him.** If all we do is talk to Him, how can we truly listen to what He has to say?

Psalm 4:4
"Stand in awe, and sin not:
commune with your own heart upon your bed, and be still."

Psalm 62:5
"My soul, wait thou only upon God; for my expectation is from him."

When did you last stand in awe of Him? In His presence is a peace that passeth all understanding. As we rest in Him and wait patiently for Him to work His will within our lives, we will find that He is Good.

Lamentations 3:25-26
"The LORD is good unto them that wait for him,
to the soul that seeketh him. It is good that a man should both hope
and quietly wait for the salvation of the LORD."

Jesus told the apostles to rest for a while
after they had returned from preaching the Gospel.

Mark 6:30-31
"And the apostles gathered themselves together unto Jesus, and told him all things, both what they had done, and what they had taught. And he said unto them, Come ye yourselves apart into a desert place, and rest a while: for there were many coming and going,
and they had no leisure so much as to eat."

Christ knew that the disciples needed to rest, but He also knew where they could find true rest…in Him. **When we choose to rest in Him, miracles can happen in us and through us.**

Bible Reading
Ezekiel 37-38 | Mark 16 | Psalm 123

A Desert Place.

Mark 6:31
"And he said unto them, Come ye yourselves apart into a desert place, and rest a while: for there were many coming and going, and they had no leisure so much as to eat."

It has been said that we should come apart before we fall apart. Christ invited the disciples into a desert place to rest; but in order to rest, they had to come apart. **In order to separate ourselves, we must often depart into another place.** The disciples could find no place of leisure due to all the people around them. Where could they go? Christ has reserved a desert place for them to rest, and He would go with them. **Sometimes the Lord will send us to a desert place, in order for us to get alone with Him.**

Mark 6:34
"And Jesus, when he came out, saw much people, and was moved with compassion toward them, because they were as sheep not having a shepherd: and he began to teach them many things."

News had spread so much about Christ, and His miracles, that they could not get alone for long. He was moved with compassion toward the people, and saw them as sheep in need of a Shepherd. He began to teach them, and they listened. **Oftentimes, it is in a desert place where we can learn the most from the Lord.** Does the Lord have to bring us into a desert place, in order to get our attention, so that we will listen to Him?

Mark 6:38
"He saith unto them, How many loaves have ye? go and see. And when they knew, they say, Five, and two fishes."

Christ can work miracles within a desert place. After the disciples had rested a day with Him, they saw Him feed the 5,000 with just the lunch of a little lad. The disciples brought the loaves of bread and fishes to Him, and saw Him bless then brake the bread. He then handed the food to the them to set before the people. After they were all filled, it was the disciples that took up the miraculous twelve baskets of fragments. One for each of them to remember the miracle that had just taken place.

When the Lord brings us into a desert place, we can feel uncertain and confused; but He always has a purpose. **If you find yourself in a desert place, rest in Him and allow Him to fulfill His purpose in your life.**

Bible Reading
Ezekiel 39-40 | Hebrews 1 | Psalm 124

Evaluate Your Faith.

Luke 8:25
*"And he said unto them, Where is your faith? And they being afraid
wondered, saying one to another, What manner of man is this!
for he commandeth even the winds and water, and they obey him."*

The disciples were in a storm, and they were fearful. Christ was with them, and yet they still had fear they would perish because of their situation. They awoke the Master and were rebuked because of their lack of faith as He brought peace to the sea. **Sometimes we need rebuked for our lack of faith as the Lord is working to still the storm in our lives.** Evaluate your faith today.

No Faith - Complete disbelief is disobedience.
Mark 4:40
*"And he said unto them, Why are ye so fearful?
how is it that ye have no faith?"*

Little Faith - Partial belief is still disbelief.
Matthew 8:26
"And he saith unto them, Why are ye fearful, O ye of little faith? Then he arose, and rebuked the winds and the sea; and there was a great calm."

Misdirected Faith – Belief in the wrong object is disbelief.
Psalm 118:8
"It is better to trust in the LORD than to put confidence in man."

True Faith - Complete belief that God is Able.
Luke 8:47-48
*"And when the woman saw that she was not hid, she came trembling, and falling down before him, she declared unto him before all the people for what cause she had touched him, and how she was healed immediately. And he said unto her, Daughter, be of good comfort:
thy faith hath made thee whole; go in peace."*

The faith of the Woman With An Issue Of Blood stopped Christ in His tracks. May we all have faith that gets the Lord's attention.

Evaluate your faith today.

Bible Reading
Ezekiel 41-43 | Hebrews 2 | Psalm 125

Unbelief

Matthew 13:58
"And he did not many mighty works there because of their unbelief."

Unbelief Has A Cost
They had the opportunity to see many mighty works done in Nazareth;
yet, they missed out because of their unbelief.

Mark 6:5-6
"And he could there do no mighty work, save that he laid his hands upon a few sick folk, and healed them. And he marvelled because of their unbelief. And he went round about the villages, teaching."

Does God marvel at our unbelief?
**If we choose not to believe,
He will find someone who does and they will receive the blessing.**

What have we missed out on because of our unbelief
that God could do a mighty work in our lives?

Unbelief Can Be Changed
Mark 9:24
"And straightway the father of the child cried out, and said with tears, Lord, I believe; help thou mine unbelief."

This father had faith in Jesus but admitted that he still had some unbelief within his heart. Christ not only cast the spirit from the man, but He compassionately took him by the hand, lifted him up, and delivered him to his father. He asked for grace and His grace was sufficient.

Our unbelief can be changed when we bring our need to Jesus.
His grace is sufficient to meet our every need.

Bible Reading
Ezekiel 44-46 | Hebrews 3 | Psalm 126

Matthew 14:31
"And immediately Jesus stretched forth his hand, and caught him, and said unto him, O thou of little faith, wherefore didst thou doubt?"

This was not the first time that Peter had doubted the Lord. He had been in this situation before. Peter had seen the Lord deliver him and the other disciples as He calmed the Sea of Galilee after they awoke Him in the boat. Yet, here we find Peter doubting that the Lord could take care of him. **Peter often serves as a reminder to us that our flesh sometimes gets in the way of our faith.**

Even though we have seen the Lord deliver us time and time again, sometimes our flesh causes us to doubt that He can do it again.

What makes us doubt?
Sometimes we doubt ourselves.
Sometimes we doubt in our situation.
Sometimes we even doubt our Saviour.

Peter had asked the Lord for help. How fast did Jesus deliver him? Did He wait until Peter had almost drowned? No, He immediately stretched forth His hand.

When we call upon the Lord to help our situation, He immediately comes to our rescue. We may not see the solution right away, but the Lord can give us peace as He works behind the scenes of our life for His will to be done.

He can work a miracle out of a mess.
He can make a way when there is no way.

Mark 9:23
"Jesus said unto him, If thou canst believe, all things are possible to him that believeth."

There's no need to doubt Him now!

Bible Reading
Ezekiel 47-48 | Hebrews 4 | Psalm 127

Peace.

John 14:26-27
*"But the Comforter, which is the Holy Ghost, whom the Father will send
in my name, he shall teach you all things, and bring all things to your
remembrance, whatsoever I have said unto you. Peace I leave with you,
my peace I give unto you: not as the world giveth, give I unto you.
Let not your heart be troubled, neither let it be afraid."*

When trying to go to sleep, a comforter can warm us and create a peaceful relaxing atmosphere for us to get some rest. In times of distress and doubt, a warm comforter wrapped around us brings exactly what its name entails…comfort.

When Jesus Christ departed from the earth after raising from the dead, He left us the greatest Comforter of all, the Holy Spirit. He brings peace to our weary souls in time of trouble. Notice how we receive Him, *"whom the Father will send in my name".* We cannot be given the Holy Spirit without Jesus. There is no peace without Him.

If Jesus can calm the stormy seas, He can comfort you. The Prince of Peace brings us the peace of God, a peace which is beyond our understanding.

He Keeps Us In Peace
Philippians 4:7
*"And the peace of God, which passeth all understanding,
shall keep your hearts and minds through Christ Jesus."*

He Keeps Us In Perfect Peace
Isaiah 26:3
*"Thou wilt keep him in perfect peace, whose mind is stayed on thee:
because he trusteth in thee."*

Worry can bring sleepless nights filled with fear that the comforter upon our beds cannot erase. Only when we release our hold of the situation and allow the Lord to carry our burden for us can we begin to feel His peace again. That Still Small Voice speaks to our troubled souls and brings peace where fear had reigned.

You can exchange your troubled and fearful heart
for the peace that only He can give.
He wants to give you peace today.

Bible Reading
Daniel 1-2 | Hebrews 5 | Psalm 128

Questions.

Luke 5:22
"But when Jesus perceived their thoughts, he answering said unto them, What reason ye in your hearts?"

We often have questions for what we go through on a daily basis. Who? What? When? Where? How? Why? **Many questions can run through our mind when we do not understand what is going on around us.**

Jesus Christ asked many questions within Luke's Gospel that we can benefit from. Unlike us, He already knew the answers to the questions He asked; however, **He asked them for a reason.**

Luke 2:49 - *"How is it that ye sought me?"*
Luke 6:3-4 - *"Have ye not read so much as this…?"*
Luke 6:32 - *"For if ye love them which love you, what thank have ye?"*
Luke 6:39 - *"Can the blind lead the blind?"*
Luke 6:41 - *"And why beholdest thou the mote that is in thy brother's eye, but perceivest not the beam that is in thine own eye?"*
Luke 6:46 – *"And why call ye me, Lord, Lord, and do not the things which I say?"*
Luke 8:25 - *"Where is your faith?"*
Luke 8:30 - *"What is thy name?"*
Luke 8:45 - *"Who touched me?"*
Luke 9:18 – *"Whom say the people that I am?"*
Luke 9:20 – *"But whom say ye that I am?"*
Luke 14:28 – *"For which of you, intending to build a tower, sitteth not down first, and counteth the cost, whether he have sufficient to finish it?"*
Luke 18:8 – *"Nevertheless when the Son of man cometh, shall he find faith on the earth?"*
Luke 18:41 – *"What wilt thou that I shall do unto thee?"*
Luke 24:38 – *"Why are ye troubled? and why do thoughts arise in your hearts?"*

There is a reason for the questions you have; He already knows, and He is waiting to help you. **Seek the answers to your questions within the pages of Scripture, and ask Him to show you what you need today.**

Bible Reading
Daniel 3-4 | Hebrews 6 | Psalm 129

John 12:21
"The same came therefore to Philip, which was of Bethsaida of Galilee, and desired him, saying, Sir, we would see Jesus."

Many Jews were come to the feast not only to see Jesus but also Lazarus, whom He has raised from the dead. The chief priests had consulted to put Lazarus to death; because as the record spread that he was now alive, many Jews believed on Jesus.

There were also certain Greeks who had come to the feast for one purpose…to worship. They heard about the miracles Jesus had been performing, and they wanted to see Him. They came to Philip and told him of their desire. They did not want to see Lazarus; instead they said, "Give me Jesus!"

His response, after Philip and Andrew came to Him with the desire of the Greeks, is something we can all apply to our lives. We too must say in our hearts, "Give me Jesus!" If we desire to see Him and be used of Him to bring forth fruit, we must first die. **We must lose our life in order to find it, and follow Him in order to serve Him.** Read John 12:23-28 for the full context.

The world offers many things in order to distract and deter us from our God given purpose. **Decide today that regardless of what you are offered, you'd rather have Jesus.** When we live our lives to please Him, we cannot go wrong. You may be the only person that can reach someone with the Truth of the Gospel.

John 12:32
"And I, if I be lifted up from the earth, will draw all men unto me."

Lift Him up today so that others may see Him!

Bible Reading
Daniel 5-6 | Hebrews 7 | Psalm 130

John 4:14
"But whosoever drinketh of the water that I shall give him shall never thirst; but the water that I shall give him shall be in him a well of water springing up into everlasting life."

Ironing by only using heat is not effective. An iron works best when steam is involved, and steam can only be created when water is present. Trying to iron our Sunday best by relying on a hot piece of metal alone will only lead to wrinkles and frustration.

Many people call themselves a Christian because they believe in God. Some even think that is good enough to get them to Heaven, yet they are missing Something most important. Much like an iron with no water to create steam, without Jesus you will not get far.

Jesus also used water as an analogy while He talked with the Samaritan woman beside Jacob's well. He referred to the thirst that shall come again after drinking from the water of the well. He then told her of the Water He possessed that would spring up into everlasting life. Christ Himself is the Water of Life. **Once we have drank of His water, we shall never thirst again.**

Are you thirsty today? Perhaps you have never tasted the Water of Life, or you simply need the joy of your salvation restored once again.

There is no cost to this Water.
"...the water that I shall give him..."

It is freely given to anyone.
"...whosoever..."

Revelation 22:17
"And the Spirit and the bride say, Come. And let him that heareth say, Come. And let him that is athirst come. And whosoever will, let him take the water of life freely."

If you have already tasted the Water of Life, share Him with someone today and every day.

Bible Reading
Daniel 7-8 | Hebrews 8 | Psalm 131

Willing To Be Broken.

Mark 14:3
"And being in Bethany in the house of Simon the leper, as he sat at meat, there came a woman having an alabaster box of ointment of spikenard very precious; and she brake the box, and poured it on his head."

She brought what she had.
She had watched Jesus raise her brother from the dead, and Mary of Bethany did what she could to show Christ her gratitude and servitude. It may have seemed odd to bring a box full of ointment to the Saviour, but it was what she had. Mary's alabaster box was precious to her.

Mark 14:8
"She hath done what she could: she is come aforehand to anoint my body to the burying."

She was willing to sacrifice for Him.
Mary may not have had much, but the ointment she used to worship the Lord was very costly. Judas mentioned that it could have been sold for more than three hundred pence. Christ told outraged Judas to leave her alone because she had wrought a good work on Him. She sacrificed so that He might get glory, and Christ acknowledged her great sacrifice for Him.

Mark 14:6,9
"And Jesus said, Let her alone; why trouble ye her? she hath wrought a good work on me…Verily I say unto you, Wheresoever this gospel shall be preached throughout the whole world, this also that she hath done shall be spoken of for a memorial of her."

She was willing to be broken for His glory.
The Scripture tells us how the box of ointment was precious to Mary, yet she was willing to not only give it to Christ, but to brake it in order for it to be used. **When we give what we have to the Lord to be used of Him, we must be willing for Him to break us.** Sometimes we ask the Lord to use us while having a firm grasp on the things we love the most. Whether it be family, friends, or objects, we have a hard time releasing our hold on what is dear to our hearts. If you let Christ have your life, you are sure to find it. The Bible says so. If you are holding on to something that is keeping you from fully surrendering to Christ and His will for your life, there is still time to make a difference. **Are you willing to be broken so that He can use you?**

Bible Reading
Daniel 9-10 | Hebrews 9 | Psalm 132 | 351

Willing To Surrender & Sacrifice.

Esther 4:16
*"Go, gather together all the Jews that are present in Shushan,
and fast ye for me, and neither eat nor drink three days, night or day:
I also and my maidens will fast likewise; and so will I go in unto the king,
which is not according to the law: and if I perish, I perish."*

Throughout history we read of those who were willing to sacrifice their lives for the cause of Christ. Foxe's Book of Martyrs tells story after story of Christians suffering horrific deaths because they stood strong in their faith. Some even died so that we can have the Bible we do today.

Esther was willing to give her life with purpose for her people. She not only saw the need, but she also set out to do something about it. She not only surrendered, but she was willing to sacrifice whatever she had to, including her life. She could have sat still and not volunteered, but she set out to make a difference.

Willing To Surrender.
Esther was willing to surrender her own life for the cause.

Willing To Sacrifice.
Esther was willing to be sacrificed, if it was necessary,
in order to fulfill God's purpose.

There is no service to the Lord that does not require both surrender and sacrifice. A servant first surrenders to God and as a result of that surrender, willingly gives sacrificially. Jesus Christ surrendered His will to the Father and then sacrificially gave His life for us.

How much are you willing to surrender and sacrifice for Him?

Philippians 1:20-21
*"According to my earnest expectation and my hope, that in nothing I shall be ashamed, but that with all boldness, as always, so now also Christ shall be magnified in my body, whether it be by life, or by death.
For to me to live is Christ, and to die is gain."*

Esther 4:14
*"…and who knoweth whether thou art come
to the kingdom for such a time as this?"*

Bible Reading
Daniel 11-12 | Hebrews 10 | Psalm 133

Willing To Forsake & Follow.

Luke 5:9-11

"For he was astonished, and all that were with him, at the draught of the fishes which they had taken: And so was also James, and John, the sons of Zebedee, which were partners with Simon. And Jesus said unto Simon, Fear not; from henceforth thou shalt catch men. And when they had brought their ships to land, they forsook all, and followed him."

Peter's partial obedience led to Christ teaching him a lesson. He was astonished at the abundance of fish they had because he only let down one net, after disobeying Christ's command to *"Launch out into the deep, and let down your nets for a draught."*

Christ used this situation to show them their purpose, to be fishers of men. Notice that once the Master gave this revelation, they immediately brought the ships to land. They could have gone home to their parents, their jobs, and their friends; but instead *"they forsook all, and followed him."* Scripture doesn't record them questioning what it meant to *"catch men"* or how their needs would be supplied. They simply made a choice to forsake and follow Him; and their lives were never the same.

Friends To Serve With - Mark 1:16-20

Andrew and Peter left their nets to follow Him; and a little farther down the road, James and John answered the same call. These men left their fathers and everything they had; yet the Lord gave them friends to serve with, partners in the ministry. When we answer the call to serve Him, He will give us people along the way to grow and serve with.

Fully Supplied - Luke 18:28-30

Christ promised Peter that anyone who forsakes their house, family, friends, spouse, or children for His sake shall receive much more in return. Whatever we surrender for His sake, we shall receive so much more!

**Yet in order to receive these blessings,
we must first be willing to forsake & follow Him.**

"I Surrender All"
Judson W. Van De Venter

A hymn sang often out of routine,
but do we really mean the words we sing?

Bible Reading
Hosea 1-3 | Hebrews 11 | Psalm 134

In Christ Jesus.

Romans 8:38-39
*"For I am persuaded, that neither death, nor life, nor angels,
nor principalities, nor powers, nor things present, nor things to come,
Nor height, nor depth, nor any other creature, shall be able
to separate us from the love of God, which is in Christ Jesus our Lord."*

What is your need today? You may not have shared it with anyone else, but rest assured that God knows all about it. He even ordained it for your good and His glory. Throughout the Scripture we find that whatever our need, Christ is the Answer. When God saw the sin of man before the foundation of the world, Christ was the Answer. From that moment to today and throughout eternity, Christ will always be the Answer. God loves us so much He sent His Son for us. God displayed His love in Christ Jesus, and because of that love we find so much more…in Christ Jesus.

There Is Redemption. - Romans 3:24
*"Being justified freely by his grace
through the redemption that is in Christ Jesus:"*

There Is Purpose. - Ephesians 3:10-12
*"To the intent that now unto the principalities and powers in heavenly
places might be known by the church the manifold wisdom of God,
According to the eternal purpose which he purposed
in Christ Jesus our Lord: In whom we have boldness and access
with confidence by the faith of him."*

There Is A Prize. - Philippians 3:13-14
*"Brethren, I count not myself to have apprehended:
but this one thing I do, forgetting those things which are behind, and
reaching forth unto those things which are before, I press toward the mark
for the prize of the high calling of God in Christ Jesus."*

There Is A Calling. - 2 Timothy 1:9
*"Who hath saved us, and called us with an holy calling, not according to
our works, but according to his own purpose and grace,
which was given us in Christ Jesus before the world began,"*

If you search the Scriptures, you will find much more that can be found in Christ Jesus…if only we will take the time to seek them. **Everything you need can be found today…in Christ Jesus.**

Bible Reading
Hosea 4-6 | Hebrews 12 | Psalm 135

Call Upon His Name.

Genesis 4:26
*"And to Seth, to him also there was born a son; and he called his name
Enos: then began men to call upon the name of the LORD."*

After Adam's grandson, Enos, was born, men began to *"call upon the name
of the LORD."* Praise God we still have the privilege to call upon His Name
today, even when we often neglect to do so.

A Call For Salvation
Whether a prayer for salvation of our sins
or deliverance from our circumstances,
His ears are open to our cry.

Romans 10:13
"For whosoever shall call upon the name of the Lord shall be saved."

Psalm 116:13
"I will take the cup of salvation, and call upon the name of the LORD."

A Call Of Thanksgiving
We have the opportunity to call out and thank Him for all that He has done,
for what He is doing right now, and for what He is going to do.

Psalm 116:17
*"I will offer to thee the sacrifice of thanksgiving,
and will call upon the name of the LORD."*

Why can we call upon His Name today?
Because He hears us.

Psalm 116:1-2
*"I love the LORD, because he hath heard my voice and my supplications.
Because he hath inclined his ear unto me,
therefore will I call upon him as long as I live."*

Bible Reading
Hosea 7-9 | Hebrews 13 | Psalm 136

The Only Reason For The Season.

Isaiah 9:6
"For unto us a child is born, unto us a son is given: and the government shall be upon his shoulder: and his name shall be called Wonderful, Counsellor, The mighty God, The everlasting Father, The Prince of Peace."

The Christmas season is here. **The Reason for the season should be at the forefront of our minds as we prepare to celebrate His birth in the days ahead.** He is the Only Reason for this season. In this prophecy of the Birth of Jesus Christ, we see both His humanity and His deity. Christ was 100% God in the flesh, but He was also 100% man. Our finite minds cannot fully comprehend this fact, but it does not make it any less true. John 1:1,14 show us that the Word dwelt among us, full of grace and truth.

A Child Is Born - Matthew 1:16
His humanity is shown in the fact that He was to come as a child, born of a woman, just like any other human being after Adam and Eve.

A Son Is Given - Romans 6:23
His deity is displayed in that He, as God's Son, was given to us so that we might have life that is only found in Him. A gift cannot be given if it does not already exist. This Gift left His throne in Heaven to be born of woman, take upon Him the form of a servant, and fulfill His purpose to die for the sins of mankind.

Unto Us - Romans 5:15
We see that this is a personal Gift, given *"unto us"*. A child was born, and a Son was given. There was only a need for One because He is the Only One who could have came, and He came for us.

In the latter part of the verse today are five descriptions that His Name shall be called. **These were given before He came, showing that by His grace we can become His children and experience the power of His Name.**

"Wonderful" – We can adore Him.
"Counsellor" – We can be advised by Him.
"The mighty God" – We can see His Almighty strength.
"The everlasting Father" – We can always find Him.
"The Prince of Peace" – We can be assured by Him.

Rest in Him today, the Only Reason for the season.

Bible Reading
Hosea 10-12 | James 1 | Psalm 137

His Purpose.

Matthew 1:21
*"And she shall bring forth a son, and thou shalt call his name JESUS:
for he shall save his people from their sins."*

Joseph was a just man. As a carpenter, imagine him sitting in his woodworking shop as he began to think on how he was not willing to make a public example of Mary, who was found to be with child of the Holy Ghost. The verses preceding display Joseph's character, even before he fell asleep and the angel of the Lord appeared unto him in a dream. The angel comforted him, *"saying, Joseph, thou son of David, fear not to take unto thee Mary thy wife: for that which is conceived in her is of the Holy Ghost."* He then heard what His Name and His purpose would be. When he awoke from his sleep, he did not question…he simply obeyed.

Mary was to have a Son, and Joseph was to name Him JESUS. Why? Because He came to save His people from their sins. We are His people when we place our faith and trust in Him for salvation…to know the Truth of the Gospel.

John 18:37
"Pilate therefore said unto him, Art thou a king then? Jesus answered, Thou sayest that I am a king. To this end was I born, and for this cause came I into the world, that I should bear witness unto the truth. Every one that is of the truth heareth my voice."

Jesus Himself explained to Pilate His purpose for coming…*"that I should bear witness unto the truth."* **He came so that all could come to Him.**

John 14:6
"Jesus saith unto him, I am the way, the truth, and the life: no man cometh unto the Father, but by me."

How can a missionary go into a remote village where there is no church and find people hungry for the Word of God? Because Jesus' purpose in coming was so that they could know the Truth.

The Christmas season gives us the opportunity to tell others why Christmas is celebrated…because He came. **Our purpose is to tell others about His purpose.**

Bible Reading
Hosea 13-14 | James 2 | Psalm 138

God With Us.

Isaiah 7:14
"Therefore the Lord himself shall give you a sign; Behold, a virgin shall conceive, and bear a son, and shall call his name Immanuel."

Immanuel means God with us. **The Son of God left His throne in Heaven to be made flesh just like us; but He was God in the flesh, and He chose to dwell among His creation.**

John 1:1,14
"In the beginning was the Word, and the Word was with God, and the Word was God...And the Word was made flesh, and dwelt among us, (and we beheld his glory, the glory as of the only begotten of the Father,) full of grace and truth."

He felt pain when His friend died because He was a man; yet He raised His friend from the dead because He was God. He hungered in the wilderness because He was man; yet He fed the multitude with the lunch of a lad because He was God.

Colossians 2:9
"For in him dwelleth all the fulness of the Godhead bodily."

The same God that came to earth to fulfill His purpose to save His people from their sins is the same God that is reaching out His hand today.

When we are fearful, He is God with us.
When we are dismayed, He is God with us.
When we need strength, He is God with us.

Isaiah 41:10
"Fear thou not; for I am with thee: be not dismayed; for I am thy God: I will strengthen thee; yea, I will help thee; yea, I will uphold thee with the right hand of my righteousness."

When we need help, He is God with us.
When we feel alone, He is God with us.

Hebrews 13:5-6
"Let your conversation be without covetousness; and be content with such things as ye have: for he hath said, I will never leave thee, nor forsake thee. So that we may boldly say, The Lord is my helper, and I will not fear what man shall do unto me."

There is no need to fear today...He is God with us.

Bible Reading
Joel | James 3 | Psalm 139

Favoured Grace.

Luke 1:28-33
*"And the angel came in unto her, and said,
Hail, thou that art highly favoured, the Lord is with thee:
blessed art thou among women. And when she saw him, she was troubled
at his saying, and cast in her mind what manner of salutation this should
be. And the angel said unto her, Fear not, Mary: for thou hast found favour
with God. And, behold, thou shalt conceive in thy womb, and bring forth a
son, and shalt call his name JESUS. He shall be great, and shall be called
the Son of the Highest: and the Lord God shall give unto him the throne of
his father David: And he shall reign over the house of Jacob for ever;
and of his kingdom there shall be no end."*

Out of all the women ever created, God chose Mary.

"...highly favoured..."
This refers to obtaining grace. Mary had been found to be graciously accepted to birth God in the flesh. She had not known a man because the blood of man could not be involved in the redeeming of the souls of mankind. The blood of a baby comes from the father. The Holy Ghost came upon her to conceive within her the blood of the Father required to redeem us from our sins. **She had been given the special honor of literally feeling the Gift of God move within her.** Favoured Grace. God had chosen her to be the vessel who carried the Son of God into the world so that we might have life in Him. We are accepted through the blood of Jesus. **He has chosen us to be one of His.** Favoured Grace.

Ephesians 1:3-7
*"Blessed be the God and Father of our Lord Jesus Christ, who hath
blessed us with all spiritual blessings in heavenly places in Christ:
According as he hath chosen us in him before the foundation of the world,
that we should be holy and without blame before him in love: Having
predestinated us unto the adoption of children by Jesus Christ to himself,
according to the good pleasure of his will, To the praise of the glory of his
grace, wherein he hath made us accepted in the beloved. In whom we
have redemption through his blood, the forgiveness of sins,
according to the riches of his grace;"*

Mary was the first to carry the Gospel. **The Living Word grew inside of her just as God desires the Word of God to grow within us.** May we carry the favoured grace of God today to those around us.

Bible Reading
Amos 1-4 | James 4 | Psalm 140 | 359

How Shall This Be?

Luke 1:34-35

"Then said Mary unto the angel, How shall this be, seeing I know not a man? And the angel answered and said unto her, The Holy Ghost shall come upon thee, and the power of the Highest shall overshadow thee: therefore also that holy thing which shall be born of thee shall be called the Son of God."

No other woman had ever been in Mary's situation before…nor has any since for that matter, *"How shall this be…?"* Can we not relate with Mary on her confusion after receiving news that seemed absolutely impossible to occur?

Abraham and Sarah must have had similar feelings after they were promised to have a son in their old age. **How shall this be?** They even thought they had to manipulate the situation in order for it to happen. They were impatient and took matters into their own hands…and look at the outcome. Even after the birth of Ishmael, God gave them Isaac just as He had promised. **Instead of manipulating, Mary trusted.**

Just like the angel began to further explain to her how this would happen, we have been given the Word of God to give us evidence to believe that God can do the impossible.

When we are faced with what seems like an impossibility, we must remember that God has ordained the circumstance within our life, just as He did in Mary's. **He not only has a purpose, He has a plan.** Our part in it is simply to trust and obey Him, just as Mary did.

If you are questioning, "How shall this be?" today, you can rest in the example that Mary has set for us. Although she questioned what was happening, she allowed God to show her He had a plan.

Trust God's plan and allow Him
to work the impossible through you today.

Luke 1:37
"For with God nothing shall be impossible."

Bible Reading
Amos 5-9 | James 5 | Psalm 141

Be It Unto Me.

Luke 1:37-38
*"For with God nothing shall be impossible. And Mary said,
Behold the handmaid of the Lord; be it unto me according to thy word.
And the angel departed from her."*

Engaged to a carpenter, Mary was planning her wedding and new life with her future husband, Joseph. Her plans changed when Gabriel visited and declared that she had been chosen by God to bring forth the Son of God. She was an ordinary woman whom God chose to do extraordinary things through. **Mary was chosen to suffer for the cause of Christ.**

"...be it unto me according to thy word."
Mary accepted her calling. **She not only made herself available to be used, but she was also willing to bare the cost of her divinely appointed task.**

Romans 8:18
"For I reckon that the sufferings of this present time are not worthy to be compared with the glory which shall be revealed in us."

Think of the physical pain she suffered during His birth and the emotional pain during His crucifixion & death. She was the only one who was there to witness both. What pain this mother must have experienced, but she willingly accepted it in order to fulfill God's purpose in her life and even ours.

1 Peter 5:10-11
"But the God of all grace, who hath called us unto his eternal glory by Christ Jesus, after that ye have suffered a while, make you perfect, stablish, strengthen, settle you. To him be glory and dominion for ever and ever. Amen."

Mary was willing to allow the Lord to use her life for His glory.
What are we willing to endure for the cause of Christ?

May we have the faith to say as Mary did to say,
"...be it unto me according to thy word."

Bible Reading
Obadiah | 1 Peter 1 | Psalm 142 | 361

Great Things.

Luke 1:46-50
"And Mary said, My soul doth magnify the Lord,
And my spirit hath rejoiced in God my Saviour. For he hath regarded
the low estate of his handmaiden: for, behold, from henceforth
all generations shall call me blessed. For he that is mighty
hath done to me great things; and holy is his name. And his mercy is on
them that fear him from generation to generation."

Mary not only accepted the Lord's purpose for her life, she rejoiced in it. She knew that the task ahead of her was far too great for her to bear on her own. She knew it was of the Lord and for His glory.

God, Who can do the impossible, had chosen her for His will to be accomplished in the birth of His Son, Jesus Christ. Through Mary, the earthly Gospel record began. Before the foundation of the world, God had a plan that He would send His only begotten Son to be born of a woman. **He had to be born so that we could be born again.**

John 3:3
"Jesus answered and said unto him, Verily, verily, I say unto thee,
Except a man be born again, he cannot see the kingdom of God."

We must remember our need for a Saviour and place our trust in His finished work on Calvary and His resurrection. We too can magnify Him and say, *"For he that is mighty hath done to me great things; and holy is his name."*

May we rejoice today in the great things
Christ has done in our lives.

Bible Reading
Jonah | 1 Peter 2 | Psalm 143

Where Is He?

Matthew 2:2
"Saying, Where is he that is born King of the Jews? for we have seen his star in the east, and are come to worship him."

These men were searching for Jesus. They had heard of Him and wanted to meet and worship Him. It's no wonder that Scripture refers to them as *"wise men"*. **Wise men still seek Him today.**

Matthew 2:9-10
*"When they had heard the king, they departed;
and, lo, the star, which they saw in the east, went before them,
till it came and stood over where the young child was.
When they saw the star, they rejoiced with exceeding great joy."*

The star led them to Jesus. Contrary to many nativity scenes we find in stores today, the wise men did not visit Jesus at the manger. It is believed their visit occurred within the first two years after Jesus' birth in Bethlehem. Scripture called Jesus a young child, likely a toddler, during this time.

Matthew 2:11
*"And when they were come into the house, they saw the young child with Mary his mother, and fell down, and worshipped him: and when they had opened their treasures, they presented unto him gifts;
gold, and frankincense and myrrh."*

The wise men followed the star until it guided them to the house where Jesus and the family was. **When they came into His presence, they fell down to their knees in worship to Him.** Then they gave the very best treasures they had to show the honor and reverence they had for Him.

Where is Christ in our lives?

Seek Him today.
Give Him your life for Him to use for His glory.
Shine your Light today so that others may come to Him.

Matthew 5:14-16
*"Ye are the light of the world. A city that is set on an hill cannot be hid.
Neither do men light a candle, and put it under a bushel,
but on a candlestick; and it giveth light unto all that are in the house.
Let your light so shine before men, that they may see your good works,
and glorify your Father which is in heaven."*

Bible Reading
Micah 1-4 | 1 Peter 3 | Psalm 144

Is There Room?

Luke 2:6-7
"And so it was, that, while they were there, the days were accomplished that she should be delivered. And she brought forth her firstborn son, and wrapped him in swaddling clothes, and laid him in a manger; because there was no room for them in the inn."

Joseph and Mary had made it to Bethlehem from Galilee for the taxing. Mary was great with child. The Scripture does not specifically mention the pain that Mary went through or if there were complications to the birth. It simply says, *"the days were accomplished that she should be delivered. And she brought forth her firstborn son"*.

After the Son of God took His first breath upon this earth, Mary wrapped Him in swaddling clothes. These were none other than grave clothes, signifying His purpose...He came die.

Matthew 20:28
"Even as the Son of man came not to be ministered unto, but to minister, and to give his life a ransom for many."

When we go on a journey, we often find a hotel to stay in for the night. In Bethlehem there were no hotels, only an inn; however, there were no vacancies there. **They had no room for Christ and His earthly parents.** He was born and laid in a manger, a place where cattle feed. This lowly crib was the first place Christ would lay His head on this earth. His humility was evident from His very first breath to His last on the cross, where He willingly gave His life so that all may come to the Father.

The innkeeper missed out on seeing the miracle of Jesus' birth because he did not make room for Him. **We are all innkeepers who choose whether or not to make room for Jesus in our lives.** Think about what we have missed out on because we said there was no room for Him. We will invite Him in for salvation, but do we allow Him to have room in our day-to-day lives?

2 Corinthians 4:15-16
*"For all things are for your sakes, that the abundant grace might through the thanksgiving of many redound to the glory of God.
For which cause we faint not; but though our outward man perish, yet the inward man is renewed day by day."*

Is there room for Him in your life today?

Bible Reading
Micah 5-7 | 1 Peter 4 | Psalm 145

Good Tidings Of Great Joy.

Luke 2:8-10
"And there were in the same country shepherds abiding in the field, keeping watch over their flock by night. And, lo, the angel of the Lord came upon them, and the glory of the Lord shone round about them: and they were sore afraid. And the angel said unto them, Fear not: for, behold, I bring you good tidings of great joy, which shall be to all people."

Mary was the first to carry the Gospel, and the angel of the Lord was the first to preach the Gospel after Jesus had been born.

Can you imagine the fright on the faces of the shepherds as a great Light shone round about them? The glory of the Lord was shining bright for them to see, yet they were afraid. The angel brought comfort and peace, saying, *"Fear not: for behold, I bring you good tidings of great joy, which shall be to all people."*

There is Great Joy in the Gospel of Jesus Christ.
And this joy is not reserved for just a few or some…it is for all people.

Remember the joy you felt when you first accepted Christ?
If it seems lost, you can find it again.

Psalm 51:12
*"Restore unto me the joy of thy salvation;
and uphold me with thy free spirit."*

If you are fearful today, remember how the angel calmed the shepherds that night…by bringing them *"good tidings of great joy".*

Acts 20:24
"But none of these things move me, neither count I my life dear unto myself, so that I might finish my course with joy, and the ministry, which I have received of the Lord Jesus, to testify the gospel of the grace of God."

Share the Joy of the Gospel with someone today.

Bible Reading
Nahum | 1 Peter 5 | Psalm 146

Make Him Known.

Luke 2:15-20
"And it came to pass, as the angels were gone away from them into heaven, the shepherds said one to another, Let us now go even unto Bethlehem, and see this thing which is come to pass, which the Lord hath made known unto us. And they came with haste, and found Mary, and Joseph, and the babe lying in a manger. And when they had seen it, they made known abroad the saying which was told them concerning this child. And all they that heard it wondered at those things which were told them by the shepherds. But Mary kept all these things, and pondered them in her heart. And the shepherds returned, glorifying and praising God for all the things that they had heard and seen, as it was told unto them."

The shepherds could have kept the good tidings to themselves, but they made known the Good News to many people. Those that heard it could not help but wonder at what the shepherds told them. They had seen the glory of the Lord shone round about them as the angel spoke peace from the sky. They heard a multitude of heavenly host praising God, and they quickly journeyed to Bethlehem to find all that had been told to them was true. A Saviour had been born; Christ the Lord had come. They had seen Him lying in a manger wrapped in swaddling clothes. **Who wouldn't want to share such wonderful news?** What an example the shepherds set for us!

Yet we often fail to make Christ known to those around us. **We have a choice to make today: to tell of the Good News of the Gospel or keep it to ourselves.**

Scripture tells us that the shepherds returned to their field glorifying and praising God for all they had heard and seen. **When we share the Gospel, it will bring glory and praise to Him!**

Ephesians 1:12-14
"That we should be to the praise of his glory, who first trusted in Christ. In whom ye also trusted, after that ye heard the word of truth, the gospel of your salvation: in whom also after that ye believed, ye were sealed with that holy Spirit of promise, Which is the earnest of our inheritance until the redemption of the purchased possession, unto the praise of his glory."

Make Him known today!

Bible Reading
Habakkuk | 2 Peter 1 | Psalm 147

God Gave.

Luke 2:11-14
"For unto you is born this day in the city of David a Saviour, which is Christ the Lord. And this shall be a sign unto you; Ye shall find the babe wrapped in swaddling clothes, lying in a manger. And suddenly there was with the angel a multitude of the heavenly host praising God, and saying, Glory to God in the highest, and on earth peace, good will toward men."

God gave His Son to be born for you.
God's Son gave His life for you.
God gave.

John 3:16
"For God so loved the world, that he gave his only begotten Son..."

We exchange presents on Christmas because God gave us the greatest Gift through the giving of His Son, Jesus, the Christ of Christmas.

John 3:16
"...that whosoever believeth in him should not perish, but have everlasting life."

God's greatest Gift is not for only a select group but It is available to anyone who will receive Him. *"For unto you...", "...whosoever believeth in him..."* Just like the gifts we receive today, this Gift is waiting to be received...because God gave.

Now it is our turn to give.

We must give the Gospel to those around us, and they must decide whether to receive or reject Him.

Why do we celebrate Christmas? Because *"God so loved the world, that he gave his only begotten Son."* **Without Jesus there would be no Christmas.**

Celebrate with family, friends, and your church family today.
Celebrate Him.

Happy Birthday to You, our Lord
You spread Your love to the whole human race
We are all nestled in Your sweet embrace
You live in our hearts, so we sing to Your grace
Happy Birthday to You, our Lord
P. Zeller - E. Zeller

Bible Reading
Zephaniah | 2 Peter 2 | Psalm 148

Be Found In Him.

Philippians 3:7-9
*"But what things were gain to me, those I counted loss for Christ.
Yea doubtless, and I count all things but loss for the excellency
of the knowledge of Christ Jesus my Lord: for whom I have suffered the
loss of all things, and do count them but dung, that I may win Christ,
And be found in him, not having mine own righteousness,
which is of the law, but that which is through the faith of Christ,
the righteousness which is of God by faith:"*

Christmas reminds us of where our story began.
Jesus came to die so that we could find life in Him.

In order to be found, something must first be lost.

It is easy to focus on what we have lost or maybe even never received. The devil knows our weaknesses and exploits them. He wants us to dwell on the things we do not have so that we are distracted from our purpose in Christ and knowing Him. **Paul had come to realize that every thing he had lost was worth the joy of knowing Christ and being found in Him.**

Mark 8:34-37
"And when he had called the people unto him with his disciples also, he said unto them, Whosoever will come after me, let him deny himself, and take up his cross, and follow me. For whosoever will save his life shall lose it; but whosoever shall lose his life for my sake and the gospel's, the same shall save it. For what shall it profit a man, if he shall gain the whole world, and lose his own soul? Or what shall a man give in exchange for his soul?"

We must daily die to our flesh, and its desires, in order to follow Christ. Every day we have a choice: to live for ourselves or for Him. **It is only when we exchange our will for His that we truly begin to live.**

Christ gave His life so that we could find ours in Him.
Be found in Him today.

Bible Reading
Haggai | 2 Peter 3 | Psalm 149

That I May Know Him.

Philippians 3:10
*"That I may know him, and the power of his resurrection,
and the fellowship of his sufferings,
being made conformable unto his death;"*

To know Christ should be the ultimate goal of any Christian. **Knowing Christ is more than just knowing about Him.** It is knowing about Him and finding out what you know about Him is true.

Knowing Him begins with believing in Him.

Romans 1:16
*"For I am not ashamed of the gospel of Christ:
for it is the power of God unto salvation to every one that believeth;
to the Jew first, and also to the Greek."*

There is power in knowing Him. The same power that raised Jesus from the dead lives inside every truly born again Christian. Paul wanted to know what it felt like to not only live a crucified life, but a resurrected life. He longed to not be in bondage to the flesh and have victory over sin. He wanted the power of Christ to be evident in his life.

2 Corinthians 12:8-10
*"For this thing I besought the Lord thrice, that it might depart from me.
And he said unto me, My grace is sufficient for thee: for my strength is
made perfect in weakness. Most gladly therefore will I rather glory in my
infirmities, that the power of Christ may rest upon me. Therefore I take
pleasure in infirmities, in reproaches, in necessities, in persecutions, in
distresses for Christ's sake: for when I am weak, then am I strong."*

There is fellowship in knowing Him. We cannot know Him without knowing what is like to suffer. Paul wanted to know Him so much that he was willing to suffer for Him. Although Paul asked three times that his thorn in his flesh be removed, Christ saw fit that it was better for Paul to suffer. **The thorn allowed Paul to know Christ more.** If we desire to know Christ, we must follow Paul's example. We can find His strength in our weakness. **Allow Christ to use the thorns of your life to bring you closer to Him today.**

"That I may know him…"

Bible Reading
Zechariah 1-3 | 1 John 1 | Psalm 150

Delight In His Word.

Psalm 1:1-2
*"Blessed is the man that walketh not in the counsel of the ungodly,
nor standeth in the way of sinners, nor sitteth in the seat of the scornful.
But his delight is in the law of the LORD;
and in his law doth he meditate day and night."*

To delight in the Lord is to delight in His Word. A righteous man or woman desires to meditate upon the Scripture allowing the Word to guide them.

When we delight in His Word, we will desire to know more of His Word.
Psalm 119:16
"I will delight myself in thy statutes: I will not forget thy word."

When we delight in His Word, we will desire to obey Him.
Psalm 40:8
"I delight to do thy will, O my God: yea, thy law is within my heart."

When we delight in His Word, we will acknowledge our need for Him.
Psalm 119:92
*"Unless thy law had been my delights,
I should then have perished in mine affliction."*

**When we delight in His Word,
we will desire to apply His Word to our lives.**
Psalm 112:1
*"Praise ye the LORD. Blessed is the man that feareth the LORD,
that delighteth greatly in his commandments."*

Throughout this year we have delighted in Him through His Word.
May we continue to delight in His Word today and every day.

Bible Reading
Zechariah 4-7 | 1 John 2

Tried With Fire.

1 Peter 1:7
*"That the trial of your faith, being much more precious than of gold
that perisheth, though it be tried with fire, might be found unto praise
and honour and glory at the appearing of Jesus Christ:"*

We must delight in His Word so that when our faith is tried, the Word
will carry us through. **When you feel *"tried with fire,"* allow the Word to
comfort you.**

Psalm 119:92
*"Unless thy law had been my delights,
I should then have perished in mine affliction."*

Our days are few and full of trouble. **It is through the trial of our faith that
we find the character of our faith.** The fiery trial reveals in what or Who our
faith dwells.

1 Corinthians 3:13
*"Every man's work shall be made manifest: for the day shall declare it,
because it shall be revealed by fire;
and the fire shall try every man's work of what sort it is."*

He is the Potter, and we are the clay. **In the heat of the fire, the Word makes
our faith come forth as a vessel of honor, more precious than gold.**

Job 23:10
*"But he knoweth the way that I take:
when he hath tried me, I shall come forth as gold."*

Our trials give us opportunity to praise and honour the Lord, giving Him
the glory He so rightfully deserves. **Don't waste your trial today.** Allow your
situation to reveal your faith in Him, while giving Him the glory despite your
circumstance. God will get the glory but it's up to us to allow our faith to
come forth as gold so that it can be laid at His feet.

1 Peter 4:12-13
*"Beloved, think it not strange concerning the fiery trial which is to try you,
as though some strange thing happened unto you: But rejoice,
inasmuch as ye are partakers of Christ's sufferings; that, when his glory
shall be revealed, ye may be glad also with exceeding joy."*

Bible Reading
Zechariah 8-10 | 1 John 3

Finish Well.

Acts 20:24
*"But none of these things move me,
neither count I my life dear unto myself,
so that I might finish my course with joy, and the ministry, which I have
received of the Lord Jesus, to testify the gospel of the grace of God."*

The Apostle Paul recognized that his race was ending soon. He had served the Lord humbly since that day he met Jesus on the road to Damascus. There were many tears and temptations that he had to deal with along the way. He had enemies, yet he gave all that he had toward the work of the ministry. He taught the multitudes, both publicly and privately, the Gospel of Jesus Christ. **He did not know what was ahead for him, but he was willing to endure whatever the Lord had in store. He made the choice to finish well.**

Philippians 3:13-14
*"Brethren, I count not myself to have apprehended: but this one thing I do,
forgetting those things which are behind, and reaching forth unto those
things which are before, I press toward the mark
for the prize of the high calling of God in Christ Jesus."*

We do not know what the ending of this year, or the New Year ahead, may have in store, but the Lord does. There may be tears or temptations. We may even encounter some enemies, but we have a choice to make. Paul not only chose to finish his race, but he desired to finish it with joy while testifying of the Gospel of the grace of God.

What will we allow to hinder us from being a Light for Christ? Paul did not let the hindrances deter him from his God-given purpose, and neither should we. There will be discouragements, disappointments, and distractions; yet we can choose to follow Paul's example and say, *"But none of these things move me".*

1 Corinthians 15:58
*"Therefore, my beloved brethren, be ye stedfast, unmoveable,
always abounding in the work of the Lord, forasmuch as ye know
that your labour is not in vain in the Lord."*

Make the choice today to strive to finish well.

Bible Reading
Zechariah 11-14 | 1 John 4

Walk With God Every Day.

Genesis 5:21-24
*"And Enoch lived sixty and five years, and begat Methuselah:
And Enoch walked with God after he begat Methuselah three hundred years, and begat sons and daughters: And all the days of Enoch were three hundred sixty and five years: And Enoch walked with God: and he was not; for God took him."*

In the entire canon of Scripture, only two people are mentioned to have walked with God, Enoch and Noah. To walk with God meant to have a constant and familiar relationship with Him. These men had faith in God and are both mentioned in the Hall of Faith with a familiar verse in between.

Hebrews 11:5-7
"By faith Enoch was translated that he should not see death; and was not found, because God had translated him: for before his translation he had this testimony, that he pleased God. But without faith it is impossible to please him: for he that cometh to God must believe that he is, and that he is a rewarder of them that diligently seek him. By faith Noah, being warned of God of things not seen as yet, moved with fear, prepared an ark to the saving of his house; by the which he condemned the world, and became heir of the righteousness which is by faith."

To walk with God is to have faith that pleases Him, while coming to Him, believing in Him, and diligently seeking Him.

"And all the days of Enoch were three hundred sixty and five years" There are no coincidences within the Word of God. With the exception of leap years, our calendar year consists of 365 days. **Enoch walked with God and lived 365 years, and he serves as an example to us that we can walk with God every day.**

Psalm 119:1-2
"Blessed are the undefiled in the way, who walk in the law of the Lord. Blessed are they that keep his testimonies, and that seek him with the whole heart."

Endeavor to walk with God every day.
Walk with Him by spending time in His Word and His presence.

Delight in Him today and every day.

Bible Reading
Malachi | 1 John 5

Title Index

Title Index

Title Index

Title Index

Title Index

Title Index

About Us

"Delight thyself also in the LORD;
and he shall give thee the desires of thine heart."
Psalm 37:4

From this verse comes the inspiration behind the name of this ministry. It is a reminder that if we delight ourselves in Him, He promises to give us desires according to His will for our lives.

In 2012, the desire for a design ministry began. The Lord has since opened door after door to allow that desire to become a reality..."*Commit thy way unto the LORD; trust also in him; and he shall bring it to pass."* Psalm 37:5

Delight Thyself Design Ministries began as a media ministry at Teays Valley Baptist Church of Hurricane, WV in 2013. Shortly after that, the Lord began to direct us toward reaching people with the printed Word of the Gospel.

A tract ministry was born, and has since continued to grow as the Lord leads. In 2014, we began shipping tracts to missionaries across the world with little to no material with which to reach their field. Please pray with us that the Lord will continue to provide the tracts the missionaries are requesting.

We ship tracts free of charge to anyone willing to distribute the printed Word of the Gospel of Jesus Christ.

Gospel tracts customized with a church's contact information is a great way to spread the Gospel and allow others to contact your ministry. We also design custom material for Independent Baptist Churches, which helps fund the printing and distribution of Gospel tracts which are sent across the world.

We are so thankful for those that the Lord has provided to support this ministry on a monthly basis or through one time donations. If it were not for these people, this ministry could not exist today. Like the Apostle Paul, we claim Philippians 4:17 for this method of support, *"Not because I desire a gift: but I desire fruit that may abound to your account."*

If you would like to receive ministry updates, follow us on social media or send us your email address to receive our ministry newsletters.

What Can One Tract Do?

One tract was sitting in the office of the home of a young man named, Hudson. When he found it, he read over it and the phrase "the finished work of Christ" began to work on his heart about his need for salvation. He then surrendered his life to Christ, and was burdened for the people of China. This man was who we now know as Hudson Taylor, the missionary who brought the Good News of the Gospel to China.

One tract was given by a friend to a man named Joe. Over the next several months, the Lord used that tract to put him under conviction, cause him to go to church and walk the aisle to trust Christ as His Saviour. When he got up, he saw his pregnant wife beside him. She had also came forward by faith to accept Christ. This is the testimony of the parents of the founder of this ministry. One tract led to their salvation, a Christian heritage, and the start of this ministry. Without God using a man to give that one tract, this ministry would not exist today.

One tract has now yielded over 700,000 tracts to date being sent all across the world, and only heaven will reveal the fruit that remains. To God be the glory, for great things only He hath done.

Isaiah 55:11
*"So shall my word be that goeth forth out of my mouth:
it shall not return unto me void,
but it shall accomplish that which I please,
and it shall prosper in the thing whereto I sent it."*

**Will you allow God to use you
to spread the printed Word of the Gospel?**

The Bible Way To Heaven.

"Jesus saith unto him, I am the way, the truth, and the life;
no man cometh unto the Father, but by me."
John 14:6

We Are All Sinners.
"For all have sinned, and come short of the glory of God."
Romans 3:23

We Were Sent A Saviour.
"But God commendeth his love toward us, in that,
while we were yet sinners, Christ died for us."
Romans 5:8

We Were Supplied A Gift.
"For the wages of sin is death;
but the gift of God is eternal life through Jesus Christ our Lord."
Romans 6:23

We Can Simply Confess & Call.
"That if thou shalt confess with thy mouth the Lord Jesus,
and shalt believe in thine heart that God
hath raised him from the dead, thou shalt be saved.
For whosoever shall call upon the name of the Lord shall be saved."
Romans 10:9,13

It's that simple.

The Bible says… **Whosoever.**
Once you see yourself as a sinner, if you will simply *"call upon the name of the Lord"*, you can be saved from spending eternity in the Lake of Fire separated from God. You may say…"It's not for me." or "I'll never be good enough.", but God said… **Whosoever.**

God is not willing that any should perish.
That includes you.

If you have trusted Christ as your Saviour,
or would like more information, please contact us.

delightthyself.com

CPSIA information can be obtained
at www.ICGtesting.com
Printed in the USA
BVHW091102011022
648422BV00007B/23